EUROPE'S POPULIST CONDITION

Emmy Eklundh

BRISTOL
UNIVERSITY
PRESS

First published in Great Britain in 2026 by

Bristol University Press
University of Bristol
1-9 Old Park Hill
Bristol
BS2 8BB
UK
t: +44 (0)117 374 6645
e: bup-info@bristol.ac.uk

Details of international sales and distribution partners are available at bristoluniversitypress.co.uk

© Bristol University Press 2026

DOI: 10.51952/9781529236859

British Library Cataloguing in Publication Data
A catalogue record for this book is available from the British Library

ISBN 978-1-5292-3682-8 hardcover
ISBN 978-1-5292-3683-5 paperback
ISBN 978-1-5292-3684-2 ePub
ISBN 978-1-5292-3685-9 ePdf

The right of Emmy Eklundh to be identified as author of this work has been asserted by her in accordance with the Copyright, Designs and Patents Act 1988.

All rights reserved: no part of this publication may be reproduced, stored in a retrieval system, or transmitted in any form or by any means, electronic, mechanical, photocopying, recording, or otherwise without the prior permission of Bristol University Press.

Every reasonable effort has been made to obtain permission to reproduce copyrighted material. If, however, anyone knows of an oversight, please contact the publisher.

The statements and opinions contained within this publication are solely those of the author and not of the University of Bristol or Bristol University Press. The University of Bristol and Bristol University Press disclaim responsibility for any injury to persons or property resulting from any material published in this publication.

Bristol University Press works to counter discrimination on grounds of gender, race, disability, age and sexuality.

Cover design: Andrew Corbett
Front cover image: Stocksy/Akela - from alp to alp

Contents

Acknowledgements		iv
Preface		vi
Introduction		1
1	What Is the Populist Condition?	13
2	Coloniality and Exclusion in Contemporary Populism Studies	33
3	Taking Coloniality Seriously: A New Approach to Populism	52
4	Populism and Gender: Feminist Lessons on the People	75
5	Good Populisms? Inclusionary Politics on the Left	92
Conclusion		110
Notes		122
Bibliography		124
Index		146

Acknowledgements

I want to thank a number of people for their assistance while writing this book, without whom it would have been practically impossible to complete.

First of all, my lovely colleagues and friends in the Populism Specialist Group at the Political Studies Association. Ever since Yannis Stavrakakis invited me to be part of this adventure in 2016, it has been my intellectual home. While this book is rather a critical account of populism as a concept, I am certain that it will continue to be my home in the future. Special mention goes to, in no particular order, Theo Aiolfi, Thomás Zicman de Barros, Lone Sorensen, Jana Goyvaerts, Katy Brown, Aurelien Mondon, George Newth, Lazaros Karavasilis, Giorgos Katsambekis, Giorgos Venizelos, Andy Knott, Reid Kleinberg, and Juan Roch. I also want to thank Benjamin de Cleen and colleagues at the VUB for inviting me to give the keynote speech to their second conference on discourse theory in 2023, which enabled me to articulate some key details of the book. Over the years, I have also had excellent conversations about populism with María Esperanza Casullo, Mark Devenney, Emilia Palonen, Allan Dreyer Hansen, and Jenny Gunnarsson Payne.

My colleagues in the Department of Politics and International Relations at Cardiff University have been exemplary in their patience and collegiality. To feel supported in your day-to-day work environment is not common in academia, but something in which our department excels. My research sabbatical in spring 2025 was especially instrumental when finishing the manuscript. I particularly want to mention Elisa Wynne-Hughes, Martin Horton-Eddison, Haro Karkour, Rachel Minto, Marta Lorimer, Hannes Hansen-Magnusson, and Victoria Basham for giving me the space to complete this book and cheering me on. I also want to thank all of my students on my module *The Politics of Populism in Europe* over the years. In the classroom, I have been able to sound out ideas and be inspired by the underappreciated wisdom of our next generation.

I want to pay special tribute to Jonathan Dean, who sadly passed away in 2024. Jonathan and I had many conversations about this project, and I felt emboldened by his enthusiasm. Jonathan, a truly critical scholar, was himself working on the gendered aspects of populism, and his thoughts have been foundational for this book. We miss him greatly.

Martin Nonhoff has been absolutely instrumental in my understanding of Laclau, and I am still learning. Thank you also for our renewed collaboration, and for making sure that discourse theory is not only about populism. Thanks also to our striking worker team, Nye Davies and Karel Musilek, for never letting me forget about Marxism.

I also want to thank the anonymous reviewers who have read and commented on the manuscript. Your feedback has been invaluable. A big thank you to the team at Bristol University Press for pushing the boundaries in publishing and remaining committed to scholarship and social justice: Stephen Wenham, Zoe Forbes, and Izzie Green. Thank you also to my copy editor, Helen White, who has done a tremendous job with the final version of the text.

I really want to thank my excellent co-author and friend Sebastián Ronderos for his unwavering positive attitude and critical feedback. Writing is such a personal process, but it is also a joy to share with others.

Thank you to my friends who have been patiently listening to my tirades about populism. It may (or may not) stop now. Especially, Maria Hovde, Rachel Massey, Thom Tyerman, Georg Löfflmann, Elisa Wynne-Hughes, Suwita Hani Randhawa, and Gareth Price-Thomas.

To conclude, I must thank my very supportive family. My parents, Lotta and Berth, have been unequivocally positive, both about my ideas and my ability to transform them into a book. For this I am forever grateful. My Brazilian family, Henrique and Alda Lucia, have been equally reassuring and encouraging.

Finally, thank you Henrique, my soulmate and forever home. Thank you for always pushing my thinking that extra mile, and for being inspirational and caring in equal measure. And Victor, *mitt hjärtas fröjd och glädje*.

Preface

In June 2018, I attended a talk by Walter Mignolo at Tate Britain in London. Mignolo gave an overview of his views on the concept of decoloniality, and also made a few comments on contemporary politics. Mignolo explained Quijano's colonial matrix of power, and elaborated on how we could see coloniality seep through in global capitalism, in gender oppression, in racial segregation, and in epistemological and knowledge terms. All of these reactionary ideas, he argued, emanate from the colonial moment, but are still with us today: 'coloniality isn't over, it's all over'.

I think many of us would agree that we are yet to rid our societies of the ills of inequality, be those based on race, gender, or class. However, most would probably still like to think that inequality is the preference of a certain political segment, often referred to as right-wing populism or the far right. Importantly, these problems do not come from us. However, as Mignolo spoke, it became increasingly clear to me that when he spoke of coloniality as a system that still plagued Europe, he was talking not about populism but about the very central structures and institutions, the mainstream.

This, however, went against all scholarship that I had encountered on populism at the time, and it has taken me seven years to articulate this initial idea into the book that you are currently reading. It is a book about Europe and about how populism is only a smokescreen for the real problems we are facing: a continued reliance on coloniality, exclusion, and difference.

In the book I use a speech by the former EU High Representative for Foreign Affairs and Security Policy, Josep Borrell. Borrell uses the figure of the European garden to illustrate his particular flavour of European exceptionalism: 'Europe is a garden. We have built a garden. Everything works. ... The rest of the world ... is not exactly a garden. Most of the rest of the world is a jungle, and the jungle could invade the garden' (Borell 2022).

In a kind of reverse homage to Borrell, the cover of this book is a picture of the garden at Alhambra in Granada, Spain, where Christopher Columbus received royal permission from the Spanish crown to embark on his 'discoveries'. To my mind, this is the quintessential 'European garden'.

If I may, I would encourage the reader not to read this as a pessimistic damnation of European politics. While I remain highly critical of the emancipatory potential of many of our current political parties and movements, I'm also hopeful that this book will spark a discussion about what we mean when we discuss challenges to the status quo. As a starting point, populism is not the answer, but neither is political defeatism. I urge us to turn the gaze inwards instead of putting our political failures at someone else's door.

Introduction

In May 2024, elections were held to choose the new representatives to the European Parliament. Throughout the European Union, there was widespread concern mixed with an at times quite unhealthy dose of fascination with the high polling numbers of what is termed far-right parties, radical right parties, or, more indiscriminately, populist parties. The growing consensus in European media seemed to be that, while the rise of these new parties was to be criticized, there was little that could be done to counter an inevitable reaction against 'unmanaged' migration and the liberal centre. The people of Europe, and in particular the economically disadvantaged, were seen as rightly questioning the status quo, and could not be blamed for turning to promises of a better future. The comments were complete with equal measures of wishful thinking as well as selective statistics, but the conclusions were clear. Populism, in whatever definition you prefer, is here to stay. Nevertheless, there are continuous attempts to clarify that populism is essentially a threat to politics as we know it in Europe. Populism, and the far or radical right, cannot be compatible with the fundamental values of a European democracy: freedom and equality.

The narrative described earlier is by no means local to the European continent but carries a particular connotation in this empirical context. Not only do Europeans typically argue that Europe is an inclusive and tolerant place to live, but it is also seen as the very birthplace of Enlightenment values. Europeans, therefore, are not only likely to be free and equal, but the most likely, given our particular history and political environment. A good example of how this is expressed in practice is the following quote from Josep Borrell, the former EU High Representative on Foreign Affairs and Security Policy:

> Europe is a garden. We have built a garden. Everything works. It is the best combination of political freedom, economic prosperity and social cohesion that the humankind has been able to build – the three things together. And here, Bruges is maybe a good representation of beautiful things, intellectual life, wellbeing. The rest of the world …

is not exactly a garden. Most of the rest of the world is a jungle, and the jungle could invade the garden. (Borrell, 2022)

While there are certainly circumstances which are undeniable, such as the presence of democratic governance throughout the European Union and a commitment to human rights, one has to ask why Europe is such a fertile breeding ground for the populist right? Should it not, since conditions are so favourable, be one of the least successful arenas of an ideology which denies that all humans are equal?

The 2024 European elections, where new parties on the right gathered 187 of the 720 seats (European Parliament, 2024), clearly demonstrates that support for a quite 'un-European' type of politics is not coincidental or fringe. We must, therefore, ask what the relationship between European politics and exclusionary policies looks like. Is it really true that Europe is the cradle of tolerance? Is it really true that Europeans are the most concerned about freedom and equality?

This conundrum has been plaguing European political debate for years. Arguments have been ranging from complete denial (populists are just a blip in a progression towards a brighter future) to partial acceptance (populists are an unfortunate consequence of poor economic performance and badly handled migration), or complete defeatism (populism has taken over) (Mondon, 2024a). All of these arguments, however, do not recognize what this book contends to be a fundamental issue: that Europe has an inherent populist condition. Populism, and all its bedfellows (nationalism, authoritarianism, illiberalism) are thus not external to European politics, but an absolutely integral part of it (Gillespie, 2024).

The not-so-democratic liberalism

If Europe has an inherent populist condition, what does this mean for our conception of European politics as a herald of democracy and equality? This book argues that the division between populism and democracy, and equally the conflation between liberalism and democracy, is a rather spurious invention, and one which does not hold up to closer scrutiny. I thus depart from Chantal Mouffe's assertion that liberalism and democracy are 'joined at the hip' (Mouffe, 2018), for a more critical disentanglement of the two topics. Over the last couple of years, it has become commonplace to argue that the policies of right-wing populists have been 'mainstreamed', somehow indicating a malicious takeover of our dear democratic society by threatening forces (Brown et al, 2021; Gillespie, 2024; Mondon & Winter, 2020). It has been rightfully argued that what is usually called the 'centre' or 'centrist policies' have moved right on the political spectrum over the past 20 years in most OECD countries. Thus, the movement has been mapped meticulously, but it fails to recognize one fundamental part of the mainstreaming literature. Contrary to popular understandings of the topic, most studies argue not only that the liberal centre and the right-wing populists are moving closer together, but that the liberal centre never possessed the democratic qualities so often ascribed to it (Mondon, 2024). This line of reasoning is highly compelling, and one which will be further developed in this book.

Only a short look into the basic tenets of liberalism can quickly dispel any doubt about liberalism's democratic credentials. Unlike what many textbooks want to tell us, the founding fathers of liberalism were fundamentally committed to preserving inequality. A simple example is John Stuart Mill, who coined the famous term 'the dictatorship of the majority' (Mill, 1972). In his writings, Mill cautioned against letting 'the masses' access the democratic process, for what would then happen to the private property of the landed nobility? Far from being concerned with democratic rights, Mill was concerned with good government, and he was convinced that this could not be achieved by letting a group of uneducated tribes make the decisions of the country. This quote demonstrates the deep disdain for 'the people' which was the grounding thought of liberal ideology.

Such anti-democratic leanings of liberalism are well documented, but more attention needs to be paid to the colonial underpinnings of our liberal modern society. Instead of trying to see populism as an external threat which adventures the European commitment to freedom and equality, in Chapter 1, I argue that we must engage with the concept of coloniality to understand how Europe's populist condition is permanent. In fact, we cannot understand the European 'People' without its colonial 'Other', which is one of the key premises of this book.

In Chapter 1, I offer another story of how European democracies came about. Drawing on decolonial theory, I argue that Europe's political history cannot be seen as disjointed from the process of colonization, as the two have developed concomitantly. In particular, this book questions the assumption that individuals in European democracies compete for an empty space of power. Rather, we must recognize that the Enlightenment in Europe did not bring about a 'fair game' of democratic decision-making, but that the goalposts only moved. Whereas political power was previously ordained by God, the age of Man introduced competition between the worthiest humans. However, this did not mean the elimination of the need for a hierarchy between the worthy and unworthy of political office – a hierarchy which was constructed with the introduction of the colonial Other, the Savage (Dussel, 1977; Wynter, 2003). This opened the door to a whole new world of distinctions between those who could be counted as political subjects (white, male property owners) and those who could not (women, slaves, the poor), along the justification that the former were more rational, more civil and, therefore, more liberal. As such, the open competition only remained open for those who met the new criteria: abiding by a certain European rationality and acting in a civil manner.

While we have thankfully seen some changes from the early Enlightenment, decolonial theory argues that the social hierarchies so fundamental to Europe's history are still relevant today. In Chapter 1, I trace how historical and contemporary liberalism still abide by most of the 'rules' put in place by Enlightenment theorists to ascertain suitability for political power. Rationality, civility, and a commitment to liberal values are still seen as paramount for 'good governance', with little regard to how these categories are highly gendered and racialized (Eze, 1997; Lugones, 2007; Mills, 1999) This book thus contends that since liberalism itself is based on an exclusionary and rather violent view of political affairs, why are we seeing populism as the main threat to a democratic and equal society?

What does populism mean in Europe?

In most scholarship on populism in Europe, the phenomenon is treated as an outside to European politics, and at times wholly antithetical and un-European. Importantly, there is almost no discussion of coloniality and its importance for the study of populism.

When discussing populism, there is a wealth of research which claims to either explain what populism is, or at least define it. Frustratingly, however, much of contemporary scholarship is in open dispute with other branches of the field. While some would like to define populism as an ideology (Mudde, 2004, 2007), a strategy (Weyland, 2021), a political style (Moffitt, 2016), or a discourse (Laclau, 2005), there are also discussions about whether the main focus should really be about the definitional problem, and not rather about how populism works as a proxy for legitimizing a radical political outlook on the right (Mondon, 2022; Mondon & Winter, 2020). It is indeed true that populism studies in general struggles to unite on a definition, and, in addition to this, the term 'populism' has taken on a life of its own, being used liberally by commentators and media outlets to describe almost any type of newcomers to politics. We can see how several, very disparate, projects have acquired the populist label, making the term rather more confusing than analytically helpful.

While these debates are indeed helpful, and necessary for any type of academic field, they are also repeating a certain narrative which sees populism as something distinct from 'normal', 'mainstream', or 'formal' politics. Such a distinction, however, must be put into question when the type of politics that is referred to is in power or occupies a large part of the political agenda. Since this is now the case in Europe (and in many other parts of the world as well), it is time to accept populism as the norm, not the exception. In this regard, the discursive approach to populism is closest to reality. For the discursive approach, populism is not something which only happens on the extremes of the political spectrum, but it is a possible constellation for any political project. Populism, Laclau argues, is essentially the creation of any political identity, meaning that it can emerge anywhere and anytime (Laclau, 2005). He also argues, controversially, that there can be no political debate without populism, since any real questioning of the status quo will necessarily involve a populist challenge.

There are, however, still some blind spots in populism research, which I will describe in Chapter 2. Since it has become increasingly difficult to argue that populism is a fringe phenomenon, the field has also started to recognize that, maybe, there are not so many differences between the People and the Elite (Benquet & Bourgeron, 2022; De Cleen & Ruiz Casado, 2024; Rojas-Andrés et al, 2024; Schoor, 2019). There is a lingering scepticism about whether populism really is a true challenge to the status quo. What about the increasing evidence that economic and political elites are, in fact, quite favourable towards populism (Ausserladscheider, 2022, 2024; Slobodian, 2025)? While populists sometimes do challenge the mainstream in terms of rhetoric and style (Aiolfi, 2022; Moffitt, 2016), does populism indicate a challenge to our current political order? This book will argue that if our main discursive order is seen as one produced by coloniality, what we call populism in Europe does not challenge the status quo. Rather, the movements and parties that we call populism indicate what could be labelled 'modernity on steroids', a natural conclusion of coloniality.

Naturally, this perspective is not universally accepted, but it asks questions in the search for a better understanding of the rise of populism in Europe. This discussion touches upon a more normative aspect of the field: is there any positive conceptualization of populism, one which is compatible with a commitment to equality? Much of the recent scholarship on left-wing populism would answer in the affirmative. The longstanding tradition of left populism in Latin America has over the past decade also permeated European politics, where we have seen the rise of a number of left populist initiatives (Biglieri & Cadahia, 2021; Casullo, 2019; De La Torre, 2017). It is immediately evident to any observer that these are different to right-wing populisms. On the left, populism often operates without the strong opposition to migration, it criticizes financial elites rather than other ethnic groups, and it has a strong commitment to democratic participation (Gerbaudo & Screti, 2017; Kioupkiolis, 2016; Markou, 2017). As such, it is undeniable that left-wing populism functions on a different premise than its right-wing counterpart. There are several explanations for this: some would argue that since populism is simply a thin ideology, the thick or host ideology would naturally shape the policy preferences of the party in question (Halikiopoulou et al, 2012; Mudde & Rovira Kaltwasser, 2012). The Laclauian field would gravitate towards an explanation which does not believe that 'thick' ideologies come before populism. Rather, since populism in simply an articulation of a political identity, it can take on both right-wing and left-wing positions (Mouffe, 2018).

There are several questions remaining regarding left-wing populism and its progressive potential. First of all, the field is not particularly keen to discuss the rather critical account of also left populist movements in Latin America (Ianni, 1972). Such accounts point to how populism sooner or later will be broken down by inherent class conflict and that any 'harmonious' class relations are simply cosmetic. The elite (the bourgeoise) will eventually favour their own material benefit. These accounts chime well with contemporary European Marxist takes on left populism (Lazzarato, 2021; Žižek, 2017). While this book is sympathetic to such a perspective, it still maintains that coloniality remains too absent from discussions about the progressive potential of left-wing populism. And, populism studies in general has identified that the People–Elite distinction may not be as strong as previously thought; more work is needed to fully appreciate the common histories of liberalism and populism in Europe.

Moving beyond the discursive approach

This book will thus argue that even in its most inclusionary and radical form, European populism perpetuates coloniality and its exclusionary logic. The reason for this, I argue, is twofold. One problem relates to how we conceptualize populism in theory, and another relates to how we see contemporary incarnations of populism as expressions of the political and true challenges to the status quo.

First, as I will show in Chapter 3, discourse theory harbours a continued reliance on world views which read our differences as automatic grounds for conflict. For instance, Carl Schmitt's influence over Laclau and Mouffe should not be underestimated. Schmitt, an early-20th-century political theorist, was also a prominent member of the Nazi party. While contemporary political theorists claim that it is possible to borrow 'the good things' from Schmitt, I enquire as to whether it is possible to cherry pick from a theory which proved so central to Nazism. Did his political views not influence his theories (Suuronen, 2021)?

Rather than emphatically rejecting any association with the most murderous and violent ideology of modernity, scholarship on populism has been surprisingly lenient on Schmitt. Mouffe (2005, 2018) uses Schmitt to construct her theory of agonism, where she blends fascist assumptions about natural differences with liberal 'a seat at the table' logic. Differences, however profound, can be overcome. Talking with the right-wing populists is the only way forward, Mouffe claims, in order to address their 'legitimate concerns'. Thus, she funnily enough aligns herself with scholars such as

Matthew Goodwin, who are not particularly known for their respect for left-wing politics, and are often seen as pandering to the far right (Goodwin & Eatwell, 2018). But the commitment to antagonism as violent conflict runs deeper than this. Even though antagonism could be read as something else, it is almost always read as an irreconcilable difference between ethnic groups, classes, or nations. The current body of literature on populism does little to move beyond the narrative that humans belong to different groups, and that this difference is what makes society impossible – a commitment to social hierarchies steeped in coloniality.

Second, Chapter 3 questions the assumption that populism offers a new type of politics simply because they do politics differently. It contends that populism, in its current forms, cannot be seen to introduce 'new' political subjects into the mix, and does not challenge the status quo. By returning to Laclau's concept of heterogeneity, it is not clear how populism would constitute what is termed 'the political', par excellence. As such, Chapter 3 interrogates whether populism in Europe, in its current theoretical and empirical form, offers a roadmap to a democratic society. Does its foundational commitment to difference as conflict steeped in coloniality become incompatible with a future based on equality?

Combining fantasy and coloniality

As such, we need a new approach to populism in Europe, one which takes coloniality seriously. At the end of the day, we need to understand why populism is so popular, both as a concept and as a political alternative. How can we explain the diverging demands and wishes of the European people? How can Europeans at once pride themselves on their inclusive character, but simultaneously vote for policies that are nothing of the sort? This book contends that psychoanalytical theory can help us explain these desires more fully. Psychoanalysis has become a rather fashionable lens through which we can explore political events (Glynos, 2008; Mandelbaum, 2020; Ronderos & Glynos, 2023). Even though psychoanalysis was initially developed as a theory of the individual, significant steps have been taken to develop this into a theory of collective identities. Laclau has been instrumental in this development, but is not alone. Such theories have focussed on the desire to belong, to form part of a community, and how this is central to any individual identity formation (Stavrakakis, 2002).

In recent work, the emerging field of critical fantasy studies has taken on this challenge and produced a wealth of relevant work on how the affective must be at the centre of any explanation of political life. These studies focus on how the role of fantasy shapes political opportunity (Ronderos & Glynos, 2023; Zicman de Barros, 2022). Bringing in a valuable and novel perspective, these studies use the logics approach developed by Glynos and

Howarth (2007), which has recently gained renewed attention with the increased focus in the field of populism studies on the emotional aspects of politics, and in particular populist politics (Bonansinga, 2020; Eklundh, 2020; Salmela & von Scheve, 2017).

Critical fantasy studies does not make the mistake so commonly committed by scholars on emotions and populism (Skonieczny, 2018; Widmann, 2021); emotions (and in particular affect) are not seen as disjointed add-ons to 'normal' political life. Rather, the affective is the absolute essence of what makes the political possible. It is due to our affective attachments that we care about politics in the first place, and there is no possibility of even imagining political identities without them. Importantly, therefore, we are not ranking political actors based on how emotional or affective they are. Since there are no political identities without affect, populists are not more emotional than others. Rather, this is simply a slur directed at populists to belittle their political agenda.

Instead, the concept of fantasy can help us understand European populism – as a concept and as a political alternative – much better. As Žižek has argued, fantasy is the structure that we use to compensate for our inherent ability to fully realize ourselves (Žižek, 2008). However, fantasy also works to cover up the underlying mechanisms of impossibility – Europe wants to be equal and inclusive, but knows that it is not. Žižek takes the example of the Jew as the ultimate Nazi fantasy, which, according to him, served to cover up class antagonisms in Germany (Žižek, 2015). While this is a highly compelling analysis, there is a need to move beyond class and introduce the decolonial perspective to understand Europe's fantasies, and what roles they play.

This book will argue that the function of the populist is simply a way to demarcate an inside and outside of politics – a fantasy of separation between the populist and the mainstream. Drawing on decolonial theorists who are also using psychoanalysis (Fanon, 2021; Mbembe, 2019), the book argues that the European mainstream continues to uphold the fantasy that Europeans are rational and superior, based in a colonial mindset. For this to be true, all the cruel realities of European politics must be externalized – enter the populist. As such, even though there are often very few differences between the mainstream and the populist, we need to believe that there are, in order to tell the story that Europeans are inherently good.

In the last two chapters of the book, I use several interfaces of coloniality (gender, rationality, and the nation-state) to illustrate that the lines between populism and the mainstream are highly porous. I pay particular attention to left-wing populism, for two reasons. First, to interrogate the argument that left-wing populism offers a true challenge to the status quo, even if right-wing populism does not. Second, since left-wing populism is in many ways seen as the least likely area where coloniality will surface.

Coloniality and gender

Another field which has of late become paramount in the study of populism is the contribution of feminist literature. Many of the criticisms of populism and the far right more generally are based on commonplace feminist understandings of politics, and how this can and should be read through a gender lens. The problem with populism and its relationship to gender is that it is by no means straightforward. In fact, we get quite contradictory signals from populist actors on their stances on feminism and gender. On the one hand, European right-wing populisms are keen to argue that they promote gender equality, given that this, according to them, is a fundamental European value. Nevertheless, there are countless examples of how right-wing populists in Europe promote clearly chauvinist policies, such as trying to get women to stay home with the children and away from the labour force, as well as controlling the bodies of mostly Muslim women and what they wear.

Another issue relates to the women within right-wing populist movements. These women, it is argued, pose another conundrum: how can women vote for something so obviously against women's rights (Mudde & Kaltwasser, 2015)? How can women, such as Marine Le Pen and Giorgia Meloni, stand at the forefront of an ideology which sees women as inferior to men, or at least as so biologically different that their social position has to become affected? This has been explained and studied at length within gender studies, where the concept of femonationalism (where women are the main instigators of a nationalist logic) can explain the prominent position of women within these movements (Keskinen, 2018; Kinnvall, 2015). There are signs, of course, that the voters of such parties are predominantly male, but one should not ignore the trends that an increasing share of women vote for right-wing populists (Spierings & Zaslove, 2015, 2017).

The topic of LGBT rights and issues is also central when discussing gender and populism. Contradictorily, European right-wing populists often claim to support LGBT rights, and posit themselves as the enlightened modernists versus the alleged old-fashioned and conservative immigrant communities. The right-wing populist becomes the defender of the modern European order and cannot be accused of promoting inequality. All of this, obviously, must be taken with a pinch of salt. As has been proven by recent research (Turnbull-Dugarte & López Ortega, 2024), right-wing populists are not deeply committed to protecting LGBT rights, but are using it mostly instrumentally to garner electoral support. The rise in support for LGBT rights can be seen particularly when such support is lacking among other ethnic groups.

With such diverging trends, the debate around gender and populism often becomes muddled and does not fully reflect the explanatory power which feminist theory possesses. In Chapter 4, I argue that there are two fundamental lessons which must be learned from feminism, and which significantly help us better understand the relationship between populism, gender, and the European democratic system. The first lesson relates to the feminist critique of European democracies and their inherent chauvinist and unequal tenets. European states, feminists argue, cannot be seen as a promoter of gender rights, or even as a neutral arbiter, but must be conceptualized as fundamentally reliant upon gender inequality. This ranges from the very basics of feminist political economy, where the capitalist system is seen as profiting over women's unpaid labour in the home, to the recognition that states around the world promote a militarized masculinity which legitimizes mass killings and violence for 'the good state' (Connell, 1990; Sachseder & Stachowitsch, 2023). The second, drawn from decolonial feminist theory (Lugones, 2007), is that patriarchy as we know it cannot be detached from its colonial heritage. Critically engaging with the traditional (male) decolonial theorists, decolonial feminists argue that gender (not sex) must be at the forefront of any decolonial analysis. Only then can we explain the variations in experiences between women of difference places and from different backgrounds, and only then can we understand how the mainstream also perpetuates colonial patriarchy (Mendoza, 2015; Segato, 2022). Gender politics, thus, is simply another interface of the coloniality.

These arguments are fundamental to this book. If we are investigating if there is indeed any distance between the populist positions and the mainstream, a quick look at feminist theory can tell us that the distance is not particularly large. If violence and exclusion form a central part of any state or nation building, and indeed of our own democratic societies, then it is not difficult to employ the same analytical tools to understand the appeal of populism. Interestingly, however, much of the scholarship on populism tends to argue that toxic masculinity is a particular occurrence among populists, and that mainstream politicians are much more civilized and equal. This is contrary to much of feminist scholarship, where masculinity is a core lens through which we understand the political game (Hemmings, 2012).

Instead, this book argues that the mainstream and populism are both situated in the same discursive order of coloniality, where unequal gender relations are central. The fantasy of separation between the populists and the mainstream are working overtime to sediment that Europeans are benign and equal. Importantly, it carries the fantasy that Europe is a gender-equal paradise.

Coloniality and the nation-state

The second interface of coloniality which will be discussed relates to how political communities in Europe (populist and mainstream) are reliant on the nation-state. In particular, they are committed to an exclusionary political subjectivity steeped in coloniality. While these observations may seem quite gloomy, we should take stock of what is for many seen as the solution, or at least a positive development, namely left-wing populism. This version of populism, it is claimed, defies the exclusionary and violent logics of the right and must be seen as distinct. There is an abundance of scholarship specializing in describing this distinctiveness, which argues that left-wing populism operates with a wholly different conceptualization of the 'People' (Gerbaudo & Screti, 2017; Kioupkiolis, 2016).

Is it undeniable that there are important policy differences between right- and left-wing populism (Eklundh et al, 2024; Mudde & Rovira Kaltwasser, 2012), and it is therefore quite difficult to speak about 'populist' policy in any meaningful fashion. Those who try often end up conflating right-wing populist policy preferences with populism in general, providing more confusion than clarity. Nevertheless, it is accurate to say that many left-wing populists tend to have a less hostile outlook on migration and often take issue with the neoliberal economic world order, which they see as unjust (Bortun, 2024). That said, we can also find examples which do not conform to these stereotypes, such as the M5S in Italy which has been promoting a hostile environment against immigrants (Gerbaudo & Screti, 2017), or similarly the left-wing support for Brexit, so-called Lexit (Worth, 2017).

There have been several successful cases of left-wing populism in Europe in the past decade, such as Podemos in Spain, Syriza in Greece, La France Insoumise in France, and the M5S in Italy. This is a very wide range of different political actors, and while they do share some commonalities, their political programmes differ significantly as well. What is of most interest to this book is how the political identities of these parties suffer from similar problems in their articulations as other European parties in the centre and on the right. While there is a recognition that equality is a key pillar for their political ideology, there are also deep tensions in who should be regarded as a political subject, and antagonistic relationships are often constructed along the same lines as for other, more right-wing, political parties. In practice, this has meant an adoption of similar rhetorical figures such as the nation or patriotism, but always with a clarification that the political content of such terms is different on the left (Custodi, 2020; Custodi & Padoan, 2022).

But is it really different? Can we, if we consider the heritage of how political identity has been constructed in Europe, find an articulation of the 'People' which affords us an indisputable commitment to equality? In Chapter 5, I make the case that this is not currently possible. This chapter demonstrates that several factors — the violent history of liberal democracy in Europe, the problematic conceptualization of populism, the narrow understanding of antagonism as a conflict between the People and something which is external to it, and the chauvinist elements of European democracy — make an inclusionary and equal populism impossible. This becomes particularly evident when looking at what happens when conditions are most favourable for such a thing to happen: why does Mélenchon so strongly believe in the French republican values (Kleinberg, 2023), why does Podemos talk about patriotism (Custodi, 2024), why did the M5S want to limit migration into Italy (Gerbaudo & Screti, 2017)? My answer to this is simple: left-wing populists are more European than they are left wing and struggle to escape coloniality. The fantasies about the civil and superior European are also present in left-wing populism, which exhibits strong ties to rationality, to managed borders, and to a concept of the People reminiscent of the Nation.

This book could be read as a complete damnation of populism, both as a concept and as a political alternative. And in some ways it is, since it refuses to accept a narrative about European politics which does not take coloniality seriously. Taking coloniality seriously has several implications. First, it has theoretical implications for discourse theory, and in particular for Laclau's works on populism. If we take coloniality into consideration, populism in its current form can no longer be seen as an expression of the political. Second, it has implications for political and academic debate, where a stronger recognition of the common histories of populism and liberalism (and their common elitist heritage) makes the term populist highly unsuited for describing any challenge to the status quo, the neoliberal consensus, etc. Third, it has implications for progressive politics. If populism is tightly intertwined with coloniality, is it compatible with a progressive agenda?

This book encourages us to consider two paths ahead. Either we can keep the concept of populism as a possible challenge to the status quo, but we must then recognize that most of the cases of 'populism' in Europe today do not actually challenge the status quo of coloniality (by which the term becomes rather vacuous). Or we must discard the concept of populism altogether and accept that it is tainted beyond salvation and cannot be read in a progressive way in European politics. The choice is ours.

1

What Is the Populist Condition?

To say that democracy in Europe is under threat is not particularly controversial today. We are convinced that we live under a particularly European system of political decision-making which is fundamentally equal and democratic, and this is ultimately a moral good. Populists are often seen as antithetical to this order and perceived as threats. We can see the threat in several opinion pieces and op-eds which discuss into oblivion what we should do with the populists, how they can be combatted, and how we can win this challenge of popular dissent (Galston, 2018; Mounk, 2018). For instance, David Remnick, the editor of *The New Yorker*, in the wake of Trump's 2016 election, argued that 'people can behave foolishly, recklessly, self-destructively in the aggregate' (Remnick, 2016). This is not limited to public debate, but is also the subject of intense academic inquiry – which is the best way to preserve democratic systems under threat (Müller, 2016)? Similarly, Yasha Mounk's book *The People vs. Democracy* is a thinly veiled critique of popular participation in democratic decision-making (Mounk, 2019), where the populist voter is castigated as a problem for democracy. These commentators thus join a long and prominent line of anti-populist sentiment which sees political participation as a potential ill, not a *sine qua non* for a democratic society. In sum, the problem formulation is clear: populists are dismantling the European way of life.

When scratching the surface of this discussion, it often becomes evident that what we are discussing is not simply democracy, but liberal democracy in particular. This elision of democracy with a particular political ideology (liberalism) seems natural and mostly goes unquestioned (Berman, 2017). In fact, such is the hold of liberal thought in contemporary European politics that the two seem inseparable, and any criticism of liberalism also becomes a critique of democracy (with some exceptions; see Mudde (2007)). The flourishing area of illiberalism studies is largely focussed on how any articulations of illiberalism are also threats to democracy – even though the two are seen as distinct entities, there is an empirical overlap in the analysis.

The populists threat is therefore not only anti-democratic, but also illiberal (Galston, 2018; Laruelle, 2022; Zakaria, 1997).

What emerges are distinct lines in European politics between the liberal *inside*, which is good, and the illiberal, populist *outside*, which is evil and threatening. This narrative is firmly positioning populism as something radically un-European – the story we are told about Europe is not one of xenophobia, violence, or misogyny, but one of equality, inclusion, and strong institutions to protect these values. Nevertheless, some uncomfortable realities are disturbing this narrative. As described in the growing literature on the mainstreaming of right-wing populism (Brown, 2024; Brown & Mondon, 2020), it seems as though the liberal centre (consisting of both centre-right and centre-left parties and governments) is not particularly reluctant to implement policies which have been labelled populists. This poses a conundrum. If liberalism is drastically opposed to populism, why are we seeing the increasing amount of time and money spent to protect Europe's borders? How has the increasingly hostile environment towards immigrants in European countries come about? How can we explain the backlash against the advances of feminism, as seen in the vilification of the trans community? Is this all the fault of populism? Can we make sense of populism and liberalism as strange bedfellows, or are they not so strange, after all (Heinisch & Werner, 2024)?

This chapter will present an alternative explanation. Instead of seeing all the ills of European politics as an external problem, as a threatening takeover from the outside, the chapter will explore what I define as *Europe's populist condition*. This chapter will argue that what European politicians and commentators spend many hours labelling populist (and therefore external to European politics) is an entirely European affair. Democracy in Europe is not the neutral vehicle towards equality which it makes itself out to be. By examining the often brutal history of how modern democracy came about in Europe, it will become evident that the commitment to equality is more an afterthought than a central tenet. In this sense, liberal democracy in Europe emanates from a distinctly elitist world view, which sees only a few as worthy of political office. The concomitant relationship between colonization and the development of the modern European state is also no coincidence – as I will argue, the latter is dependent on the former for its justification that European peoples are more suitable for governing than the wild savages of the colonies.

In essence, the People, in European democratic thought, could not be envisioned without being connected to a particular territory. However, not only were the People connected to that territory, but they were also its rightful masters, due to certain characteristics thought to be connected to Europeans: rationality and civility. Civility, the capacity to act in a civilized manner, is a key concept when understanding democracy today. It is often connected with liberal democracy, which is supposed to favour rational dialogue between citizens and therefore circumvent a recourse to violence (Habermas, 1984). What is often forgotten is that the very concept of rationality played a fundamental role in colonization (Eze, 1997; Mills, 1999). The justification for the subjugation of other peoples was made with reference to capacity of rational thought, and thus inflicted unspeakable violence throughout the world. Colonial conquest was justified with the argument that indigenous peoples were unable to manage good forms of governance and only Europeans could provide this and were therefore the rightful masters of territory in the colonies. The populist condition, in this sense, harbours a strong belief in the merits of European superiority and civility, when, in fact, this myth has contributed to the suffering of so many.

This chapter will begin by outlining the elitist foundations of liberal thought, with a special focus on how liberalism has not, for the most part, worked towards equality but rather against it. The unquestionable support for social hierarchies within liberalism (be those based on race, gender, or class) cannot be seen as diametrically opposed to the populist versions of the same. While the undemocratic nature of liberalism, and in particular neoliberalism, has been heavily debated, there is a curious absence of discussions of why it is that liberalism retains such an approach, with a few notable exceptions (Gillespie, 2024; Mondon, 2024). Instead of seeing our current problems of democratic deficits and inequality as problems of *implementation*, this chapter argues that they are by *design*. This design, furthermore, can be explained by engaging with the concept of coloniality.

To this end, in the second section, the chapter will introduce the concept of coloniality and explain how this can help us better understand why populism and liberalism are not such an unlikely pairing. In the third section, the chapter will engage with contemporary liberal theory to demonstrate that the liberalism of old is also the liberalism of today – the main tenets of the ideology have not softened, and the issues around colonial thinking are still present. Overall, the chapter aims to dispute the claim that liberalism works in favour of the people and contends that there is an inherent elitism in liberal thought.

The elitist foundations of liberalism

When learning about liberalism, be that in school or at university, the story often begins with a recognition that we owe our freedom to this ideology. The narrative is constructed around the idea that no modern and democratic society could possibly exist had it not been for liberalism and its disciples (Rawls, 1999a, 2005). When we do discuss the potential problems of liberalism, they are seen rather as exceptions to the rule, or problems of implementation, not design. As such, we could conceive of problems with neoliberalism and inequality (Bruff, 2014; Bruff & Tansel, 2019). There is also a growing body of scholarship which connects the rise of right-wing populism with the failures of neoliberalism per se (Mattei, 2025; Slobodian, 2025). The problem with such scholarship is that there is a lingering notion that liberal democracy *in toto* may be saved. Advocates of the liberal paradigm could still argue, as they often do, that these critiques do not detract from the main merits of the liberal promise. The issue with this narrative, I argue, is that the liberal promise is itself flawed, and rests upon a conception of popular power which is incompatible with equality.

The liberal promise tells us that there is an empty space of power, and that this empty space must be filled. We as citizens are able to determine who our leaders are and hold them to account. It also tells us that the decision of who should be in power is one that *should be made* and not one that has already been made. In fact, liberalism has historically made great advances to restrict democratic involvement, not expand it. Liberalism is, therefore, not at odds with elitism.

The belief that we can choose our own leaders was developed during the Enlightenment, when increased questioning of both political and religious doxa enabled a perspective to see power in the hands of man and not God (Rancière, 1999). This substantial shift in political philosophy instilled an inherent uncertainty in society – who shall rule and why? As Rancière has argued, this uncertainty is what makes democracy fragile, but is also the fundamental condition for a just society.

However, when taking a closer look, the goal of liberal thought does not seem to reveal a desire to keep the place of power open, but rather to close it down (Mehta, 1999). As Landa has argued, 'liberals, for the most part, doggedly resisted the expansion of democracy to the masses, and insisted on limited, propertied, democracy, so to speak' (Landa, 2012, p 275). At the forefront of this anti-popular thinking stand Mill (1972) or Tocqueville (2009), who see in democratic development not a promise of emancipation, but a threat to social stability and progress. They argue that the rule of the masses is simply another form of despotism. John Stuart Mill's concept of the tyranny of the majority (Mill, 1937, 1972) has gained renewed traction in recent years, signalling an increased worry among the elites that the People are not fit to rule. In today's language, we would refer to this as deeply authoritarian, a label more commonly associated with populism and illiberalism than liberalism itself. Such authoritarian tendencies are no strangers to contemporary politics, as pointed out by Hall in the 1980s (Hall, 1988, 2017; Katsambekis, 2023; Knott, 2020). Mill, who is often considered a beacon of liberal democracy, should be read with a careful eye that also pays attention to the very undemocratic nature of his proposals. For Mill (1972), there is a need for government to retain stability by limiting the impact of democratic decision-making. Importantly, herein lies the nexus between the property-owning class and liberal thought – good government will protect the former with support of the latter. What has later been termed economic liberalism is, in fact, very close to political liberalism.

That economic liberalism has an innate authoritarian side, as argued by the growing scholarship on authoritarian neoliberalism (Bruff, 2014; Bruff & Tansel, 2019), can be further corroborated by the unwavering support of neoliberal economic policies by the far-right in Europe and beyond. Consider, for instance, the very close links between French businesses and Le Pen, *The New York Times* endorsing Bolsonaro in Brazil, or the policy choices by the Austrian FPÖ, recent electoral winners in the 2024 Austrian general elections (Ausserladscheider, 2022, 2024). Similarly, we can observe how many right-wing populists are supported by big financial actors (Benquet & Bourgeron, 2022). As such, we are beginning to see a different story emerge, where liberalism is not a counterforce against the elites, but rather the very elites themselves. Importantly, there is emerging scholarship which demonstrates that the neoliberal politics of financial elites exhibit clear ideological affinities with right-wing populism (Mattei, 2025; Slobodian, 2025).

As is commonly argued, one of the core threats against democracy is that populists mislead the electorate and act as demagogues, as demonstrated by the growing literature on anti-populism (Galanopoulos & Venizelos, 2022; Moffitt, 2018; Stavrakakis et al, 2018) and misinformation (Farkas, 2023). What is often disregarded are the blatant admissions of esotericism in liberal thought, as described by Landa (2012). The goal with political communication is not to speak to the entire electorate, but to design political speech so as to 'perform the miracle of speaking in a publication to a minority, while being silent to the majority' as so aptly put by Leo Strauss (quoted in Landa, 2012, p 278). Similarly, many would like to argue that the most liberal countries today abide by the highest standards of transparency and honesty, as so often demonstrated by the Freedom House Index (Freedom House, 2024). The index, which has gained international acclaim and respect, ranks countries around the world and how corrupt they are. Funnily enough, the index does not operate with any external point of reference in measuring corruption, but simply measures how corrupt countries are perceived to be (which is a different thing altogether). Unsurprisingly, the level of perceived corruption tends to increase proportionally to the level of authoritarian tendencies, indicating that the index supports a correlation between democracy and transparency.

In sum, we can see that liberalism is by no means a guarantor against inequality, and is, in fact, often working to sediment social hierarchies. We are thus faced with a rather problematic situation where the differences between liberalism and populism are fading. Where does this leave us? How can we understand the connections between liberalism, populism, and elitism today? How can we make sense of the fact that actors which are painted as so different are, in reality, quite similar? Later, I posit that using coloniality as a cipher to read the links and overlaps between liberalism, elitism, and populism can make this conundrum make sense.

Introducing coloniality

Many of the critiques of liberalism mentioned earlier are common knowledge, and by no means a new discussion. In addition to these critiques, however, we must read another layer of how democratic thought developed in Europe, and how the field of democratic theory has been shaped in the face of colonialism. Only then can we fully begin to appreciate how populism and liberalism function in this context. This chapter is not an exhaustive overview of colonial history, nor is it a particularly novel contribution to decolonial theory, but it is to be read as an imperative for academic and public debates on populism to also take coloniality into account. It is impossible, I argue, to discuss democracy in Europe without discussing the colonial legacy, which is a fundamental part of who Europeans think they are. As will be developed in Chapter 3, there are psychoanalytical figures that we can use in order to better understand how the European political identity is so strongly intertwined with a sense of superiority, but, for now, let us focus on the substance of that claim – what is it that makes Europeans feel superior and how does this affect the view of political subjectivity and, ultimately, democracy?

Let us begin at the slew of events which all contributed to the rather monumental changes which happened in 15th-century Europe. This is not an attempt to describe these in their entirety, which has been done well by many others (Maldonado-Torres, 2008; Mignolo, 2011; Pitts, 2005); we can simply focus on a few. One of them is world-making, where the limits of the universe were changing, both literally and figuratively. Central to this change was a renegotiation of how Europeans interacted with the continent's 'others', often termed as the barbarians. In Medieval Europe, based on the Latin definition of the word 'barbaria', which was a common denominator for any foreigners or strangers, the term also carried a connotation of being uncivilized and badly mannered. This normative value is imparted in a word which was primarily onomatopoetic – the language of the Gauls sounded like 'bar bar' in the ears of the Romans.

The connection between heritage and manners is what lays the foundation of what is to come: the conflation between civilisation and European Christianity (Kundnani, 2023). This, however, must be nuanced by the fact that Renaissance scholars, such as Machiavelli, were convinced that European strength lay in its prominence of man over God, as later developed by Nietzsche (1996). This is a historic minefield, however, where some scholars would argue that this alleged secularism simply replaces one political theology with another (Maldonado-Torres, 2007), and that Machiavelli, for all his talk of separation of Church and State also remained conspicuously interested in witches and other supernatural phenomena (Bartelson, 1995). One cannot, as such, claim a definitive point where modernity started, where the rise of man replaced God. The modern claim to universality is, however, what becomes a central point for European world-making, that European values and customs could be said to represent a superior mode of being, for all peoples of the Earth. In order to fully understand the breadth and depth of the influence of colonial conquest on liberal thought, we must engage with the concept of coloniality, as explained by Mendoza:

> decolonial thinkers suggest that slavery, forced labor, and the rightlessness of colonized peoples exist in dialectical relation to liberal notions of liberty, equality, justice and free labor. The colony is both the condition of possibility and the proving ground of the Western nation-state, and rights-bearing citizenship tethered to men of property. In other words, the freedom of the European and the colonial settler depends on the unfreedom of the colonized. (Mendoza, 2015)

Coloniality is a term developed by Quijano (2007, 2000) and later reworked by decolonial scholars such as Mignolo (2011), Dussel (1977, 1994), and Maldonado-Torres (2007). Coloniality enables us to see the development of race and the modern state in the light of colonial conquest, and as a direct co-constitutive element of it. Quijano thus departs from many scholars working on colonialism from a Marxist perspective and makes the claim that colonialism created a division of labour not only based on geography but also on the construction of race. Coloniality, as different to colonialism or colonization, indicates how this is an ongoing process and not, like many argue, a thing of the past. Coloniality, the mindset of colonialism, is still a fundamental part of society today (Quijano, 2000). For decolonial theory, the racism, exclusion, and inequality that European states have favoured during modernity is not disjoint from the colonial experience, but rather wholly dependent on it, indicating the 'dark side of modernity' (Maldonado-Torres, 2007, p 244; Mignolo, 2011). Even though both Quijano and Mignolo recognize that race and racism has looked different throughout the centuries, there is still a common core to the desire to create hierarchies between peoples. This hierarchy certainly exists in economic terms, but runs deeper than simply conceiving of political subjects as subjects in the wage-labour relation (Grosfoguel, 2007). Rather, for decolonial theorists, and in particular Quijano, these relations are connected:

> Coloniality of power is based upon 'racial' social classification of the work population under the Eurocentered world power. But coloniality of power is not exhausted in the problem of 'racist' social relations. It pervaded and modulated the basic instances of the Eurocentered capitalist colonial/modern world power to become the cornerstone of this coloniality of power. (Quijano, 2007, p 171)

Thus, for Quijano, we must also look to other areas of social and political life to fully understand the impact of coloniality (Mignolo, 2007; Quijano, 2007). This has given rise to what is termed the *colonial matrix of power*, which consists of four interrelated domains: 'control of economy (land appropriation, exploitation of labour, control of natural resources); control of authority (institution, army); control of gender and sexuality (family, education) and control of subjectivity and knowledge (epistemology, education and formation of subjectivity)' (Mignolo, 2007).

The decolonial inquiry into the underlying assumptions of modern thought continues with an attack on phenomenology, Descartes, and the *ego cogito*. Both Dussel and Maldonado-Torres, the latter inspired by the former, are wholly unconvinced of the presumed 'neutrality' of the division between mind-body and endeavour to situate Descartes' thinking in its colonial context. We must, they argue, engage with how the mind-body distinction cannot be disjoint from all the hierarchies that follow in its wake (weak/strong, European/non-European, man/woman, civilized/uncivilized, rational/emotional, colonizer/colonized, white/black). The at first sight innocuous division has social and political implications and has justified violent oppression since its inception (Eklundh, 2020).

Dussel argues that instead of the *ego cogito*, we should define modern subjectivity by the *ego conquiro*: 'This ontology does not emerge from nowhere. It emanates from a previous experience of domination of other men, from cultural oppression of other worlds. Before the ego cogito, there was the ego conquiro (and "I conquer" is the practical foundation of "I think therefore I am")' (Dussel, 1977, para. 1.1.2.2, my translation).

This, argues Maldonado-Torres, is an 'unquestioned ideal of self' (2007, p 245). When considering Descartes' development of the *res cogitans* (a thinking thing), Maldonado-Torres and Dussel encourage us to notice how its creation could not have happened without the firm conviction of the white man's superior cognitive qualities. It becomes symptomatic of a world in which the colonized savages were seen as incapable of rationality such that the foundation of being, the beginning of phenomenology, would have to be situated in the most likely place, 'at home'. As such, the 'barbarian' was the obligatory context of all reflection on subjectivity, reason, the *cogito* (Dussel, 1994, p 133). The experience of the European, white man becomes the universal, the measure with which we could understand the world.

The conviction of the superiority of the European mind is intertwined with an equally strong 'Manichean misantropic scepticism' (Maldonado-Torres, 2007, p 246). For Descartes, the only way to fully find certainty, and to prove the existence of the *ego cogito* (and God), was to approach knowledge with scepticism, with rigour, and without former beliefs (Broughton, 2003). However, Dussel and Maldonado-Torres are convinced that this is preceded by a fundamental scepticism about the humanity of the colonized peoples and their ensuing inferiority. The mind-body distinction and all of its related dichotomies (European/non-European, man/woman, civilized/uncivilized, rational/emotional, colonizer/colonized, white/black) must be thought of together and not as disjoint political ciphers. The natural conclusion of misanthropic scepticism (that there is a fundamental difference between humans) explains the continued refusal of centuries of liberal political philosophers to recognize humans as equal – it is, as Maldonado-Torres argues, a 'worm at the very heart of modernity' (Maldonado-Torres, 2007, p 246).

Another key element of the strife towards superiority within modernity lies in what Wynter refers to as a new epoch in the wake of the Copernican revolution (Wynter, 2003). As described previously, the Renaissance and later modernity brought with it an empty space of rule which was no longer filled by an omnipotent God. With the rise of man, the growing scholarship of the humanists, such as Pico della Mirandola, found a way to rehabilitate the power of humans in relation to God. Instead of being weak pawns in a game designed by higher powers, humans were now beginning to be have some power over their own fate, what Wynter terms an 'epochal de-godding' (Wynter, 2003, p 277). Instead of an ever-present God with the power (and will) to intervene at any time, God in Copernican times was a caring God, who had created the world for the sake of man (*propter nos homines*). However, Wynter's and Dussel's understanding of the empty space created by the removal of God as the superior authority over state matters is very different from that of Nietzsche, or even contemporary democratic theorists such as Rancière (1999) or Lefort (1988).

Indeed, most of our modern understandings of democracy rest on the assumption that there is no 'given' authority, that divinity, nobility, or wealth do not afford legitimacy of power. The ensuing discussion, the crux of democratic theory, is to decide who can legitimately occupy the space of power. This, argues Wynter (following Jacques Le Goff, 1992), is a misreading. The divide between the Spirit and the Flesh, the justification for the limited powers of man, was not simply an abstract figure, but also a geographical reality (which can be seen in the distinction between Holy Land/Unholy Land). The habitable/unhabitable division between different zones of the Earth was, by all means, an incarnation of the Spirit/Flesh separation. What happens to this distinction when man becomes a master of his own fate and when it becomes evident that humans also live beyond the sea? According to Wynter, the need for a space of otherness, for humans bound by Original Sin, does not abate, but only changes places. Instead of incorporating *all* of humanity, the Flesh is now represented in the colonized. As such, Wynter sees a change in cosmology which is necessary for man-centrism (Wynter, 2003, p 280). In the end, the rise of man is inseparable from the 'discoveries' of the Americas – man could only master his own fate if there is another division between Flesh and Spirit, that between civilized and uncivilized people. In this sense, there never was an 'empty' space of power, because the fact that man could occupy that space in the first place was always contingent on distinctions between men (Dussel & MacEoin, 1991). The conqueror becomes the authority on the sake of his superior qualities.

Decolonial theory contains a strong critique of gender as another form of oppression (Segato, 2010, 2015). This critique has been advanced by decolonial feminists such as Lugones, who argues that we cannot 'keep on centering our analysis on the patriarchy; that is, on a binary, hierarchical, oppressive gender formation that rests on male supremacy without any clear understanding of the mechanisms by which heterosexuality, capitalism, and racial classification are impossible to understand apart from each other' (Lugones, 2007, p 187). Lugones identifies concomitant problems in contemporary scholarship: white feminists do not take coloniality seriously, and decolonial scholars do not always take gender seriously. The only way forward is to join the two together. These insights have enabled the development of decolonial feminist scholarship, which rejects the idea that gender can be studied without also studying race or capitalism. There are other feminist theories, most notably in postcolonial feminism (Spivak, 2011), that differ from the decolonial approach. Primarily, postcolonial feminism does not believe that capitalism or the modern state system developed the same way in the colonized world as it did in Europe, whereas decolonial theory is much quicker to argue that capitalism as we know it could not have been possible without colonization (Mendoza, 2015). For the purpose of the arguments made in this book, however, both posit a healthy alternative to the mainstream literature on the gendered politics of populism, even though decolonial theory serves as a main source of inspiration.

Decolonial feminism is not a monolithic field and contains several different interpretations both of coloniality and gender (Schiwy, 2007). Quijano is by no means the end all, and is heavily criticized by feminist scholars for treating gender as a biological reality and not as a social construct, and is therefore regarded as closer to the more Eurocentric idea of gender (Mendoza, 2015). It must also be noted, of course, that the most recognized names in decolonial studies (Dussel, Quijano, Maldonado-Torres and Mignolo) are all men (Velez & Tuana, 2020). Similarly, there is some debate on whether patriarchy and gender hierarchies were non-existent in the colonies prior to the arrival of the Europeans (Lugones, 2007) or whether there were indeed some form of gendered social relations but that these were made worse by colonization (Segato, 2022). Regardless, however, there is agreement that a particular form of gendered politics is associated with coloniality, and that this is concurrent with the other forms of violence committed in the name of European superiority. As such, it sees gender as much broader than Quijano's idea of 'sex' or the 'sexual', and that there are gender relations which need not be governed by coloniality (Lugones, 2007, p 189), but at the same time there are hegemonic understandings of gender, primarily through the lenses of dimorphism, heterosexuality, and patriarchy. Lugones aims to keep Quijano's understanding of race and coloniality but wants to develop what she terms the modern/colonial gender system. We are still operating on the basis that modernity/coloniality functions across labour, sex, collective authority, and intersubjectivity. As such, Quijano presents coloniality as 'a conception of humanity ... according to which the world's population was differentiated in two groups: superior and inferior, rational and irrational, primitive and civilized, traditional and modern. Primitive referred to a prior time in the history of the species, in terms of evolutionary time' (as cited in Lugones, 2007, p 192), but the gender aspect of this needs to be specified. Lugones here draws on the concept of intersectionality (Cho et al, 2013) to argue that it is indeed only when we fuse race and gender that we can fully understand current power relations. We cannot comprehend the reality for women by solely looking at their racialized identity – their gender is likely to exacerbate inequality. Importantly, this is a product of coloniality – with the introduction of the European state system came the exclusion of women from spaces where they had previously been included (Oyěwùmí, 1997, p 123): 'the transformation of state power to male-gender power was accomplished at one level by the exclusion of women from state structures. This was in sharp contrast to Yoruba state organization, in which power was not gender-determined.' As such, there were two simultaneous processes of inferiorization, one of non-whites and one of women. The binaries of civilized/uncivilized and rational/emotional must thus be differentiated between genders, not simply race. Colonization therefore also meant the destruction of social relations not based on patriarchy.

This is fundamental for understanding the development of political subjectivity in Europe. It becomes vital to understand that we are not simply dealing with an open discussion of who is most suited to rule (as liberal democratic thought often positions itself), but that this discussion has already concluded. When reading the founding fathers of liberalism, their rather limited commitment to democracy and political participation is therefore not particularly surprising – it is simply another articulation of the necessity of the rule of European man.

The colonial underpinnings of liberalism

We can see the traces of coloniality clearly within liberalism. In particular, one cannot understand the rise of modern Europe without the concept of race and gender, as per Quijano's colonial matrix of power. Racial and gender categories, and the social hierarchies that they produce, are the fundament upon which European democracy rests, and has done since its early inceptions.

The racial aspect of liberalism is acutely present, but constantly overlooked. In Hobbes (1991, p 89), the state of nature is not a fictional segment of imagination, but the very real living conditions of the 'savage people in many places of America'. The state of nature, and man's capacity to overcome it, was never disjoint from the context in which it was developed, where the white man ruled superior. Colonial conquest was made possible by liberal reasoning, and vice versa. John Stuart Mill contended that the very possibility for society rested on the fact that some people are civilized, and some are not (Mills, 1999, p 66). Mill was of course influenced by his more radical father, James Mill, and still supported his father's crude assessment of the Indian peoples (Pitts, 2005, p 133). Much like many of the liberal philosophers at the time, Mill considered the people of the colonies backwards (he often refers to them as 'children'), and while he did not subscribe to biological determinism, he firmly believed in a national 'character' which determined the outcomes for societies. But, there is always a possibility of improvement, primarily through a despotic and civilizing rule (Pitts, 2005, p 139).

This can be clearly seen also in other founding fathers of liberal thought. For instance, John Locke was keen to distinguish between peoples and peoples, and it must also be noted that he was an investor in the Royal Africa Company, known for its trade in slaves. Locke emphasized the beneficial nature of colonization, where the white man essentially rescued the savages from a much worse fate – the knowledge and capacity of European men would contribute to administration and general order in society (Williams, 1995, p 103).[1] A similar argument was made by Rousseau, who as a contractualist was in many ways more supportive of democracy than Locke, but was convinced that Europeans were superior due to their use of wheat and iron, completely oblivious to the fact that wheat is not a native European crop, and that metallurgy (though not with iron) was significantly more advanced in the Inca and Aztec empires. Rousseau confirmed that the regressive societies outside of Europe were such because 'both metallurgy and agriculture were unknown to the savages of America, who have therefore always remained savages' (Rousseau, 1984, p 116). Such a perspective is also not simply a thing of the past, but similar discourses are found in books such as *Guns, Germs and Steel* (Diamond, 2019), where the case is made that

Europeans are indeed a more successful people (not a race), due to fortunate weather conditions and particular skill sets (Restall, 2003).

The gendered aspects of liberal thought are glaring, and it is particularly evident in contractualism. While there are significant differences between them, most Enlightenment political thought struggles to understand the woman as a political subject. In the end, they get themselves into knots to argue that women are, at the same time, too feeble to be thought of as true parties in the social contract, but all the while fully capable to enter into the marriage contract. While Hobbes constitutes an exception in arguing that a conjugal contract is also a political contract (Hobbes, 2009, p 121), others are less optimistic about the capacities of women. Pufendorf for instance, is convinced of the natural occurrence of marriage, which is always consensual, since 'the man enjoys the superiority of his sex' (Pufendorf, 2005, p 853). Locke, on the other hand, is very clear that men and women are different, since he excludes women from the category of the individual (which is otherwise such a fundamental category in liberalism). This may seem contradictory to some, who contend that Locke did see women as capable of owning property. However, as astutely argued by Pateman, Locke still perceives the subjectivity of women as part of the state of nature. As such, the submission of women in the marriage contract is a natural phenomenon, and not a political event. Even Rousseau, who otherwise is quite at odds with many of the conclusions of Hobbes, Pufendorf, and Locke, agrees that 'civil order depends on the rights of husbands over their wives' (Pateman, 1988, p 53).

Pateman thus brings out the inherent contradiction in contractualism: women are at the same time able and unable to enter into contracts and be regarded as political subjects. They are unable to form social contracts in civil society, but expected to enter conjugal contracts in the private sphere (upon which the civil sphere rests). The contradiction, says Pateman, emanates from a general implicit assumption in social contract theory about property. For most of the contractualists, the basis of contract presupposes an exchange of property (in its widest sense) between individuals. This property is not simply material goods, but equally one's body and labour. The importance for the social contract is that such an exchange must assume that the exchanging parties recognize each other as property owners, that is being able to control their bodies and labour: 'a necessary condition of such protection is that each individual recognize the others as property owners like himself. Without this recognition others will appear to the individual as mere (potential) property, not owners of property, and so equality disappears' (Pateman, 1988). While this may work in an employment relation, which is a social contract, it is more difficult to employ the same logic to the marriage contract or, for that sake, slavery. Here, social contract theory runs into difficulties, when it maintains that a contract is between equals, but still realizes that what it produces is a contract of subordination. As such, while it is clear that contracts should be between equals and should be entered into voluntarily, the reality of the marriage contract and the slave contract cannot, in any way, be described in these terms. While some, like Rousseau, rejected the slave contract as a social contract in theory (even though he clearly supported the view of slaves as inferior, as discussed previously), he was fully on board with the marriage contract.

Similar lines of reasoning follow liberal thought later on. The works of one of the giants of liberalism, Immanuel Kant, also have a significant racial component. Kant makes a brilliant move, which builds on the concept of civility and rationality in early modern thought. Where Descartes simply created the mind-body distinction as a philosophical figure, Kant makes full use of this when developing his political theory. The rise of rationality as intrinsically central for democratic governance is game-changing and, as I will explain in subsequent chapters, a fundament of European democracies today. However, Kant's political thought is more blatant when it comes to who can be afforded rationality and draws the – at the time uncontroversial – conclusion that rationality is a quality of the white man. This provides the ultimate justification for colonization: savages would be better off managed by a European white man who had his full faculties. Kant does not mince his words when contending that 'so fundamental is the difference between the black and white races of man, it appears to be as great in regard to mental capacities as in colour' (Kant, 1960, p 111). Kant's racial hierarchies came to influence much of later racial biology (Eze, 1995), but even though this field has been discredited and debunked, the assumptions around a capacity to reason and political subjectivity still linger. It can of course be argued that no such racial discrimination exists in modern liberal democracies, but the tendencies to invalidate political action by ethnic minorities, such as Black Lives Matter or the pro-Palestine demonstrations, carry clear analogies with Kant's racial hierarchies. The repeated claims that these actions are either 'too violent' or not civilized enough echo the underlying tenets of racism. For instance, in the wake of the Black Lives Matter movement, *The Washington Post* argued that the actions of the movement could not be taken seriously, partly due to looting, but also the general incivility of the protesters, such as their way of dressing (Reynolds et al, 2015).

The changes to political philosophy in the transition into modernity were ground-breaking, but over the centuries democratic theory would come to nuance and refine the increasingly unpopular assumptions that some are better suited to rule than others. Much of post-Enlightenment political philosophy has focussed on rationality as a key quality for any political subject (Eklundh, 2019) and rejected what has often been termed the 'hysteric' plebs. Interestingly, the central focus on rationality echoes the early modern and Enlightenment writings on civility as a key feature of political life.

In the 19th century, when resistance to the squalid conditions for most people in the early days of industrialization grew at a steady pace, there was a renewed interest in the concept of the tyranny of the majority. The majority, it was said, could under democratic conditions rob legislators of their law-making powers, and further wreak havoc in the careful balance between rulers and ruled. The answer was simple: resistance to state and market power was not only a nuisance, but even pathological. Individuals who fought for equal rights should not only be prosecuted, but medically treated for their conditions. This was the birth of crowd psychology, which to this day influences common assumptions made about certain political actors, often those who are outside the political establishment. Crowds were, according to French theorist Gustave Le Bon (1960), primitive and highly damaging for individuals and society alike. Civility, and therefore the right to participate in democratic decision-making, in other words, was out of reach for most people, and bestowed on the property-owning classes. Similar thoughts can be seen in Schumpeter's disdain for the common man who partakes in collective action – 'he becomes a primitive again' (Schumpeter, 1976) or even in later American political science, with the arrival of rational choice theory and the claims to a 'civic culture' (Almond & Verba, 1963).

Contemporary liberalism and the spectre of coloniality

Over the years I have had countless conversations with commentators and political theorists about the problematic origins of liberal democracy, and how we must all come to recognize the injustices committed in the past. Most of the time, this is an uncontroversial point – even Boris Johnson, perhaps one of the more outspoken fans of British colonial history, has argued that the end of the British Empire was 'fundamentally a good thing'.[2] Nevertheless, he also represents a large share of the British population (43%) who consider the British Empire and colonialism in a positive light (Stone, 2016). This raises the question of whether the racism so fundamental to the colonial projects has really softened over time, and whether the liberal democracy we are now so fond of is not tarnished by these assumptions? Many would contend that while things are sometimes bad, they are still better than before. In a recent blog post, public intellectual Anand Menon, director at research institute UK in a Changing Europe (and of British Asian descent), argues that despite the recent race riots in the UK in summer 2024, we are miles ahead of where we were (Menon, 2024).

As such, we are faced with a conundrum once again: if liberalism and liberal democracies are such strong defenders of equality, why are we experiencing such rampant racial and gender inequality? Why is populism so successful in Europe, which should by the same logic be the least favourable environment for such movements? The short and somewhat depressing answer is that liberal democracies in Europe are not particularly concerned with equality, and that the slow progress (and sometimes regression) is due to a refusal of liberal theory to fully engage with the racial question, with gender, or with coloniality.

Nowhere is this more obvious than in the works of John Rawls, probably the most influential liberal theorist of the 20th century. Political philosopher Charles Mills has taken on the mastodon task of mapping the presence (or rather absence) of the concept of race in Rawls' work. Much of the racial discussion boils down to the lingering commitment to rationality, and how this is tied to the affordance of political subjectivity – if you are not rational, then you cannot participate in political deliberation. Rawls, and his many followers, does not recognize how rationality has historically simply been a question of skin colour or gender (cf. Kant, mentioned earlier), and how the current incarnations of rational thinking often seem to benefit some political actors over others (Eklundh, 2020). Rawlsians and contemporary liberals would rather argue that rationality today is race- and genderless, but seem to be oblivious to the notion that the simple statement 'I don't see colour' is itself racist (Morrison, 1992).

According to Mills, Rawls suffers from racial amnesia. In one of his most coveted works *A Theory of Justice* (Rawls, 1999a), he does not even mention American slavery, only briefly discusses the possibility of slavery and serfdom, and makes some references to the non-racial slavery in ancient Rome (Mills, 2017, p 142). The concept of race does appear, but only as a 'fixed natural characteristic that cannot be changed' (Rawls, 1999a, p 84). Rawls tried to make amends in *Political Liberalism*, and discusses race and slavery more in-depth, but largely as a historical phenomenon. In *The Law of the Peoples* (Rawls, 1999b), there should be ample opportunity for Rawls to engage with racism and colonialism, seeing that this book is about international relations. Unfortunately, Rawls seem to regard the most significant racial crimes, such as the Holocaust and the slave trade, as 'unique' (Rawls, 1999b, p 19), not recognizing the work of scholars who have demonstrated racial thinking as integral to European state-building (as discussed previously). As Mills points out 'he refers briefly to the "empire building" of European Nations, but makes no reference to the genocide of non-European peoples as part of this process' (Mills, 2017, p 145). In fact, there are no references in any of his main works to Native Americans, or to the transatlantic slave trade (Mills, 2017, p 149).

As such, it is quite obvious that race and racial inequality is not the main point for Rawls; he rather bases his analysis of inequality on an idea of the European working class, who is mainly conceived of as white (Mills, 2017, p 152). In Rawls' universe, the European experience seems to be spared from racial exclusion, which, as we know, is a highly problematic and inaccurate statement (Bhambra, 2017). As argued by Bhambra, the constant exclusion of ethnic minorities in the working class bears witness of a methodological whiteness, something which we can clearly notice in Rawls, but also more generally in the discussion of the working class in Europe (Mondon & Winter, 2018).

Mills argues that Rawls justifies these absences in two ways. First, he claims that since he is working with the 'classical' tradition, it is impossible to import issues such as race and gender since these do not form part of the ideal, and are only seen as blips in the implementation of a fair system, which in analytical political theory is called partial compliance or non-ideal theory (Rawls, 2001, p 66). This is, to put it mildly, a very surprising assessment, and simply erases how centuries of racial and gender discrimination were integral to the design of liberal democracy, as mentioned earlier. As argued by a wide range of scholars, the principles for the white population also gave us plenty of information about how the non-white population should be treated (Mills, 2017, p 153; Pitts, 2005).

Second, Rawls only aims to 'present certain principles of justice and then to check them against only a few of the classical problems of political justice as these would be settled within ideal theory' (Rawls, 2001, p 66). He is essentially arguing that since race and gender discrimination do not form part of a just society, they are not part of ideal theory. The problem, says Mills, is that ideal theory's main function is to suggest ways forward to a better and fairer society (Mills, 2017, p 155). But when Rawls is talking about ideal theory, we get the impression that we are concerned with the *ideal* ideal, which bears little resemblance to our current reality. The *ideal* ideal, says Mills, presupposes that we can construct a new society from scratch without race as a social function. While this may be laudable, it is also wholly impossible: 'ideal theory represents an unattainable target that would require us to turn back the clock and start over. So in a sense it is an ideal with little or no practical worth' (Mills, 2017, p 158). In sum, Rawls is ignoring our non-ideal history and all of its injustices: 'what is ideally called for under ideal circumstances is not, or at least is not necessarily, what is ideally called for under non-ideal circumstances' (Mills, 2017, p 158).

Similar critiques against Rawls, but regarding gender, have been made by Pateman (1988), who traces how Rawls employs the Kantian idea of reason to construct the original position of political subjects. For Rawls, as for Kant, the individual sheds their worldly attributes and becomes a sexless, raceless being. Behind the veil of ignorance, there is only reason. Therefore, when we make claims about how people act as political subjects we can, says Rawls, 'view the choice in the original position from the standpoint of one person selected at random'. The problem, argues Pateman (an argument later employed by Mills as well), is that the examples which Rawls uses to support his theory are nothing of the sort. Rawls repeatedly claims that political subjects have 'descendants' or that they are 'heads of families' (Rawls, 1999a, p 139). As Pateman eloquently puts it: 'he merely takes it for granted that he can, at one and the same time, postulate disembodied parties devoid of all substantive characteristics, and assume that sexual difference exists, sexual intercourse takes place, children are born, and families formed' (Pateman, 1988, p 43). If seen through a decolonial lens, it becomes obvious that Rawls thus falls foul of the same universalizing mission as Descartes: the original position is chosen at random, but, unsurprisingly, this position is that of a white man. Rationality and reason cannot be decoupled from their speaker.

Another key figure in liberal thought, Jürgen Habermas, struggles with similar issues. Just like Rawls, Habermas is convinced of the procedural advantages of what he terms communicative action (Habermas, 1984). The common good can and will be agreed on through mutual recognition of our interlocutors as rational, and whether their claims can be deemed valid. Habermas thus draws on the same Kantian heritage as Rawls.

The problem, as has been pointed out by several scholars (Casullo, 2020; Chatterjee, 2004), is that even though both Habermas and Rawls allegedly work in the abstract (the model of communicative action can work anywhere and is a general theory), there is an implicit assumption about how we can recognize rationality when we see it. Even though the procedure should, in theory, be able to be applied to any cultural or ideological context, it becomes evident that there is a particular context, culture and ideology which serves as the blueprint: European liberal democracies. The theory is therefore more substance than form, at the end of the day. As such, Habermas also commits the errors of an assumed universality – similarly to Descartes who based his whole oeuvre on the experience of the European white man, Habermas has clear articulations about what rationality looks like, in the wild. While this is less obvious in his earlier work, in *Between Facts and Norms* (Habermas, 1996), the full force of Habermas' assumptions comes to light:

> First, a robust civil society can develop only in the context of a liberal political culture and the corresponding patterns of socialization, and on the basis of an integral private sphere; it can blossom only in an already rationalized lifeworld. Otherwise, populist movements arise that blindly defend the frozen traditions of a lifeworld endangered by capitalist modernisation. (Habermas, 1996, p 371)

It becomes clear that Habermas harbours no doubts about the necessity of liberalism for a fully working society, and that this liberal culture is also an example of a 'fully rationalized lifeworld'. On the other hand, we are to understand that non-liberal societies and cultures are those caught in 'frozen traditions'. We are thus made aware that the lifeworld has a place; the non-rationalized societies exist somewhere. One need not look far to understand which examples Habermas is referring to here: countries outside the Western world who have failed to embrace liberalism and capitalist modernization. These are also the places that can fall prey to populism, which Habermas, like so many others, posits at the opposite end of the political spectrum. Habermas explains that in the absence of a liberal public sphere, there is a risk of an 'accumulation of indoctrinated masses that are seduced by populist leaders' (Habermas, 1996, p 382). As such, even though the model of communicative action purports to retain neutrality regarding the substance of the public good, it is deeply embedded in a context where European rationality is seen as the superior mode of governance.[3] Habermas thus repeats the same liberal mantra as we have seen before: the liberal public sphere enables us to legitimately fill the empty space of power. There is little acknowledgement that if the empty space of power can only be legitimately filled by processes which are favourable to the European liberal context, then there is no 'empty' space of power in the first place. What is sold as an open competition has already been decided.

As such, the heritage of liberalism and its questionable democratic credentials lives on in its contemporary incarnations. To argue that racial and gender discrimination do not form part of a just society has functioned to silence discussions on these very topics – critical race theory, for instance, is labelled as cultural Marxism and gender theorists are attacked from so-called gender-critical feminists (who oppose trans rights). In this climate, it is difficult to see how liberalism is the ultimate defender of democracy and equality and how populism would be categorically different.

Conclusion

In this chapter, I have argued that the characterization of populism and the liberal mainstream as strange bedfellows is wholly mistaken. By tracing the fundamental rejection of equality throughout liberal political thought, both in theory and practice, I have demonstrated that liberalism is not, and never has been, a guarantor of a democratic society. Instead, much of what we consider the 'ills' of contemporary democratic society can be traced down to the axioms of liberalism. In particular, the chapter has emphasized that the problem with liberal democracy is not simply one of implementation, or of corruption and co-optation, but one of design. Nor is it a problem local only to neoliberalism. Turning to the concept of coloniality, I have pointed to how the very development of modern subjectivity (and therefore also of statehood and political identities) has been marred by a wish to keep some elements of society excluded from the democratic 'People'. This means that the distinction that is typically made between liberalism and elitism is also put into question. Both of these perspectives can be traced to a colonial view of European superiority, based on the civilized Peoples of Europe. In this light, recent political events are not so strange. The rise of right-wing populism and the mainstreaming of right-wing policies is not something that is foreign to the European core – the intellectual and political heritage, on which European democracies rest, is largely in line with what right-wing populism proposes. A return to a distinction between peoples and peoples is only just that, a return.

This has far-reaching consequences for how we view populism. If, as argued earlier, the very foundation of the European liberal centre is agreeable to constructing a hierarchy between desirable and undesirable political subjects, if it is unwilling to face the fundamental racial and gender injustices which have built our contemporary states, then how can we conceptualize the 'populist' as something external and threatening to democracy? Is it not the case that the threat to equality comes not from any external force, but from within the European mainstream?

In the next chapter, I will map how the field of populism studies is still in the grip of the liberal narrative: it struggles to free itself from a commitment to the assumption that liberal democracy has promoted an equal society. Much of this is because there are similar silences in populism studies as there are in liberal political thought. There is no strong conceptualization of coloniality, of how liberalism has developed in conjunction with colonialism, and how the questions of race and gender need to be centre stage for any fruitful analysis of our current political conjuncture. However, there are important differences in the focus of the debate. Whereas some may be less disturbed by the conclusions of this chapter – that liberalism is elitist at heart – it may be more controversial to argue that populism, too, is marred by an elitist mindset.

2

Coloniality and Exclusion in Contemporary Populism Studies

Over the past few years, the number of works on populism has exploded. From being a term that was only used occasionally, it is now commonly used throughout political science research, not to mention public debate (Hatakka & Herkman, 2022). In the wake of this exponential rise, we can see certain trends in how populism is treated. There are varying views on how populism is defined, and how it relates to the European democratic project. This chapter will not be engaging in simply a definitional discussion of populism, and will not primarily focus (once more) on the by now rather familiar debates on whether populism is a strategy (Rueda, 2021; Weyland, 2021), ideology (Mudde, 2004, 2007), discourse (Laclau, 2005), or style (Moffitt, 2016; Ostiguy, 2017). Nor will this chapter engage with whether populism is a nominal or an ordinal problem (as argued by Ostiguy (2017). These discussions, while worthwhile and central to the field, do not grapple with the question most important to this book: what if populism is actually the European mainstream? This chapter investigates how populism studies conceptualize democracy, and what relationship populism has with 'European' democratic values. It traces how populism studies have very diverging answers to this question, ranging from seeing populism as diametrically opposed to democracy, to seeing populism as simply another form of doing politics. What is common to all of these perspectives is a general unwillingness to discuss the violent and exclusionary history of European politics, as described in the previous chapter. Populism studies do not, on the whole, talk about colonialism, or how the field is situated in an empirical context which does not particularly favour equality.

This chapter will place a particular emphasis on the least likely offenders of this oversight. While we may expect such silences from some areas of populism studies, the more critical segments of the research should be well placed to engage with the fundamental inequality at the heart of European political thought. However, and as I will demonstrate, this is not necessarily the case, and the silences about colonial violence and the integral flaws of liberal thought are present in mainstream and critical scholarship alike. Importantly, there is a lingering 'myth of civility' – that there indeed is a democratic liberal culture in Europe – which haunts the field and embeds it in the elitist discourse of liberalism.

Furthermore, this chapter discusses the mistaken idea that populism in its current incarnation is at complete odds with elitism. As will be demonstrated later, throughout populism studies we can discern an unwillingness to recognize that what we often term 'the People' is, in fact, the 'Elites'. By not discussing coloniality, or how the exclusionary elements of liberalism completely align with populist politics, we cannot feasibly argue that the People are anything but yet another articulation of the unequal power relations in Europe. As such, it is only by understanding that the 'populist condition' means a constant favouring of the Elites that we can truly start to grasp the empirical realities of European politics today.

The chapter will outline how different areas of the field relate to the question of coloniality, how they treat the relationship between populism and liberalism, and where we may see ways forward to understand populism in Europe. The chapter will begin with how populism is often seen as a threat and totally antithetical to liberalism, which will largely be refuted. After this the chapter will sketch how populism can be seen as democracy's underside, as an integral part of democracy, or as simply another political identity. It will then discuss the progressive potential of populism, and point out how scholars who believe that populism can be progressive must do more to recognize the importance of colonial heritage in Europe. The last part of the chapter will connect to ongoing debates about the separation between the People and the Elites. The chapter will argue, following from the conclusions from Chapter 1, that using decoloniality allows us to see how the boundaries between populists and the elites in Europe are very porous and that the elitist elements of liberalism reign supreme across the continent.

Populism as a threat to democracy

Many would like to start describing the history of populism studies with a conference held at the London School of Economics (LSE) in 1967. Here, prominent academics gathered to discuss the phenomenon, and this has later been seen as a watershed moment, the inception of populism studies as we know it. However, this does not sufficiently recognize the very strong tradition of scholarship on populism in Latin America, which predates the LSE gathering. Seminal works published in the wake of the conference include the 'big names' of populism studies like Berlin, Hofstadter, Ionescu, and Gellner (Berlin & Hofstadter, 1968; Ionescu & Gellner, 1969).

However, many of the insights presented at the conference had already been discussed at length in previous works. Given the strong prevalence of populist movements in Latin America, there was already substantial insight on the topic. Many of these early works are highly critical of populism and argue that it threatened the much-needed modernization of the continent. For instance, Germani, while discussing the class composition of Peronism, concluded that populism was ultimately an authoritarian force and not compatible with democracy (Germani, 1979; Germani & de Yujnovsky, 1973). Similar thought can be detected in Di Tella, who also agreed that the working-class masses were highly susceptible to authoritarian manipulation from the populists (Di Tella, 1965). It is evident that these perspectives are situated in a rather archaic view of how modernization works (Biglieri & Cadahia, 2021; Casullo, 2019), whereas today we have, fortunately, a better grasp on how economic development does not automatically deliver liberal-democratic institutions. This does not prevent the influence from scholars such as Germani and Di Tella to live on in contemporary incarnations, such as the works of De La Torre and Peruzzotti (De La Torre, 2017; Peruzzotti, 2017; Torre, 2015).

This trend has continued in the analysis of populism in Europe today, where the most common and cited works on populism are often the ones that, in line with the myth of civility, clearly identify populism as a threat to democracy. When discussing populism in public and academic debates, Jan-Werner Müller (Müller, 2016) surfaces as one of the first names mentioned. Müller has come to define the field of populism studies, even though his definition of the phenomenon is highly contested. Müller begins with the assumption that populism is a negative development for liberal democracies. He argues that populist leaders play on the fears of voters, and is a particular moralistic imagination of politics, the shadow of democracy where there is a strong quest for unity and anti-pluralism. In Müller's eyes, there can be no doubt about the suggested remedy: the annihilation of the populist tidal wave, and a return to a politics that treats institutions with respect. Müller is not alone in his proposition to label populism as an essentially negative development. Norris and Inglehart, in their recent book (Norris & Inglehart, 2019), argue that while populism can be seen as a symptom of a larger crisis of democracy, their definition also carries negative connotations. Populism is primarily treated as the symptom of malaise and is the expression of a sick society and not of a healthy democracy. This is further sedimented by an array of works which asks what we should do to counter populism, and how it remains a threat to liberal democracy (Rummens, 2017; Urbinati, 2019). From this perspective, it becomes evident that there is a well between the populist idea of democracy and the liberal idea. Rummens goes completely at odds with most decolonial theory when arguing that it is only populism which signifies a 'closure of the empty space of power' (Rummens, 2017, p 559).

As argued in Chapter 1, liberalism itself never constructed an empty space of power, since this was always tainted by restrictions on who could be counted as a political subject, along gender and racial hierarchies. This does not prevent Rummens from arguing that liberal democracies remain open and pluralistic. Rummens thus upholds the liberal myth of that the external legitimation of power really is open, and not tainted by privilege or class. Conversely, it also claims that populism is simply the rule of the unworthy, and that populists are largely illiberal (Mudde & Rovira Kaltwasser, 2012), since it conceives of the People as a homogenous entity and is thus hostile to the protection of minority rights (Rummens, 2017, p 562), an argument also reinforced by Habermas (1996). As such, Rummens confirms that even though there may be traces of democratic thought in populist movements, these rapidly descend into authoritarian thinking once in power. It becomes blatantly obvious that Rummens, Müller and Urbinati do not consider Europe's history of liberalism, and how it in most cases has not offered any 'empty space of power'. Rather, as was demonstrated in Chapter 2, liberalism has a clear elitist dimension, where some are seen as more worthy than others. As such, populism is not so much a threat against liberalism as an open ideology, but a threat against ingrained power relations. Other areas of this field engage with the alleged emotional side of populist politics (Valentim & Widmann, 2021; Widmann, 2021), playing into an age-old trope which argues that populists are (somehow) more emotional than other political actors. This follows another key aspect of coloniality, what I term the 'hegemony of rationality' (Eklundh, 2019, 2020). Rationality, as we have seen in the discussion on liberal thought in Chapter 2, becomes yet another tool for elites to exclude the People. What is interesting is that much of the current scholarship on populism and its alleged emotional character readily reproduce the narrative by Rummens, Urbinati and Müller, that populism is, essentially, a threat to democracy.

Populism as the underside of democracy

There are many other, more nuanced takes on the populist phenomenon, which are not so quick to dismiss populism.[1] However, they are still captive in the colonial frame. The perhaps most widely used interpretation in academic circles is that of Cas Mudde, who has argued that populism is a so-called 'thin' ideology that can be paired with a more 'thick' ideology,[2] such as conservatism or socialism (Mudde, 2004, 2007). Mudde's definition has become the dominant definition of populism in academic circles and is used widely in research that wishes to understand how parties on the left and the right use common tropes (representing the pure People against a morally corrupt Elite) in order to gain electoral advantages. Such studies include both parties on the right (Froio & Gattinara, 2015; Gifford, 2015) and the left (March, 2017). Importantly, however, populism for Mudde is more than simply a political style, consisting of an ideological core, however thin. This ideology could, in theory, be paired with any other thick ideology, meaning we could have liberal populism, but in practice both Mudde and others who apply his framework are largely focussed on the radical right (Stanley, 2008; Zanotti & Turnbull-Dugarte, 2022).

Populism, in this interpretation, signifies a challenge to the mainstream and should be seen as distinct from 'ordinary' democratic politics. In Mudde's view, populism comes as a wish for something which is beyond the present, and that can provide a better form of politics. This perspective, however, has been challenged by a large portion of critical populism studies, which identify populism as an internal component of democracy. Katsambekis has challenged the focus on morality, arguing that there is an implicit understanding of mainstream politics as somehow freed from moralistic discourse, whereas populists are seen as overly moralistic (Katsambekis, 2020). As such, the ideational approach also believes populism to be more emotional (moralistic) and less sophisticated than other, thick, ideologies. These conclusions can be compared to similar thinking around rationality and civility (what forms part of a civic culture) and thus echoes the colonial mindset.

There is, however, also a burgeoning portion of the literature that contends that populism is, and always has been, part and parcel of democratic politics. Populism is not an anomaly, but the very expression of popular sovereignty. Arditi argues that populism is a symptom of democratic politics, and is closer to Rancière's understanding that politics is the enactment of disagreement (Rancière, 1999). However, this symptom is not a direct reflection of democracy (or disagreement) but should be thought of as an 'internal foreign territory' (Arditi, 2005, p 94) or an internal periphery of the democratic order. The concept of symptom, in this sense, comes from Žižek's reinterpretation of Lacanian thought through Marx as 'a particular element [of a structure] which subverts its own universal foundation' (Zizek, 2008, p 47). Populism, accordingly, is characterized as a crucial part of democracy (its very core) but should not be equated with a pristine homogeneity of democratic practice. Arditi encourages us to consider how populism, albeit internal to democracy, can also bring unwanted consequences (as a de-centred core). There is, according to him, a gap that separates populism from democracy, and there is a constant potential pivot to authoritarianism within populism, as embodied in the charismatic leader (Panizza, 2005, p 30). Democracy, thus, for Arditi, cannot be equated with populism, as the latter carries with it 'a fantasy of a unity without fissures' and this 'is present in the populist temptation to confuse the government with the state, which amounts to a perversion of representation' (Arditi, 2005, p 96). For Arditi, it seems as though a version of democracy that is freed from a 'fantasy of unity' exists. Equally, there seems to be a concept of political representation which is different from populist representation. This representation, wherever it exists, does not seem to be subject to the exclusionary patterns of its populist equivalent – real representation is not subject to authoritarian tendencies. Arditi thus supports the figure of the double bind of populism: one democratic and one undemocratic. Throughout Arditi's work, there is a commitment to a democratic ideal that is tightly intertwined with a liberal idea of political subjectivity, and which does not sufficiently acknowledge the undemocratic, colonial, and authoritarian practices of European democracy.

Populism as an inevitable part of democracy

There are scholars that are more inclined to argue that the distance between the European versions of liberal and mainstream democracy and populism is not that great. Like Arditi, Panizza contends that 'populism reminds us of the totalitarian ghosts that shadow democracy' (Panizza, 2005, p 30). Nevertheless, he also argues that all modern democratic societies are a compromise between democratic and non-democratic forces, thus recognizing that there is an inherent problematique in the European democratic ideal. Panizza's work moves towards the collapsing of the opposition between the internal and external forms of democratic practice, which is an advantage compared with the crude view that populism is an exception in European politics. But neither of them fully elaborates how the concept of populism – imaged as the decentred core of modern democracy – relates to the commitment to the myth of civility that accords contours of coloniality to modern European political thought. Both theorists search for ways in which the core of democratic representation could be re-centred, avoiding the drawbacks of the populist ghost, labelling much of European populism as the opposite of the mainstream.

A similar issue, but with a markedly different political undertone, can be detected in Canovan's work. In her widely renowned book *The People*, Canovan masterfully draws out the essence of populism in many ways, explaining the intricacies of popular power. Canovan impresses on us that populism is indeed how we renegotiate the power of the People, where such power may seem insufficient (Canovan, 2005). The account of how populism has been a key feature of democracy for centuries is compelling, but the argument, much like others in populism studies, still suffers from significant blind spots caused by the overt or tacit adherence to the Eurocentric myth of civility. While populism is far from being equated with extremism in Canovan's work, there is a lingering notion that the form of liberal democracy presented in the Western world is unequivocally just, even though it may exhibit, as she terms it, a 'privileged boundedness' in the construction of 'The People'. The privileged boundedness refers to the fact that the People are not universal and always signifies a certain political community that is excluding others. Canovan, for instance, sees the United States as one of the least ethnic forms of nationalism globally: 'The most civic and least ethnic of all is of course American nationhood, in which a population drawn from remarkably diverse ethnic and national origins is united in a collectivity of formidable solidarity' (Canovan, 2005, p 46). Further, she contends that the USA has a 'remarkable capacity to integrate diverse ethnic groups' (Canovan, 2005, p 46).

Canovan here betrays a noteworthy sense of positivity regarding American nationhood, which is surprising but not uncommon. The social contract of the Americas, in the United States and elsewhere, cannot be seen without recognition of who this contract was intended for. As eloquently explained by Mills and Eze, not only do we need to recognize the injustices committed to the native population of the Americas, but we need to subsequently understand how the social contract and nationhood were reliant upon these injustices (Eze, 1997; Mills, 1999, 2017). The 'formidable solidarity' described by Canovan seems less obvious when looking at how Native Americans and African Americans have been treated as less human, and to this day remain disenfranchized due to both political and economic inequality. Canovan, a few pages later, is not oblivious to this fact, as she also explains how the definition of the People is by default exclusionary (Canovan, 2005, p 60). Drawing on Rousseau, she explains how 'this privileged boundedness, which seems so offensively inconsistent with the universal principles professed by liberal democrats, is at the same time the political precondition of those universal principles themselves' (Canovan, 2005, p 61). Canovan here beautifully illustrates how the distance between the exception, the exclusionary populist, and the supposedly inclusionary mainstream liberal democrats is nothing but a chimera. The argument comes to its full conclusion when Canovan describes how demographic change through migration, 'a sudden influx into (say) Australia of twenty million people from a non-democratic political culture would certainly cause violent conflict and might destroy democracy altogether' (Canovan, 2005, p 64). As such, Canovan supports the argument that populism is part of the mainstream, but she is also acutely aware and supportive of the exclusionary underpinnings of the mainstream, relying on the concept of democratic culture as a civic culture (Almond & Verba, 1963). However, she does not elaborate on how the colonial experience has been central to the formation of modern forms of political subjectivities, nor does she engage with how this historical heritage limits the notion that populism is an exception.

Populism as just another political identity

Other theories come closer to recognizing the essential links between the exclusionary European political subject, populism, and mainstream democratic practice. For Laclau, every political identity, whether class or an ideology, is not a given circumstance that simply has to be accepted, but an articulation. An articulation, contrary to a Marxist idea of class, is a fluid construct that cannot be predetermined. Importantly, however, the conclusion that identities are fluid does by no means indicate that they are happenstance; identities are contingent upon their historical constructions, and always work in contexts, never in a vacuum. Furthermore, the relation between identities and the wider contexts is not neutral. Laclau argues that identities are always constructed in an antagonistic fashion. Taking cues from psychoanalysis, all identities (whether on an individual or collective level) are examples of the Lacanian split subject (Laclau, 2005). As will be further developed in Chapter 3, Lacan's influence pushes Laclau to see societal relations in general, and not only populist ones, as built on division. The division is ingrained in any political subject due to a constitutive lack; there is always an empty space in a political subject that cannot be filled, but the desire to entirely fulfil one's identity is never fading. However, Laclau's concept of antagonism is more complex than simple ideological differences. He argues that identities always comprise what he terms logics of equivalence and difference. Collectives are formed in spite of the differences of certain groups, and the equivalence among them is all based on what they are lacking.

Laclau's concept of hegemony can help us better understand how populism can be seen as the generalizable form of politics in modernity, but also how we must question its violent underpinnings. According to Laclau, the universal presence of the constitutive lack makes any political identity potentially populist. Importantly, this also means that the difference between populists and non-populists is only present temporarily, and as an ever-changing challenge against the status quo. Similar to Panizza and Arditi, Laclau argues that populism is both a threat to the current order and a possibility for something new to be born; it is both subversive and a radical reconstruction (Laclau, 2005). Crucially, though, 'populism never emerges from an absolute outside and advances in such a way that the previous state of affairs dissolves around it, but proceeds by articulating fragmented and dislocated demands around a new core' (Laclau, 2005, p 177). This makes it essential to query and recognize the vestiges and contingencies of the colonial heritage for this new which is yet to be born, but that so often resembles the old status quo. It is vital to acknowledge that both populism and mainstream politics are subject to this contingency. As such, we must acknowledge that the myths of coloniality and civility are either not addressed or sometimes reproduced in some of the central figures of populism studies across several theoretical traditions.

Populism with progressive potential

There are significant empirical studies on how left populism is different from right-wing versions (Agustín, 2020; Casullo & Ostiguy, 2017), and how this impacts the discussion on populism as the exception or as part of democracy (Mudde & Rovira Kaltwasser, 2012). However, this discussion forms part of a longstanding debate on whether populism can, indeed, further progressive movements. Such a discussion was very prominent in Latin America in the first half of the 20th century, when the continent was experiencing many populist movements: quite a few from the left, but also many from the right. This led to the belief that such an impetus was the result of a popular uprising against the elites, which would be emancipatory at its core. This was not particularly the case, however. As was observed already by Jaguaribe, it is a misunderstanding to argue that mass movements are automatically left wing (Jaguaribe, 2013; Ronderos & Zicman De Barros, 2020). Jaguaribe makes the argument that the first examples of populism in Brazil came from the right, and even when the label was subsequently adopted by other politicians, such as Adhemar de Barros, they were still seen as a compromise on the values of the left.[3] Here Jaguaribe follows what Marx had already observed more than a century earlier in his Eighteenth Brumaire: that the lumpenproletariat can deliver a reactionary leader, like what happened with Louis Bonaparte (to be further discussed in the next chapter) (Cowling & Martin, 2002; Ronderos & Zicman De Barros, 2020). A similar line of reasoning was put forward by Ianni, who argued that populist movements must be divided into a popular part and an elite part (Ianni, 1972). Importantly, Ianni was convinced that even though populism might manage to transcend class politics momentarily, there will always be a reckoning between diverging class interests. More recently, similar views can be seen in the works by Portantiero and De Ipola who also reject that populism can be compatible with socialism (Portantiero & De Ipola, 1981).

Funnily enough, these insights from the early examples of populism Latin America seem to be largely absent in the current debate about left-wing populism in Southern Europe. One of the most notable scholars on left-wing populism is Chantal Mouffe, whose recent works include *For a Left Populism* (2018). In particular, in studies on the new left-wing populism in Southern Europe (which will be further developed in Chapter 6), there is growing consensus around the specificities of the left-wing populists, and how their politics focuses on protecting the People from an oppressive Elite. This can be seen in studies on the Spanish party Podemos, where scholars have argued that Podemos stands for an inclusionary form of populism that resists neoliberal globalization and promotes equality (Iglesias, 2015; Kioupkiolis, 2016). We can also see it in studies on the Greek Syriza (Markou, 2017; Stavrakakis et al, 2018), something which will be further elaborated in Chapter 6. It is important to recognize that Mouffe is one of the key founders of radical democratic theory and is widely thought to have transformed the field, paving the way for the perspective on populism as a logic, later developed by Laclau (2005). In her recent works, however, Mouffe specifies how this logic can (and must) take the shape of a left-wing alternative to right-wing populism, and that the articulation of the People cannot be left to the exclusionary ideology of conservatism.

To this end, Mouffe proposes several key theses: that left populism broadens the scope of democracy; that there is a need for a populist moment to break the logic of neoliberalism; that the articulation of the People should take place on the left, rather than on the right, and that left-wing populism will propose a radical break, rather than a rupture, in order to further equality (Mouffe, 2018). Mouffe's diagnostic skills are impeccable. Indeed, there has been a preponderance of right-wing parties claiming to speak for the People, and the left has many times failed to propose political programmes which resonate with the populace on a similar level as, for instance, the xenophobic rhetoric against immigrants. Nonetheless, there are some areas in need of further development. As mentioned earlier, radical democracy was founded in order to counter the narrative of class reductionism. In 1985, after the birth of new social movements, and the clear challenge from the neoliberal narrative, there was a need to reformulate the promise of the left, to include democratic struggles beyond the roles assigned by production. To expand the political subject of the People beyond the working class has been one of the most promising and theoretically exciting developments in left-wing political theory for a long time, and has led to the embrace of feminist, LGBT, environmental, and anti-racist groups by the left. The interesting thing with left populism, however, is that it is still largely situated in the field of economic inequality. Much of this can be seen in the rhetoric against neoliberalism. While Mouffe, following Foucault (2003), recognizes that it is more than an economic ideology – 'neoliberalism also connotes a whole conception of society and of the individual grounded on a philosophy of possessive individualism' (Mouffe, 2018, p 12) – the majority of the grievances described are related to socio-economic status, and often related to the economic crisis and the disappearance of the Keynesian welfare state. This perspective, however, betrays a view of Western European countries which promotes an idea of an equal society, when this was and is so often not empirically accurate. Mouffe claims that the decline of popular sovereignty has happened over the past 40 years, thus disregarding the deeply undemocratic practices of Western democracies present in the post-war period. The loss of popular sovereignty, it seems, can only be experienced if one was included in that sovereignty in the first place. It shows a desire for a past steeped in racial hierarchies, gender discrimination, and violent immigration practices.

Mouffe seems to argue that the problem in modern democracies has somehow started with neoliberalism, and, to be fair, she is not alone in this interpretation which has become largely hegemonic in critical thought (Lazzarato, 2021; Mattei, 2025; Slobodian, 2025). She says that with the arrival of neoliberalism, the 'agonistic tension between the liberal and the democratic principles, which is constitutive of liberal democracy, has been eliminated' (Mouffe, 2018). Neoliberalism, in other words, is the reason why we have seen a depoliticization of issues which were previously at the heart of a democratic society: the tensions between freedom and equality. Nonetheless, this raises questions around how popular sovereignty and equality were conceived of before the arrival of neoliberalism, and there are questions remaining around what popular participation was in, for instance, the post-war period in Europe.

In addition, there is an interesting tension in how Mouffe relates liberalism to democracy. On the one hand, Mouffe argues that democracy need not depend on liberalism, and that there is a democratic tradition which is independent from liberal thought. This tradition holds equality and popular sovereignty as its main values, instead of the liberal rule of law, separation of powers, and defence of individual freedom (Mouffe, 2018, p 14). The relationship between the two, according to Mouffe, is 'only a contingent historical articulation' (Mouffe, 2018, p 14) and it should be possible to conceive of a democratic society separate from liberalism. While I am in full agreement on the latter, the former needs further scrutiny. To what extent can we argue that Western European democracies are separate from liberalism, and is it possible to preserve some of the democratic values embedded in our institutions while discontinuing others (such as the protection of individual freedom)?

On the other hand, and rather confusingly, Mouffe suggests that radical democracy will not signify a break with core liberal-democratic principles. The strategy of left populism 'seeks the establishment of a new hegemonic order within the constitutional liberal-democratic framework and it does not aim at a radical break with pluralist liberal democracy and the foundation of a totally new political order' (Mouffe, 2018, p 45). She further states that the new collective, the new People, will 're-establish the articulation between liberalism and democracy that has been disavowed by neoliberalism, putting democratic values in the leading role' (Mouffe, 2018, p 45). As such, left populism does not propose a complete reworking of the liberal order. It is also obvious that there must have been a more just system which preceded neoliberalism, which would be more akin to a traditional liberal order, balancing between freedom and equality.

Left-wing populism, for Mouffe, seems to simply be a way of reconfiguring a system whose principles are sound. The basic tenets of liberal democracy are not questioned per se, but the problem is seen as one of implementation. What is needed is a creation of a new hegemonic order, but 'it does not require a "revolutionary" break with the liberal-democratic regime' (Mouffe, 2018, p 36). There is also a key reliance on the narrative that liberalism itself need not be the main problem; the problem is the neoliberal cousin that has destroyed the economic prospects for many of the European middle classes. The 'radical' break envisioned here by Mouffe is thus less concerned with questioning the foundations of modern political subjectivities.

Mouffe's work is thus embedded in civility and coloniality. She argues that while right-wing populist demands are many times dangerous, the right-wing populist voter should be rehabilitated. We must, according to Mouffe, 'recognize the democratic nucleus at the origin of many of their demands' (Mouffe, 2018, p 22), framing the question as if the problem were to be found in the form (incivility) of the demands, rather than the content itself. While Mouffe does not agree with the demonization of immigrants, she nevertheless argues that 'the struggle to recover democracy needs to start at the level of the nation state' (Mouffe, 2018, p 71), and that it is 'qua citizens that a social agent intervenes at the level of the political community' (Mouffe, 2018, p 65). She is thus reinforcing the very structures which make migrants the excluded parts and furthering the strength of the European nation state – a format pioneered via the colonial experience (Anderson, 1983) and therefore entangled in the symbolic tapestry of coloniality – as the preferred societal order. It is remarkable that a theory which claims to be based on progressive politics still demonstrates such an unwavering commitment to the very structures that make equality impossible. To argue that the far right is based on a 'democratic nucleus' exhibits a surprising naiveté about what the far right wants. Ultimately, however, it becomes very telling that liberalism is seen as a promoter of equality and a possible vehicle for democratic politics. In addition, Mouffe does not discuss the concept of coloniality, and how it can be relevant to understand how populism and liberalism alike are unable to escape from the elitist underpinnings and structures of European politics.

There are several other works in the field which attempt to salvage populism from the right, from various angles. Stavrakakis (2017), for instance, is similarly to Mouffe convinced about the emancipatory potential of populism, even though his works are less keen to recognize any democratic nucleus of right-wing populists. Marchart is also optimistic about the possibilities of left-wing populism, even though, as he acknowledges, these can be co-opted by right-wing forces (Marchart, 2018). Biglieri and Cadahia take this line of reasoning one step further and argue that populism cannot ever be right wing. They make the claim that all right-wing populisms should rather be referred to as fascisms, and that these are largely incompatible with a Laclauian idea of populism since they are tied to a quest for homogeneity and do not recognize the inherent heterogenous nature of any 'truly' populist project (Biglieri & Cadahia, 2021). They therefore buy wholeheartedly into Laclau's claim that populism is the quintessential expression of the political. As will be further discussed in Chapters 3 and 5, there are, however, remaining questions about the practical examples of populism and their political consequences. Even though we may identify populism as the political on an ontological level, do contemporary examples of populism support this statement?

Performing the 'People' and the 'Elite'

In recent debates, a new perspective on populism has emerged which refutes the rather stale debates on whether it is a strategy, ideology, or discourse. In what is essentially an offshoot to the discursive approach, the socio-cultural approach to populism argues that we can understand populism as a style. The authors of this approach, including Ostiguy (2017), Casullo (2020), Moffitt (2016) and Aiolfi (2022), do not argue that this is simply a question of rhetoric, rather this approach speaks in favour of seeing populism as a performance, where politics must be seen as a wide array of actions and words (Sorensen, 2021). This approach offers a valuable turn to practice within populism studies, since it incorporates non-linguistic elements in the analysis of political actors, where the works of Casullo have been particularly enlightening (Casullo, 2020). Similarly, the works of Sorensen have demonstrated how populism is never only a rhetorical figure and must be understood as a performance (Sorensen, 2021). Nevertheless, there are clear echoes of the previous approaches and, thus, similar blind spots. The socio-cultural approach also places rather strong dichotomies between populism and the mainstream, between People and the Elite and therefore lacks a critical focus on the People–Elite distinction. Even though the analysis of the so-called 'bad manners' of populists can seem initially convincing (who could disagree with the claim that Trump has 'bad language'?), we must dig deeper to see how these dichotomies (Ostiguy, 2017) once again make the connections between populism and elitism invisible. Ostiguy and Casullo, for instance, argue that populism on the right and on the left are different since one is punching up (left wing) and one is punching down (right wing). This, however, simply argues that there are different conceptualizations of the elites on the left and on the right (Casullo & Ostiguy, 2017).

Even if the socio-cultural approach does not place overly normative hierarchies on the populism-elitism division, the simple analytical presence of this distinction says it all. The approach does not sufficiently engage with the fact that such distinctions have been used in order to shut people out from the political arena, rather than including them (Eklundh, 2020).

The concept of coloniality is rarely touched upon, which obscures how populism is much closer to liberalism than previously thought. Further, the approach remains focussed on the form of populist expressions (even though these go beyond text). What remains underdeveloped is an engagement with the practice of populist politics (Eklundh & Ronderos, 2025), what type of society does it promote, and is that radically different from the liberal mainstream?

Questioning the 'People'–'Elite' distinction

There is nascent scholarship in the field which is more attuned to understanding the connections between populism, liberalism, and elitism (Karavasilis, 2025). Much of this is in line with decolonial understanding that liberalism does not offer an 'empty space of power', meaning there is no open and fair competition over who should rule. If elitism is indeed not foreign to populism, current scholarship which constantly pushes the People–Elite distinction as a primary tenet of populism must be put into question. This has been done very successfully by, for instance, Schoor, who argues that there are strong overlaps in the rhetorical figures used by populists and elitists alike (Schoor, 2019). Schoor demonstrates that populist politicians, such as Donald Trump, Boris Johnson, and Thierry Baudet, all portray themselves as the 'good' elite against a constructed 'bad' elite. This breaks down much of the assumed knowledge about the anti-elitism of populist parties and actors. Similar thoughts have been advanced in the growing literature on techno-populism (Hartikainen, 2021; Kioupkiolis & Pérez, 2018), which argues that populism can, at times, justify its own existence with reference to expertise and experience, which goes against most of the scholarship on how the anti-elitism of populists should result in a rejection of experts. Similar views are also present in the works of Caiani and Della Porta, who, in their analysis of the extreme right in Italy and Germany, found that while there was opposition to the current political elites, the concept of elites as such was not rejected, and was rather seen as a desirable feature of a future society (Caiani & Della Porta, 2011).

In addition, Paget introduces the concept of elitist plebeians to further explain how populists may act when they are in power. Using the example of Magafuli in Tanzania, Paget has also noticed the cross-pollination between the People and the Elite. This relates neatly to the work of Venizelos, who has also pointed to how populism is, as we have seen so many times, not an underdog phenomenon but the very highest echelons in society (Venizelos, 2023). Another very compelling argument is made by Bortun, who argues that we must consider the material interests of populist parties, and how they often promote the interests of the capital class (Bortun, 2024), which echoes insights from early Latin American scholarship on populism (Ianni,

1972; Jaguaribe, 2013) about how the revolutionary potential of populism is, sooner or later, compromised by diverging class interest.

Furthermore, the work by de Cleen and Ruiz Casado introduces the concept 'populism of the privileged' in order to indicate the rather spurious definitions behind the terms 'People' and the 'Elite' (De Cleen & Ruiz Casado, 2024). This builds on quite extensive scholarship in the field which questions the claim that populism emerges due to economic inequality and ensuing political disenfranchisement. We must engage with how political and economic elites support populist projects (Benquet & Bourgeron, 2022; Slobodian, 2025). It has, by now, been emphatically debunked that people vote for populist parties due to economic inequality alone (Mondon & Winter, 2018; Norris & Inglehart, 2019; Rooduijn, 2018). Instead, various other explanations are on offer, such as the rise of xenophobia and racism (Mondon & Winter, 2018) or the *perceived* economic inequality among some segments of the middle classes (Norris & Inglehart, 2019). In sum, it is clear that the definitions of the 'Elite' are as vague as the definitions of 'the People'. De Cleen and Ruiz Casado see this as an excellent opportunity to advance the claim that the 'Elite' must be understood also from a sociological perspective, and that the 'demands' so often studied in populism research are socially constructed, not a given (De Cleen & Ruiz Casado, 2024, p 1014). While this is clearly the aim of the discursive approach to populism, we have seen an increased debate in the field which seems to treat the demands of populist actors as legitimate grievances (cf. discussion on Mouffe's work, mentioned earlier).

As such, de Cleen and Ruiz Casado put forth that the populism of the privileged must be analysed as a 'specific form of populism'. They indicate that this particular variant can be thought of as either by, with, or for the privileged, indicating the multifaceted nature of populist politics. In particular, they are keen to explain what they see as an *ad faciem* contradiction: how is it possible that a discourse claiming to represent the People is actually implementing the politics of the Elite? In order to solve the puzzle, the sociological approach to privilege helps the authors somewhat along the way. By seeing privilege as not merely economic income, but also comprising social status, education, ethnic origin, etc., we are able to begin to see between the lines of the at first so black and white People–Elite dichotomy. Without unreservedly accepting his class analysis, Ianni's scholarship is extremely instructive (Ianni, 1972). Populism can, and must, be interrogated for what type of society it produces, not simply whether they say, on paper, that they are anti-elitist. Even if populism may, for a moment, indicate a joining of forces from various segments of society, analysis cannot stop there. Rather, we must question the practices, consequences and outcomes of populist politics (Aboy Carlés, 2023), as further will be elaborated in Chapters 4 and 5.

Following a similar line of reasoning, this book argues that the affinities between the People and the Elite are not at all surprising nor contradictory: the populism of the privileged is the only type of populism that we have in Europe. If we take the concept of coloniality seriously, it becomes obvious that populism in its European incarnations is built on the superiority of Europeans *tout court*. Importantly, that superiority is not limited to economic wealth – as argued in the previous chapter, the economic wealth of Europeans was only made possible due to the construction of racial superiority (a sociological category, if you will). All the different forms of privilege that we can think of – be those class, education, gender, sexuality, religion – must be situated within the colonial matrix of power. It is only when we begin seeing that these different types of privilege are connected that we can fully understand how populism operates in Europe, namely at its political core. Importantly, populism typically does not reject the exclusionary politics in Europe but acts as its main proponent. Crucially, this is not done *in opposition to* the mainstream or the status quo, but *in conjunction with* the mainstream and the status quo. Variations exist across the continent, of course, but what de Cleen and Ruiz Casado have identified as a possible anomaly, seems, at the end of the day, to be the norm. Populists and non-populists alike are, by all accounts, steeped in Europe's colonial history

This leads us on to another very common argument in the populism literature, that what we are currently witnessing is a mainstreaming of right-wing populist ideas into the political centre. This thought has been championed by a variety of scholars (Brown, 2024; Brown et al, 2021; Brown & Mondon, 2020; Katsambekis, 2023), who have, quite successfully, demonstrated that so-called mainstream parties often adopt the rhetoric and policy proposals of the far right. What is important to note here is that these scholars most often do not use the term 'populism' to indicate what they view as a primarily far-right agenda.

Nevertheless, this scholarship offers valuable lessons for how the mainstream and the far right are constructed, and how this affects our discussion on the People–Elite distinction. First and foremost it is vital to recognize the very empirical dimension of this work, which has demonstrated beyond all reasonable doubt that we have seen a significant turn to the right over the past 20 years in the Western world (Mondon & Winter, 2018). Such a turn, it is argued, must be explained by an increased willingness to sympathize with far-right demands. For instance, the excellent work by Mondon and Winter investigates how such a turn to the right has been justified with reference to 'the People' and that far-right views and perspectives must be headed if voiced by 'ordinary people' (Mondon & Winter, 2020, p 147). Much like the scholarship mentioned in the previous section, Mondon and Winter debunk the idea that 'the People' are really very ordinary: voters of populist parties come from all socio-economic bands, and cannot be said to belong to the poorest in society.

There is also a constant reminder for Mondon and Winter that liberalism, instead of acting as a guarantor against injustice and inequality, is actually very much to blame for the racist and exclusionary society that we see today. Mondon and Winter distinguish between what they term 'illiberal' and 'liberal' racisms, and even though there are differences between the two, the lingering sentiment is the same. Mondon has further developed this in what he terms 'the bulwark fantasy', which dispels the myth that liberalism protects society from evil reactionary forces (Mondon, 2024). As such, 'really existing liberalism has been a more or less active enabler rather than a bulwark' (Mondon, 2024, p 2). The term 'really existing liberalism' puts the focus on the violent nature of liberal thought, as described in the previous chapter. Liberalism, it turns out, is not an ideology based on a commitment to equality, but to the preservation of privilege, as argued in Chapter 1. The mainstreaming thesis, however, still maintains that the mainstream *imports* ideas and ideologies from the far right (Gillespie, 2024). This is contrary to the argument of this book, which contends that those ideas have been present in the liberal mainstream all along, just articulated differently. I argue that the cipher of coloniality enables us to see how the difference lies not between populists and the mainstream, but between recognizing that coloniality exists, or not.

The conclusions from the works previously discussed are very useful and really further our understanding of the problematic relationship between the Elite and the People. There are clear synergies between the works of de Cleen and Ruiz Casado, on the one hand, and Mondon and Winter, on the other. In both cases, however, there is a missed opportunity in using the concept of coloniality to fully understand the relationship between liberalism, elitism, and populism. While we are moving in the right direction and beginning to break down the assumed barriers between the three, we must consider how coloniality can help us better understand the 'strange bedfellows'. Here, looking towards the histories of populism studies is essential, which reveals that many of the early examples of populism were not compatible with a revolutionary aim (Ianni, 1972; Jaguaribe, 2013; Singer, 2009): populism is a project of the right.

As I demonstrated in Chapter 2, the death of God did not create an empty space of power which could be filled after careful consideration over worthy candidates. In fact, ever since, liberalism has worked overtime to justify why some people (who typically belong to the Elite) should continue to be in a position of power. As such, the distinctions between liberalism and elitism are easy to break down, and break them we must if we are to understand our current political landscape. Where does that leave populism? As we have learnt, populism is deeply connected both to elitism and to liberalism. While this surprises some scholars and commentators, it is to be expected. Overshadowing any possible distinctions between liberalism, elitism, and populism is the reality of the design of European politics: a design reliant upon keeping some forces as far away from the political scene as possible. Such exclusions can take many forms, as has been rightly identified by many scholars mentioned in this chapter, but all carry something in common. At the heart of the matter lies a worldview tainted by coloniality, which can express itself through race, gender, or class hierarchies, or all of them mixed together. Populists, therefore, when constructing the demos, are doing the same exclusionary work done by liberalism for hundreds of years.

Where does this leave the study of populism? As will be further developed in the next chapter, there is a small but very important part of the field which is increasingly seeing a critical engagement with the colonial frame. The work of Grattan, for instance, points to the fact that what she terms the 'open-source' coalition promise of left populism can also be a major problem, as long as 'such efforts retain the material and affective attachments to whiteness that have characterized populist moments across the political spectrum' (Grattan, 2021, p 137). Grattan details the conflicts and tensions between Black activists in the United States who want to abolish racial capitalism and the populist project of Bernie Sanders. Even though Sanders was, clearly, a better alternative for the left than many others, there are what Grattan calls 'representative failures' where marginalized groups are not represented by the populist project, due to its historical commitment and reliance upon a colonial world order. A similar argument has been made by Kleinberg, who argues that Jean-Luc Mélenchon, the left populist presidential candidate in France, has a strong commitment to French republicanism, which is often at odds with minority and human rights (Kleinberg, 2023). McKean has also pointed to how the new left populism in Southern Europe, Podemos and Syriza, do not have a thorough engagement with the question of race, and that this is mirrored in Laclau's theory of populism, which does not address this topic sufficiently, either (McKean, 2016).

Conclusion

In this chapter, I have presented an overview of populism studies and how many areas of the field largely remain in the grip of a colonial world view. In some sense, this is not surprising, since the elitist views of liberal thought are still at the forefront. As we move on to other, more critical, areas of the field, however, I have shown how there is a remaining unwillingness to break with the liberal narrative. In particular, I have shown how in the views of Canovan or Mouffe there are very problematic assumptions about the progressive nature of liberal values. As such, these thinkers do not manage to break away from the narrative that European liberalism is based on equality, which, as we saw in Chapter 1, is not accurate.

However, there is also very valuable work which is beginning to dismantle the strong divisions between populism, liberalism, and elitism, divisions which have only worked to camouflage contemporary power relations. Such work recognizes the elitist nature of populist politics and identifies how the liberal centre in many cases does not differ from what is termed populism. Further, there is scholarship which is outrightly questioning the compatibility between left populism and egalitarian principles, bringing the invisibility of class, gender, and racial hierarchies to the fore.

This nascent scholarship will form the basis for the remainder of this book, where I will argue for a perspective on populism which takes coloniality seriously. Taking coloniality seriously will mean situating populist and mainstream politics in their empirical reality and seeing how this reality is steeped in exclusionary practices, be those race-, class-, or gender-based.

To construct such an alternative, we must see the main fault lines between a decolonial approach to populism and other approaches, primarily the discursive approach. The discursive approach, as mentioned earlier, gives us the possibility of seeing populism as the generalizable form of politics in modernity, something with which I largely agree. It does not, however, discuss at any length the colonial history of Europe, and thus the theory remains largely oblivious to many of the injustices it purports to oppose.

The next chapter will engage with the main question of why we remain in the grip of the colonial mindset, and how this plays out in populist politics. We will see how an affective approach to political identities can explain much of our current predicament, but that this must be sensitive to the historical contingencies of identity construction, something which could be stronger in Laclau. We must also engage with the concept of antagonism, and question how the Schmittian heritage in radical democracy prevents us from having a true commitment to equality. Ultimately, I will explain how populism is not the exception to European politics, and, importantly, it does not manage to transgress the rigid structures of liberalism and elitism.

3

Taking Coloniality Seriously: A New Approach to Populism

In the last chapter, we saw how many areas of populism studies struggle to align the rather contradictory empirical realities of populist parties and movements. On the one hand, populists are seen as anti-elitist, but on the other hand, it is increasingly recognized that there is substantial overlap between the People and the Elites. The last chapter concluded that only by acknowledging the importance of coloniality can we understand how populists and elites are not that divergent, after all.

This does not answer one of the more fundamental questions, however: why is populism so popular as a concept and as a political alternative? What does populism as a concept *do*? This becomes even more pressing in light of the main conclusions of the last chapter, namely that populism is simply another form of politics in modernity, and one which is reliant on and contributing to unequal power relations sedimented in coloniality. Thus, we must ask why we remain in the grip of the colonial mindset. In addition, we need tools to understand the connections between populism, elitism, liberalism, and coloniality.

This chapter returns to the discursive approach and gives an explanation why it in many ways offers a useful framework for understanding populism. However, there are several silences and omissions within the discursive approach which must be taken seriously, such as the increasing similarities between the People and the Elite, and the colonial heritage in Europe. The goal of this chapter is to offer a new perspective on how populism should be understood, an approach which recognizes coloniality as one of the foundational elements of European politics. The chapter will be advocating an approach sensitive to historical contingencies while seeing them as just that, contingent. In this approach, populism does not escape the power structures of the past, it simply reinforces them, be those based on gender, race, or class. As such, populism in its contemporary European form cannot be said to be challenging the status quo, since it does not break free from the European exclusionary mindset. In this vein, it also fails to be progressive (as will be further developed in

Chapters 4 and 5). As such, the chapter will challenge the understanding that populism is an expression of the political, par excellence.

This chapter will begin with an overview of Laclau and Mouffe's approach to populism and describe the main components of this approach. Since this is something that has been done at length in the literature already, this chapter will focus on clarifying the concepts most relevant to this chapter: subjectivity, antagonism, and hegemony.

In the second part of the chapter, the new approach to populism departs from the discursive approach in two key aspects. First, it does not accept the Schmittian problem formulation and argues that Schmitt (a hugely problematic Nazi supporter) cannot possibly function as a figurehead for theories of radical democracy which advocate a fundamental commitment to equality. The rejection of Schmitt leads to a rejection of a theory of antagonism as offered by the discursive approach. This chapter argues that antagonism cannot be seen in a simple us-them dichotomy and seeing it in this limited fashion rather reinforces inequality. Second, it questions the idea that existing and historical examples of populism have been expressions of what is understood as the political. If examples of populism have failed to challenge what I have argued to be the main political order in Europe – one based on coloniality – then can we really say that they signify a moment of renewal? Are they not, simply, more of the same?

Thirdly, the chapter follows the substantial insights from critical fantasy studies which argue that political identities are always based on desire. Importantly, it does not only ask *if* we are affectively invested in a political project, but *how* we are invested in it. This becomes fundamental when understanding the grip of the populist narrative. Importantly, we must join together the lessons learned from decolonial studies with critical fantasy studies in order to fully grasp the internal workings of populism. The phantasmatic structure of populism, I argue, is the same as that of liberalism and elitism: European superiority. However, for the European mainstream liberal centre this fantasy can only be sustained if there is a clear demarcation between Europe and its violent others, be those the hysteric and xenophobic populists or the image of the Savage. The figure of the populist allows Europeans to nurture a fantasy of themselves as inclusive and egalitarian. In addition, by tapping into already present dreams and ambitions about European superiority, which have marred and shaped the continent for centuries, populism plays on the same quest for mastery as so many political projects before it.

The discursive approach: affect and identity

Laclau and Mouffe's approach to populism is becoming ever more popular and there is a growing body of scholarly work which uses this approach

(Katsambekis, 2020; Kioupkiolis, 2016; Ostiguy et al, 2021; Stavrakakis, 2014). The approach is, as shown in the previous chapter, very distinct from other approaches to populism. Much of this emanates from the psychoanalytical heritage that Laclau is keen to foster (Laclau, 2005). Laclau's thought is not, however, a unified body of work, but there are several contradictions and developments. As such, even though this chapter seeks to represent the main lessons, there will be instances in his work where different things are argued (Hansen, 2020).

Starting from his insights in *New Reflections on the Revolutions of our Time*, Laclau introduces key Lacanian concepts into his analysis. This impetus emanates from a reading of Marx which is compatible with a Lacanian articulation of the lack, where Laclau sees the possibility of society as intertwined with the ontology of the social, the political (Laclau, 1990, p 96). The reason why we can have politics at all is because signification is not pre-determined, because we cannot fully capture what anything means at any time. This application of psychoanalysis – which is essentially a theory of individual identities – to collective identities is Laclau's master move. That collective identities also suffer from constitutive lacks is really what brings the discursive approach to populism into being.

In order to fully grasp how collective identities form, Laclau turns to the empty signifier as a key concept. In one of his later essays 'Why do Empty Signifiers Matter to Politics?' (Laclau, 2007), Laclau develops how one signifier, which is tendentially empty, can function as the unifying unit for what he terms a chain of equivalence. The signifier can be anything – a word, a slogan, a person – but its meaning, its *signified*, does not have any essential content. Importantly, however, it signifies opposition to the system (Laclau, 2007, p 41), and manages to overcome the differential identities that it unites. As such, any collective identity is formed on the basis of lack. The empty signifier then assumes the role of a 'false' universal, a signifier which can act as the fullness absent from all of the different identities in the chain.

Laclau develops these early lessons more fully in *On Populist Reason* (2005). While this book deals largely with populism, it is, still, a book about collective identities, which is obvious from the very first sentence: 'the main issue addressed in this book is the nature and logics of the formation of collective identities' (Laclau, 2005, p ix). Here Laclau becomes ever clearer about his commitment to Lacan. The formation of collective identities can be explained also with regards to *why* they happen, not only *how* they happen. Laclau draws on the experience of the child in its realization that the symbolic order will never address its unachieved fullness (Laclau, 2005, p 114). What we see, however, is that this aspiration, or desire, never goes away. We are always wanting to achieve a sense of fullness, and we do so by attaching to what Lacan referred to as the *objet petit a*, which Laclau deems the 'key element in a social ontology' (Laclau, 2005, p 115). This is also how

Laclau defines hegemony: that which assumes the role of the impossible universal, even though it is a partial representation.

This representation, the partial which assumes the role of the impossible universal, is not done in a vacuum. Importantly, the identity formed by the empty signifier is done in relation to something else, which for Laclau becomes the possibility of the construction of the 'People'. In order to understand what the People is, we have to see what it is not. Crucially, Laclau does not abide by a simple A–B definition of difference. That A is not B is not a good analogy for describing how collective identities work. When we are talking about populism, there is more to the picture than simple difference: it is when B becomes the impossibility of the fullness of A that antagonism occurs. It is worthwhile to quote Laclau at length from *On Populist Reason*:

> So from the very beginning we are confronted with a dichotomic division between unfulfilled social demands, on the one hand, and an unresponsive power, on the other. Here we begin to see why the plebs sees itself as *populus*, the part as the whole: since the fullness of the community is merely the imaginary reverse of a situation lived as a deficient being, those who are responsible for this cannot be a legitimate part of the community, the chasm between them is irretrievable. (Laclau, 2005, p 86)

Importantly, Laclau argues that 'there is no populism without affective investment in a partial object' (Laclau, 2005, p 116). The natural conclusion of this argument is that populism is part and parcel of any identity construction, which indicates the connection between populism and politics. Even though this seems counterintuitive (or controversial) to some, Laclau insisted that the possibility of politics, that we have a particular which represents the universal, is the precondition of politics, but also the very foundation of populism per se. Laclau, then, perhaps controversially, argues that politics as such becomes the formation of populist demands. Populism, therefore, is not any specific type of movement, but a political logic.

One of the key developments of Laclau's later works concerns the introduction of social heterogeneity and floating signifiers. This is something which forms the backbone of the theory of populism, but it is often not the central focus of works that use Laclau to analyse populism today. Social heterogeneity and floating signifiers introduce more movement in Laclau's rather formulaic theory and will be vital for understanding Europe's populist condition. Laclau argues that the People–Elite relation, an antagonistic frontier, is by no means a static construction:

> As we can see, the categories of 'empty' and floating' signifiers are structurally different. The first concerns the construction of a popular

identity once the presence of a stable frontier is taken for granted; the second tries conceptually to apprehend the logic of the displacements of that frontier. (Laclau, 2005, p 133)

The floating signifier thus makes movement in the system possible. There can be competing discursive constructions which challenge the current antagonistic relation. This can be seen, says Laclau, in the movements of voters between the left and right, for instance. The second challenge to the static system is that of heterogeneity, which challenges the assumption that 'every unfulfilled demand can incorporate itself in the equivalential chain that is constitutive of the popular camp' (Laclau, 2005, p 139). This is not always the case, and we must consider demands which are not subsumed in the antagonistic frontier.

This connects to another fundamental development in *On Populist Reason*: Laclau's idea of social heterogeneity. Instead of thinking that all identities could fit into the antagonistic frontier, Laclau recognizes that there are demands which sit outside of the antagonistic relation. Laclau thus wants to introduce another element that 'cannot be incorporated into the equivalential chain because it clashes with the particularistic aims of demands which are already links in that chain' (Laclau, 2005, p 139). Laclau draws on Hegel to explain that this concerns 'peoples without history', who are entirely outside of historicity, or what Lacan referred to as the *caput mortuum*, the 'residue left in a tube after a chemical experiment' (Laclau, 2005, p 139). Marx also draws on Hegel to construct his concept of the lumpenproletariat (Stallybrass, 1990). Unlike the proletariat, which has a clear role and position in the social system, the lumpenproletariat is different:

> Within a history conceived of as a history of production, the working class would be the agent of a new stage in the development of productive forces, and the term 'proletarian' was used to designate this new agent. In order to maintain its credentials as an 'insider' of the main line of historical development, however, the proletariat had to be strictly differentiated from the absolute 'outsider': the lumpenproletariat. (Stallybrass, 1990)

It should be noted here that the definition of the lumpenproletariat in Hegel and Marx is far from normatively neutral. Hegel came as far as proposing that the 'excess population' should emigrate to overseas colonies. Engels continues this with 'the lumpenproletariat, in the big cities, is the worst of all possible allies. This rabble is absolutely venal and absolutely brazen' (Stallybrass, 1990, p 89). Laclau, however, sees that the very constitution of the proletariat needs a 'constitutive outside' that is not the antagonist – the lumpenproletariat plays a much more important role in history than we might like to imagine. As such, he does not agree with Hegel that these are people without history; they are rather what make political identities throughout history possible. He further contends that 'antagonism presupposes heterogeneity because the resistance of the antagonized force cannot be logically derived from the form of the antagonising one. This can only mean that the points of resistance to the antagonising force are always going to be external to it' (Laclau, 2005, p 150). Heterogeneity, in other words, is thus central to the articulation of any political identity and precludes any complete homogenization of the People (sometimes regarded as evidence that populism cannot be right-wing, since the right is essentially a movement based on homogeneity (Biglieri & Cadahia, 2021, p 39). The political, in essence, for Laclau becomes the attempts at homogeneity which are always interrupted by heterogeneity. It is when the heterogenous elements disturb the equivalential chain, when the empty signifier becomes a floating signifier, that the political appears. This is comparable with Rancière's notion of politics and the police, as the introduction of the 'part that has no part' (Rancière, 1999), or what Gramsci referred to as the 'war of position' (Gramsci, 2005). Laclau also recognizes that his conclusions are largely comparable with those of Bataille, who also thinks of the heterogenous as the possibility of the formation of new political frontiers. Bataille – like so many other of Laclau's influences – uses the example of fascism, and argues that it created a political identity for those who had no obvious part in society, and who is lured by 'mystical thinking of primitives' (Bataille & Lovitt, 1979, p 128), which will be discussed later. And it is here that Laclau presents his at times controversial conclusion that the political, in this sense, becomes synonymous with populism. Populism here indicates the very movement of heterogenous elements and the creation of new frontiers.

Problems with antagonism: conceptual, analytical, political

In order to fully be able to critically interrogate the People–Elite distinction and understand the contaminations and overlaps between the two, we need a renewed focus on what antagonism means. Antagonism is one of the core concepts in discourse theory and constitutes the cornerstone of how political identities are formed. In order to avoid any lingering essentialism of the political subject (such as in Descartes or liberal thought, as described in Chapter 1), Laclau and Mouffe argue that the difference which constitutes the subject is not neutral, but antagonistic. While this book fundamentally agrees with the claim to non-essentialism by Laclau and Mouffe, there are several remaining problems with antagonism. I argue that these problems can be seen on a conceptual/ontological, empirical/analytical, and ethico-political level, and that they are all connected to coloniality.

Before delving into the discursive approach to antagonism, we must engage with some of the influential thinkers on the topic. For instance, Carl Schmitt is a rather substantial influence on Laclau, and for Mouffe the influence is absolutely central. Schmitt's conceptualization of the political and of antagonism must be put into question here, as it shapes the world view radical democratic theory. As a political legal theorist of the early 20th century who became a figurehead for the Nazi party in Germany in the 1930s, it is not directly obvious why his writings are so central to Laclau and Mouffe.

For many, Schmitt is simply an inspiration when it comes to the realization that society is based on conflict, or on a friend-enemy relation. However, to take only this rather narrow lesson from Schmitt does not recognize his *oeuvre* as a whole, which is essential. Schmitt was not only writing about antagonism and society, but was a key source of intellectual development for the Nazis. Even though there has been significant scholarship discussing whether or not Schmitt was a 'real' Nazi (Mehring & Steuer, 2019), this becomes rather secondary in the light of how his work has been received and used.

For Schmitt, the friend-enemy relation is what defines the political. Importantly, however, this relation must, by default, have a potentiality of all-out war, or else politics cannot exist: 'a world in which the possibility of war is utterly eliminated, a completely pacified globe, would be a world without the distinction of friend and enemy and hence a world without politics' (Schmitt, 2007, p 35). As such, while Schmitt recognizes that war is not a permanent state, it must remain a potentiality. Schmitt also realizes that war must not only take place between states, but can also be directed against the 'enemy within', which later became a key tenet of the Nazis against the Jews. Schmitt constantly retains that his theory is a neutral one, and does not comment on the desirability or ethical aspects of war. It must be argued, however, that a theory which sees war as inevitable and total peace as impossible has a strong normative foundation. For Schmitt, humanity cannot co-exist in peace, since 'every human is symbolically a combatant' (Schmitt, 2007, p 33).

Schmitt has become a key thinker of the radical right, both among his contemporaries and today (Mehring & Steuer, 2019), but his works are also very popular outside these circles. Many key theorists, such as Habermas (2006) and Derrida (1988), have made a clear demarcation between their own works and his, arguing that Schmitt stands for a dangerous neonationalism. Others, however, such as Mouffe (1999, 2005) and Agamben (2005), have tried to incorporate some of his key theses into their own. Mouffe has repeatedly argued that we must think 'with Schmitt against Schmitt', often recognizing the problematic aspects of his works, but still wanting to use Schmitt's anti-liberal thought to develop her own (Mouffe, 2005, p 2).

My objective is to think with Schmitt, against Schmitt, and to use his insights in order to strengthen liberal democracy against his critiques. By drawing our attention to the centrality of the friend/enemy relation in politics, Schmitt makes us aware of the dimension of the political that is linked to the existence of an element of hostility among human beings. (Mouffe, 2005, p 2)

The problem is that when Mouffe says that she will think with Schmitt against Schmitt, she still accepts his primary problem formulation that human relations are essentially conflictual. Even though her conclusions do not land in that the 'enemy within' (namely the Jews) should be fought in civil war, she does not break away from the idea that human beings cannot live peacefully due to their difference. Such a perspective, I argue, is more reminiscent of coloniality than of any progressive politics.

The difficulty to salvage Schmitt has become more pronounced as time goes on. The more we learn about his writing and political leanings, the more it becomes obvious that his perspective is not compatible with equality. In a recent study of Schmitt's diaries between 1933 and 1936, Suuronen demonstrates that Schmitt, far from being distanced to the racialized politics of Nazism, in fact is a key proponent of them (Suuronen, 2021). His rejection of liberalism is what enables his development of a racially pure German state led by the Führer. Drawing on Foucault (2003), Suuronen points out that Schmitt makes the final move from the sovereign power to biopower, and argues for the 'the elimination of the biological threat to and the improvement of the species or race' (Foucault, 2003, p 256). This, in other words, is what Schmitt refers to by the friend–enemy relation and is the only solution to degenerative liberalism. Suuronen also points to Schmitt's opening statements to the conference 'Jewishness in legal science', which Schmitt organized in 1936, where he explains his guiding principles:

> The first comes from Hitler's Mein Kampf: 'By fighting off the Jew, I struggle for the work of the lord.' The second comes from Hans Frank: 'The racial legislation is finished; but it remains the task of our relentless education to uphold the awareness of the Jewish danger among the German people.' The third principle is derived from the Nazi martyr Theodor von der Pfordten: 'For decades you have watched idly and indifferently how the flood of non-German endeavors loosened the structure of the state and penetrated our science with its deadly poison.' (Suuronen, 2021, p 356)

Anyone who would like to argue that Schmitt's theories are 'neutral ground', or that his theory of antagonism could somehow be separated from his personal politics, must engage with how racial division is really what brings about the theory of antagonism in the first place and which becomes synonymous with the political. Schmitt is not a neutral bystander whose theory was hijacked by the Nazis – rather, Hitler's anti-intellectualism made it harder for Schmitt's views to be heard, yet he prevailed. The friend-enemy relation in other words, has a heritage which has not been sufficiently recognized, but which comes from the same racialized thinking, which was so acutely present in early liberal thought, as mentioned in Chapter 1.

This does not seem to prevent contemporary scholars from utilizing this distinction, and from it gaining significant traction in populism studies. A quick search on Google Scholar for the term 'populism' along the friend-enemy relation delivers 64,100 results, indicating that it is a common way of seeing how populism works. This is not to say that the discursive approach as a whole accepts this articulation, but, as I will demonstrate later, there are lingering questions to answer regarding how Laclau conceptualizes antagonism, in particular, and how populism becomes the prime example of the political.

Conceptual problems with antagonism

Firstly, antagonism in Laclau is *conceptually* problematic, which stems from how he considers the limits of discourse. Here we are concerned with the ontological status of antagonism, which has profound consequences for the ontological status of populism. According to Stäheli, the relation between a discourse and its exterior is 'necessarily antagonistic' (Stäheli, 2004, p 234), and points to how Laclau explains this in *Emancipations*: 'antagonism and exclusion are constitutive of all political identities' (Laclau, 2007, p 52). However, it is also vital to recognize that the antagonist poses a fundamental threat to the possibility of the discursive order – here Laclau uses the deconstructive argument as developed by Derrida (2006; Laclau, 2005, p 86) to point out how the condition of possibility is also the condition of impossibility. The political identity is only possible due to the Other, but the Other is also what negates the possible fullness of said identity.

In *New Reflections on the Revolutions of Our Time* (1990), Laclau develops the concept of dislocation, to indicate the instability of meaning which makes identities possible in the first place. Dislocation could, at least on paper, provide the roadmap for how difference could be conceptualized in a non-antagonistic fashion. On some level, dislocation assumes a deeper ontological status than antagonism, and is rather closer to Derrida's structural undecidability (Hansen, 2020, p 537). However, as Hansen has rightly pointed out, there are diverging takes from Laclau on the relationship between dislocation and antagonism. In some places, there seems to be a significant difference between them, where dislocation simply indicates the instability of signification and identification. If this is true, then not all collective identities are constructed around an antagonistic frontier (Thomassen, 2019). On the other hand, Laclau's earlier works are ripe with statements which indicate the primacy of antagonism for social relations, which Žižek even argued was his strongest contribution to the field (Žižek, 1990, 2008).

The argument that antagonism is a central part of the understanding of the political has also been developed by Marchart, who contends that 'whatever occurs in our social world, it has to pass through the medium of antagonism' (Marchart, 2018, p 25). Marchart is thus unconvinced about the ontological claim of dislocation and favours an interpretation of Laclau which returns to the more Schmittian heritage. Even though Marchart does not equate antagonism with the friend-enemy relation, he still argues that there is a 'spectral presence of a ground that remains absent but exerts an uncanny presence of moments of conflict and contingency' (Marchart, 2018, p 171). The natural conclusion of this world view is that antagonism should, as argued by Mbembe, be seen as a particular European ontology – one which favours conflict over difference (Mbembe, 2019, p 64). Mbembe further contends that the political, for Schmitt, goes far beyond disagreement and ultimately entails a 'politics of annihilation', which can be seen throughout European history, be it the Holocaust or current migration policies. As such, 'this conception of the political is the almost natural outcome of Western metaphysics' long-standing obsession with, on the one hand, the question of Being and its supposed truth and, on the other, the ontology of life' (Mbembe, 2019, p 63). It is also important to remember the very physical and violent underpinnings of antagonism: 'In Schmitt's world, which has become our own, the concept of enemy is to be understood in its concrete and existential meaning, and not at all as a metaphor or as an empty and lifeless abstraction.' (Mbembe, 2019, p 49). It is thus difficult to argue, as has been done by some, that 'political struggle does not see the "physical" elimination of the adversary, but rather the transformation of the position they occupy within a given relation of forces' (Biglieri & Cadahia, 2021, p 28). Rather, the primacy of antagonism indicates how there is still a strong commitment to the Schmittian 'political', which one could refer to as 'ontological militarism' (Furtado, 2023).

It is paramount to point out that antagonism in Laclau is by no means identical to that in Schmitt. As mentioned earlier, the poststructuralist ambition to understand subjectivity in the face of the Other is based on an understanding of difference, not necessarily conflict. However, the way that the Schmittian (and at times Gramscian) conceptualization of antagonism has found its way into radical democratic theory is rather interesting. This becomes particularly apparent when Laclau discusses the differences between left-wing and right-wing populism. The example of voting patterns for the Front National (now the Rassemblement National) becomes a case in point, where it has been shown repeatedly that many voters of the FN had previously voted for the Communist Party in France, what we could call 'atypical logics' (Laclau, 2005, p 88). For many, it is surprising to see such a movement, but Laclau argues that the 'ontological need to express division was stronger than its ontic attachment to a left-wing discourse which, anyway, did not attempt to build it up any longer' (Laclau, 2005, p 88). This is what Mény and Surel (2000) have termed 'left-lepenism' (gaucho-lepenisme) or 'workers-lepenism' (ouvriero-lepenisme).

Laclau thus draws the conclusion that the presence of antagonism overrides any commitment to political values – we are more interested in creating frontiers along friend-enemy lines than we are in realizing the world we want to live in. As such, the echoes of Schmitt's understanding of politics are clear, where we cannot imagine a world without the defining feature of conflict and antagonism. Even though Laclau himself is much more careful and nuanced, the logical conclusion of an ontological commitment to social division is unequivocally similar to Schmitt's work. When Laclau states that 'antagonism and exclusion are constitutive of all identity' (Laclau, 2007, p 52), he also clarifies that this is not simply a matter of difference, but a difference which 'poses a threat to all the differences within that context' (Laclau, 2007, p 52). Antagonism, then, is not simply difference, but a threat to the very existence of the subject, completely in line with Schmitt's argument.

This leaves us with several questions: why is the discursive approach so committed to the friend-enemy relation? And how can a questioning of this relation help us better understand populism today? I argue that a simple way of understanding the appeal of Schmitt is coloniality, or, rather, the absence of a discussion on coloniality. What Laclau sees as a tension between the ontic and the ontological can be explained by a limited scope of antagonism as an ontological order. What we must look to is to how the development of the Other has served as a justification for hierarchical difference for centuries. As such, antagonism, or irreconcilable difference, is a remnant of the classical liberal example of elitism. The justification for some people to rule instead of others was made through a construction of difference based on racial and gendered lines and continues to shape political thinking to this day. By realizing that difference as a threat is not a neutral analytical vehicle, we can further understand how populism, as a theoretical concept, is nothing but a re-articulation of the liberal quest for domination.

Analytical problems with antagonism

Secondly, there are several *analytical* and *empirical* issues with how the concept of antagonism is currently applied, and how much it helps us understand the specificities of populism. According to Laclau, and most works that use his theories, populism marks an antagonistic frontier against the liberal centre, the establishment, the status quo. Populism in this sense becomes a challenge to the current order, and regardless of what we may think about the political aims of populist actors, many analyses affirm that populism is a threat to the current order, and that it subverts contemporary norms. This depiction of contemporary populism, I argue, is deeply problematic. As I will discuss in Chapters 4 and 5, populism does not offer much in the way of a challenge, either on the left or on the right. In practice, contemporary populisms in Europe do not indicate examples of the political.

The influences that Laclau takes from Marx and Bataille are central. For Marx, heterogeneity manifests itself as the lumpenproletariat (Cowling & Martin, 2002; Stallybrass, 1990), political subjects which cannot be subsumed under the proletariat–bourgeoise relation. The lumpenproletariat is that which can be seen as a 'irreducible remainder', which is a necessity for any identity formation. Bataille used the same figure when trying to explain the rise of fascism, and argued that due to economic shocks, the homogeneity of the social was threatened and gave rise to the fascist movement among the workers (Bataille, 1997). Importantly, heterogenous elements escape the antagonistic relation and cannot be said to be recognized as political subjects; they are the subaltern, or the Hegelian people without history (Laclau 2005, p 139).

This becomes central for understanding populism for Laclau. In his idea, populism happens when heterogenous elements create a new chain of equivalence in order to form a new counter-hegemonic frontier and become part of the antagonistic relation. This, I argue, may be correct on an ontological level, but the ontic examples of that which we call populism do nothing of the sort. Rather, we should be encouraged to think about what Thomassen has said about antagonism, which is that is means rather the closure than the opening of a system: 'on closer inspection, however, the antagonistic relation does not actually threaten the identity established through the chain of equivalence' (Thomassen, 2019, p 45). With antagonism, in other words, we are not dealing with a questioning of the field of discursivity, but of an articulation of identities within the system: 'antagonism can be seen as a way of suppressing and externalizing heterogeneity. It can be seen as a way of establishing coherence and closure. As such, antagonism is ideological: it is a strategy to achieve closure and to suppress its ultimate possibility' (Thomassen, 2019, p 45).

It thus becomes difficult to argue, like some scholars do, that there is inherent progressive potential in populism (Biglieri & Cadahia, 2021; Marchart, 2018; Mouffe, 2005; Stavrakakis, 2017). While this could be *theoretically* possible, it is problematic to detach theoretical developments from empirical realities. It is telling, I argue, that most of the inspirations for Laclau's theory of populism are ones who try to explain the rise of fascism. Schmitt, Bataille, Gramsci, and to some extent Derrida were all concerned with how fascism came to power, how it was made possible. Can we, feasibly, argue that those insights can be directly transposed to favour a left-wing agenda? And, most importantly, if we consider coloniality, did fascism really challenge the political order in Europe, or was it simply, as argued by Mann and Meister, an expression of the inherent genocidal nature of European politics (Mann, 2012; Meister, 2009)?

As discussed in Chapter 2, this also poses questions for the part of literature on populism which considers it a transgression, which seems to mean a challenge to the discursive order (Aiolfi, 2022; Moffitt, 2016; Ostiguy, 2017; Zicman de Barros & Aiolfi, 2025). I contend that the performative transgressions made by populists pale in comparison with their support for the colonial order. As such, the way populists speak, dress or in any way 'perform' politics cannot detract from the main question of whether they are challenging or reinforcing existing social hierarchies. In other words, being transgressive is not synonymous with being subversive (Glynos, 2008, 2021).

If we look at populism in practice, the idea that it introduces heterogenous elements into the antagonistic relation becomes rather dubious. This will be further developed in the subsequent chapters, but we can already now point to how populism, in most cases, reaffirms a People–Elite relation which is not rejecting many of the existing power relations; it is not subversive. A quick look at how right-wing populists embrace neoliberal economic policy, or how populist parties left and right rearticulate forms of masculinity provides us with a notion of how populism, rather than disrupting the system or transgressing any boundaries, ends up sedimenting the order already in place, an order based on coloniality. As such, we have serious analytical problems with the discursive definition of populism, in that the examples most often used do not fit the theory available. I argue that if we look at the system as a system of coloniality – not of only capitalism or liberalism – these forces appear less disruptive and anti-systemic, and more like products of the reigning ideas. While it is indeed true that capitalism and liberalism form part of coloniality, only focussing on the two proves insufficient. As such, while Žižek (2017) and Lazzarato (2021) make valid points about how populism fails to further a left-wing agenda, for them it is capitalism, not coloniality, which is the main culprit.

In Figure 3.1, I have illustrated populism's place in a system of coloniality. Instead of seeing the construction of the People as a radical move to introduce new elements into any equivalential chain, I argue that current incarnations of populism are rather reaffirming the status quo and the liberal order. In order to read our present, I argue that we need the cipher of coloniality. Only when accepting that populisms do not challenge the liberal order can we begin to fully grasp populism in Europe. Coloniality is present both on the ontological and ontic levels. Ontologically, the commitment to the friend-enemy relation as the basis of politics echoes the colonial mindset.

Figure 3.1: The discursive field of coloniality

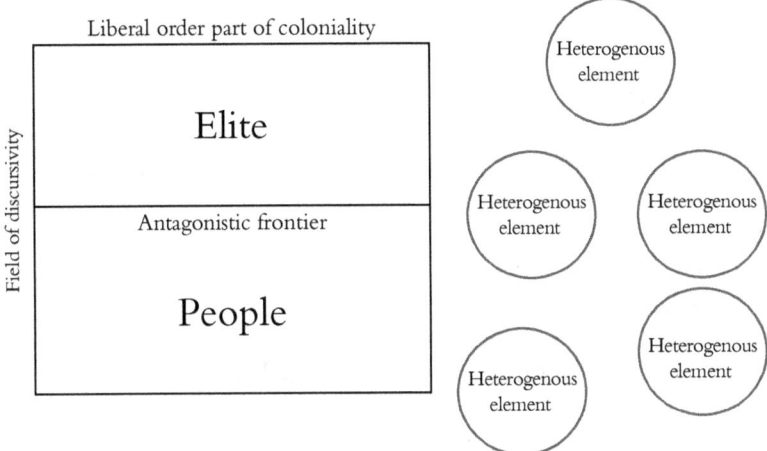

It is only by seeing man as the *ego conquiro* that we can understand why conflict is so central both to Enlightenment theories and to right-wing ideologies. This is what they have in common. Our current world order only works if European Man replaces God and is the more deserving political subject. European Man, as we have seen in previous chapters, is today represented by the lingering dichotomies in politics which favour rational over emotional, masculine over feminine, civil over savage.

Coloniality also works on the ontic level. As I will demonstrate in Chapters 4 and 5, current incarnations of European populism do not manage to break free from the colonial mindset. Even the most progressive of populisms are caught in a structure where citizenship is the basis for political participation, where we have to be 'realistic on migration', and whose political leaders emulate masculine logics. All of these, as Quijano would say, are parts of the colonial matrix of power (Quijano, 2007).

Ethico-political problems with antagonism

Thirdly, there are ethico-political issues with the way that the discursive approach handles antagonism. These issues stem from the points mentioned earlier about the ontological and ontic problems with antagonism in the discursive approach. While it may seem harmless to construct an approach based on antagonism, there are very real political consequences for doing so. Here I agree with Marchart when he argues that there is no fundamental difference between ontological questions and political questions – the two go hand in hand (Marchart, 2018). The commitment to reading difference as antagonism has repercussions outside of political theory. If we let theorists such as Schmitt dictate how the world should be read, we run a real risk of reproducing the same type of society that Schmitt saw as desirable, which, clearly, is not based on any radical commitment to equality.

On an ontic level, it is telling that political movements which do so little to challenge the fundaments of a modern-liberal society, like populist movements do, are still afforded the status of heterogenous elements – they are thought to have revolutionary and emancipatory potential. We are oblivious to the fact that the underlying assumption (that we are fundamentally different) is also what underpins a modern, liberal society. There is therefore no substantial challenge coming from what is today termed the populist camp. Importantly, the commitment to difference, rather than equality, is what characterizes and unites both European liberal democracies, as well as populist movements.

It is also equality which becomes the major loser in the process. By succumbing to a world dictated by difference as antagonism, it is nigh on impossible to argue the fundamental equality between humans. Contemporary political debate, both inside and outside of academia, thus loses sight of that which should be central to our enquiries: that all human beings have an intrinsic equal value. This is also what Laclau's politics constantly reaffirmed, and it is therefore unfortunate that the theoretical insights do not always work in this direction. This becomes obvious in the examples of populism that Laclau chooses and in how his work has been used since.

A turn to fantasy

I have so far discussed how populism, both conceptually and empirically, is situated in a system of coloniality and does not manage to break free from this oppressive order – it is not an expression of the political, in its current European form. I will demonstrate the details of this claim further in Chapters 4 and 5. However, to better understand populism in Europe, I now turn to the question of why this is the case. Why is there such a stubborn commitment to an order that most would say they disagree with? Why is coloniality still with us? And why, at the end of the day, is populism so popular, both as a concept and as a political alternative?

In order to address these questions, I will take inspiration from critical fantasy studies, which, while closely connected to discourse theory, adds an additional layer of analysis with which we can read the present situation of populism in Europe. Critical fantasy studies can help us better explain how identities such as populism are formed and how they are sustained, but also, importantly, how we engage with certain signifiers. As put by Glynos, critical fantasy studies 'offers a vocabulary within which to understand how structures that appear to be "out there" – structures of economy, biological, sex, race, etc. – can come to inhabit us, making them feel personal, intimate, and natural' (Glynos, 2021, p 97). Glynos is also adamant to affirm the 'critical' component of critical fantasy studies, relating it to the post-Marxism of Laclau and others. This critical component, he argues, should also serve as the space through which we can exert normative and ideological critique.

Building on the psychoanalytical aspects of discourse theory, as previously discussed, critical fantasy studies places a special emphasis on the role of fantasy in the creation of political identities. Here, there is an implicit recognition about the importance of affect, and how affect does not equate to studying the emotional aspects of politics (Eklundh, 2019, 2020; Stavrakakis, 2002, 2007). As such, when we are talking about fantasy, we are not simply talking about whether people are angry, happy or sad (Salmela & von Scheve, 2017; Skonieczny, 2018), but how their affective investment in certain phantasmatic structures determine their political life. Importantly, critical fantasy studies affirm that affect is not disjointed from ideological conviction (Glynos, 2021, p 98).

A fundamental tenet of fantasy concerns the idea of radical contingency, which connects to our previous discussions on how language can never capture the whole of our reality – there is a limit to the symbolic. The Laclaudian idea of dislocation expresses this very limit, as does the Derridian concept of undecidability, as previously discussed. For Lacanian psychoanalysis, this limit of the symbolic is what gives rise to the lack, the fact that we can never fully realize our own 'full' subjectivity (Lacan, 2007; Stavrakakis, 2002). This gives us the main building blocks between affect and our constant desire to grasp this ungraspable idea of Self, on the one hand, and discourse, on the other. This is where fantasy enters the scene, as the pushing of the limits of discourse (Glynos, 2021, p 99). As developed by Glynos and Howarth (2007), fantasy can be seen as another logic, one which functions in addition to the social and political logics developed by Laclau (where populism becomes the political logic par excellence).

For this book, the relevance of phantasmatic structures is central to our argument. In order to understand why coloniality – a discursive construction built on a hierarchical and conflictual construction of difference – is so popular, we must engage with what Lacan calls *jouissance*, or enjoyment (Lacan, 2007). Enjoyment serves a central function in the creation and sustention of fantasy, either in its present or absent form. Desire, in other words, is but a longing for enjoyment (Glynos & Stavrakakis, 2004). Discourses are impossible to understand without a focus on enjoyment. Importantly, fantasy does not make any truth claims, and it becomes secondary whether the fantasy represents an 'accurate' idea of society. In a world marred by post-truth, it becomes ever more central to see how the fantasies which uphold these structures are constructed. However, we must also note that phantasmatic investment is present in all discourse, whether notionally 'true' or 'false' (Glynos, 2021, p 101). What we are interested in is rather how our structures of meaning are imbued with a phantasmatic dimension.

In our context, however, we must focus on how enjoyment comes into force between identities, and how desire is restricted or confined. This has been debated at length by various scholars, such as Miller who makes the claim that we approach the enjoyment of Other as someone who 'steals our enjoyment' (Žižek, 1993). This theft becomes the fundamental element of social and political relations: we can consider, for instance, nationalism or racism as an unwillingness to accept the enjoyment of the Other. A construct such as coloniality is clearly built on a similar structure – the enjoyment of the Savage cannot be accepted, and the threat coming from the Other constitutes a theft. While there are divergences and conflicts between the psychoanalytical tradition and post- and decolonial scholars, it is important to see how the concept of fantasy can help us better understand colonial relations, as argued by Fanon (2021) and Mbembe (2019), and as will be developed later.

The concept of fantasy can help us understand European populism – as a concept and as a political alternative – much better. As Žižek has argued, fantasy is the structure that we use to compensate for our inherent ability to fully realize ourselves (Žižek, 2008). However, fantasy also works to cover up the underlying mechanisms of impossibility – Europe wants to be equal and inclusive, but knows that it is not. Žižek takes the example of the Jew as the ultimate Nazi fantasy, which, according to him, served to cover up class antagonisms in Germany (Žižek, 2015). While this is a highly compelling analysis, there is a need to move beyond class and introduce the decolonial perspective to understand Europe's fantasies, and what roles they play.

Critical fantasy studies has become an expanding field, with more studies affirming the need to look at phantasmatic logics to understand contemporary politics. Such examples include studies which investigate contemporary movements on the left and right (Ronderos & Glynos, 2023; Ronderos, 2020; Zicman de Barros, 2022). These studies focus on how political identities are formed through processes of (dis)identification and how these contain a strong phantasmatic element. For instance, Ronderos and Glynos demonstrate how the Brazilian magazine Veja exhibits a clear anti-left-populist structure in its reporting which is linked to a possible loss of enjoyment of the Brazilian middle classes. This threat comes from a potential restriction of free market policies, as enacted by the Lula government (Ronderos & Glynos, 2023). Similarly, Zicman de Barros investigated how phantasmatic structures construct political identities in the Yellow Vest movement in France (Zicman de Barros, forthcoming). Mondon has also explored how fantasy operates in public debate, and especially the idea that liberalism act as a bulwark against reactionary ideology (Mondon, 2024).

Mandelbaum has also made a substantial contribution to the field when discussing the fantasy of the nation-state and its impact on contemporary politics. He argues that unlike previous theories of nationalism which saw the nation as a construction, such as Anderson (1983) and Gellner (1983), we should think of the nation-state as a fantasy. Mandelbaum develops how ethnic homogeneity, which has never existed, becomes a source of enjoyment for the nationalist project (Mandelbaum, 2020). And, to be expected, any threat to the homogeneity of the nation is also a theft of enjoyment. Again, this is not to argue that national unity is empirically false or untrue, but rather to say that without the fantasy of national unity, it becomes impossible. Mandelbaum here draws on Edelman, who has argued that fantasy is the 'central prop and underlying agency of futurism' (Edelman, 2004, p 33). We can therefore see that there is no national identity without fantasy, but, all the same, 'failure is at the heart of the nation/state fantasy because it is the lack and void of national subjectivities that propels the fantasy of national unity, which in turn must explain and articulate its own impossibility: its inherent failure' (Mandelbaum, 2020, p 55). Similar thoughts have been expressed by Žižek (2017), when contending that populism always contains a fantasy of the people as one.

This book, however, is not about nationalism, even though nationalism certainly serves as one of the many interfaces of coloniality. What Mandelbaum terms the nation/state congruency is essentially based on one of the key aspects of coloniality: that some are more deserving to rule than others, and those more deserving represent what it means to be European. So far, we have seen that political identities in the discursive approach are based on affective investment that is not random but contingent on phantasmatic structures. In addition, the phantasmatic structure involves a focus on enjoyment, where the potential theft of enjoyment turns difference into conflict. These insights are vital for understanding how populism functions today, but also put the finger on where current explanations could be further supplanted.

Populism and fantasies of separation

In this final part, I will tie together the insights from Chapter 1, on the presence of coloniality in European politics, with a focus on the phantasmatic structures of political identity. Most of all, I will emphasize the grip of coloniality for how we study and understand populism. This grip, I argue, stems from a phantasmatic structure and must be read as such. The figure of the European populist enables two concomitant facets. First, it retains the populist as a threat to the European way of life, as a harbinger of evil, and one who steals our enjoyment. Second, it sustains the fantasy of Europe as benevolent and peaceful – and therefore superior – since violence and cruelty stems from somewhere else. These two phantasmatic facets construct an imaginary separation between the mainstream and the populist, which is only just that, a construction. It is ultimately this fantasy of irreconcilable separation between Europe and its Others which is the source of so many of the violent acts committed in its name.

Let me, before we begin, recapitulate the main tenets of coloniality. We saw in Chapter 1 how, in the transition away from a sovereign ordained by God, we did not create an empty space of power (Wynter, 2003). Rather, this empty space was quickly filled with what Dussel refers to as the *ego conquiro*, the political subject superior to the colonial Other, the savages. The legitimate sovereign, henceforth, is tightly intertwined with particular qualities attributed to the European Man, such as rationality and civility. The whole question around power, then, is not an open or level playing field – we are not debating in the 'marketplace of ideas' about the common good (as argued by Habermas), but we are simply reliving the foundational moment of European political subjectivity – the moment of conquest. Coloniality becomes the cipher through which we can read the productions of power today: man/woman, civilized/uncivilized, rational/emotional, colonizer/colonized, or white/black.

One could of course argue that such reactionary and problematic content has no place in the contemporary study of populism, but, as I showed in Chapter 2, there is a significant trend within the field to draw sharp demarcations between the People and the Elite, and not recognizing the overlaps that exist between populism, on the one hand, and elitism, on the other. These overlaps, I argue, can be explained by coloniality. The People/Elite distinction thus becomes but a façade behind which we can hide the more fundamental leanings of European politics. This façade is part of a phantasmatic structure. It is the *panem et circenses* to keep the status quo alive, an enjoyment. This restriction imposed by coloniality can be seen on three different levels.

Importantly, coloniality presupposes a separation and an inherent *conflictual relationship* between the Savage and the White Man. This fundamental conflict is also, however, what enables the possibility of the colonial subject, the *ego conquiro* (Maldonado-Torres, 2007). The very presence of the Savage as the Other which steals our enjoyment is what propels European politics forward. European culture and civilisation must be defended. This presupposes a conflictual outlook on political identities which is not neutral or unproblematic. Most importantly, it is not historical or a thing of the past. As demonstrated earlier, what was taken up by Schmitt as the inherent 'war' between peoples has come to define much of political theory today, also from the critical camp.

Mbembe explains this well when he argues that 'if the desire for apartheid is indeed one of the characteristics of our times, then actual Europe, for its part, will never again be as before – that is, monocolored. In other words, never again will there be (if it was ever the case) a unique center of the world' (Mbembe, 2019, p 63). In other words, Mbembe blames the current political situation not on populists, but on the inability of Europeans to reconcile with pluralism. This, then, is what leads to the fantasy of annihilation, of the complete destruction of the enemy.

This is a sign of what Furtado refers to as 'ontological militarism' (Furtado, 2023), which indicates how many academic fields (as well as public debate) are designed around the basic assumption that conflict is what dictates our lives. Militarism and a desire for violence, according to Furtado, is not simply one fantasy among many others, but is the ontological cipher through which we understand the world:

> Ontological militarism, which should be understood as the linguistic substratum that such metaphors reveal, consists, thus, of two central elements: (1) the attribution of heuristic privilege to war as an a priori of the social, that is, the cypher through which all social relations become legible; and (2) the foreclosure of alternative ontologies and forms of political action by investment in an assumed indistinction between war/peace and war/struggle. (Furtado, 2023, p 3)

Such insights can be directly applied to our common understandings of populism. The field has, as I have demonstrated, not managed to move beyond this founding moment of conflict and thus separation. Difference and the alienation of the subject – so influential for discourse theory – are constantly being read as conflict. This is not to say that Laclau or other discourse theorists were necessarily committed to seeing the world in a militaristic manner. Nevertheless, the incessant focus on how difference translates into conflictual relations, into antagonism, is the central focus of Laclau's work, and also what many would term his main contribution (Žižek, 1990). This also becomes excessively clear when looking at how discursive accounts of populism look today, where the antagonistic relationship is often at the heart of the matter.

As I have argued, such a commitment to antagonism as the main cipher of politics must be put into question, and we must also engage with how certain conflicts are kept alive and exacerbated due to an unwillingness among scholars and public commentators to see difference as non-conflictual. As such, we must make the phantasmatic aspect of antagonism visible, how it is constructed and sustained, which will be developed in the next two chapters. In the end, I will show that what we call populism is part and parcel of Europe. Europe has a populist condition. This may also be why scholars such as Dussel reject populism as an emancipatory project. According to Dussel, populism (in Latin America) is simply 'a process hegemonized by the national bourgeoise'. On the other hand, the 'popular' is what describes 'the movement driven by the 'people' as the 'social bloc' of the suppressed: exploited classes, ethnic and marginalized groups (my translation) (Dussel, 1977, p 71).

The fantasy of separation can also be seen in how populist movements and parties are labelled as transgressive, and therefore subversive. As will be developed in Chapters 4 and 5, the empirical examples of populism in which we currently trade, there is little evidence that these movements subvert coloniality. Many of the studies on the transgressive nature of populist politics focus on the 'bad manners' of populist leaders (Moffitt, 2016; Ostiguy, 2017) and do not pay sufficient attention to the policy choices advocated by said leaders, or how the alleged transgressions are completely in line with the liberal centre (Eklundh & Ronderos, 2025). As I have argued and has been made abundantly clear by a range of scholars, what we term populism is, in fact, very closely related to liberalism (Brown et al, 2021; Mondon, 2024; Mondon & Winter, 2020). As I pointed out in Chapter 1, this follows from a history of liberalism which is unable to escape the spectre of coloniality.

If populist movements do not, after all, transgress anything, why do we keep saying that they do? The fantasy of separation and the enjoyment embedded in this fantasy can help us understand things better. For the European mind there is a desire to be seen as a world saviour, as someone fundamentally good. This can only be achieved if European political subjectivity is purged of its violent qualities – xenophobia, colonial violence, border control, etc. The 'Populist' becomes the ideal candidate and fills the important role of externalizing the inherently violent practices so common in Europe, past and present. The Populist assumes the role of the thief of enjoyment, the one who prevents good and liberal Europeans from doing politics properly. This eclipses any debate about how the real 'Other' of Europe is not the malevolent Populist but the uncivilized Savage which the White European Man has sought to dominate for centuries.

The fantasy of separation has a natural conclusion so crucial to the European frame: mastery and domination over others. Many studies on political identities from a discursive perspective argue that our desire is to create order, to settle our subjectivity through the symbolic (Mandelbaum, 2020; Stavrakakis, 2002). While this is eminently true, we can also draw on decolonial scholarship to explain that what we desire is not simply any identity which creates order, but a very particular identity which affords us domination over others (Fanon, 2021). The creation of European Man, in other words, is not simply based on a desire to belong, but on a desire to command (Maldonado-Torres, 2008). This is due to the construction of the Savage as not simply different, but as a threatening subaltern, which constantly has the potentiality to negate civilized Man (Maldonado-Torres, 2007; Mbembe, 2019).

As has been so eloquently explained by Wynter, the humanist world view, in which God had created the world for Man's sake (*propter nos homines*) (Wynter, 2003, p 280), enabled Western intellectuals to equate humanity with the European experience. The Western Man was a universalizing force – in order to be considered human, you had to be like the Western Man. This is the inevitable connection between coloniality and modernity (Mignolo, 2011). Any other articulation of humanity, therefore, was impossible. Wynter also develops how political thought at the time was very preoccupied with explaining the qualities that Man must possess in order to be a worthy replacement of God. She argues 'that the master code of symbolic life ("the name of what is good") and death ("the name of what is evil") would now become that of reason/sensuality, rationality/irrationality in the reoccupied place of the matrix code of Redeemed Spirit/Fallen Flesh' (Wynter, 2003, p 287).

What we must note here is the coloniality adds a necessary layer of analysis to any psychoanalytical conception of identification. How can we, reasonably, think about political identities in Europe without engaging with one of the founding historical events? I argue that to understand populism and the role it plays in European politics, the desire for mastery within the mainstream cannot be ignored, and to simply repeat the, by now quite tired, distinctions between the People and the Elite closes the debate about what European politics does, and why.

Conclusion

In this chapter, I have argued that we need a new approach to thinking about populism in Europe. I have done so by making two main points. First, I have investigated how the discursive approach to populism struggles with coloniality on both an ontological and ontic level. Ontologically, there is a lingering commitment to seeing difference as conflictul antagonism, which I argue is situated in coloniality. Similarly, I have discussed how the movements which are labelled as populist in Europe do not really do what the discursive approach would argue that populism does: challenging the status quo and subverting the political order. What we call populism in Europe, I argue, is not at odds with the rather violent history and present of the continent – it is not an expression of the political.

Second, I have argued that we can use the concept of fantasy – particularly the fantasy of a separation between Europe and its Others – to fully explain what is going on in European politics and why populism has become such an omnipresent term. I claim that coloniality makes visible the common histories of liberalism, populism, and elitism in Europe – there is no contradiction between them. Through this lens, what are often termed populist movements and parties today become simply another form of articulation of the status quo – the liberal, exclusionary colonial order. I argue, however, that the fantasy of separation conceals these common histories. It paints the populist as fundamentally at odds with what Europeans think they are: equal and inclusive. Contrarily, as I have pointed out in Chapter 1, the European mainstream is far from it. The construction of the populist as the main enemy sustains the fantasy that Europe is an inclusionary place committed to equality.

In the next two chapters, I will demonstrate how the separation between the People and the Elite, between populism and the mainstream, is a phantasmatic structure. The chapters are built through different ciphers where we can see the desire for conflict and separation, and how it pervades populist and non-populist European politics alike. First of all, we will look at the gendered politics of populism. I will show how populist parties, much like their mainstream counterparts, promote a gender unequal world view, one which is based on militarized masculinities and in which politics becomes simply another articulation of the homosocial bond. Second, I will show how populist parties, particularly on the left, also struggle to leave behind a commitment to colonial ideas, the supremacy of nation-states, and seeing rationality as a superior mode of doing politics. As such, populism, instead of providing an alternative, becomes yet another instance of mainstream Europe.

4

Populism and Gender: Feminist Lessons on the People

When discussing populism and gender, we often end up in foregone conclusion: populists are terrible for any advances towards gender equality and remain a threat to women's rights in Europe and therefore to the European liberal democratic project. While there is much truth to this statement, reality proves far more complicated. It appears there is not a black and white situation where all populists are categorically rejecting gender equality as a political goal, and some try to use it to their political advantage. For instance, the Sweden Democrats claim to defend women's rights. What of the gender policies of the left-wing Podemos, which have included strengthened measures to combat violence against women? How can we explain the rather peculiar commitment to gender equality of populism left and right? At the same time, we must also recognize that many hindrances to gender equality are present within the mainstream. How then can we better understand the differences between mainstream gender politics and populist gender politics? I contend that extant literature on populism requires further development.

We could engage with Mudde and Kaltwasser's claim that 'conceptually, populism has no specific relationship to gender'; in fact, 'gender differences, like all other differences within "the people", are considered secondary, if not irrelevant, to populist politics' (Mudde & Kaltwasser, 2015, p 16). While this may seem like a fruitful approach in a first instance, it does not explain the rather chauvinist patterns of leadership within the mainstream. This is even recognized by Mudde and Kaltwasser, who admit that their 'analysis provides a somewhat muddled picture' (Mudde & Kaltwasser, 2015, p 16). The problem remains – we struggle to draw the lines between what constitutes populist politics (bad for gender equality) and mainstream politics (good for gender equality). Other commentators are equally confused and draw on the age-old horseshoe theory – that extreme right and extreme left parties eventually meet at the bottom of the horseshoe – to explain how populists approach gender. James Angelos from Politico, when analysing the German left-populist BSW, even asks 'Is Germany's rising superstar so far left she's far right?' (Angelos, 2024).

The aim of this chapter, therefore, is to help un-muddle the waters by telling a different story, by using the insights from decolonial theory and psychoanalysis, as described in Chapters 1 and 3. In this story, threats to gender equality are not foreign to European mainstream politics, and largely predate any populist movements. The rights that many women currently enjoy in European countries have been hard won, and not without struggle, and more often than not championed by socialist parties. Nevertheless, there remains a significant imbalance in gender equality, which of course differs in its nature across the European continent. It is sufficient to state, however, that Europe has not provided a gender-equal paradise.

Then why do we keep insisting that populism is such a threat to 'who we are'(Agius, 2022) as a gender-equal society? An alternative explanation can be found if we introduce the frame of coloniality into the picture. By seeing gender as simply another facet of coloniality – and the ensuing hierarchy between men and women as conceptualized by Western patriarchy – it is possible to connect the dots between populism and the mainstream. As I will demonstrate, both populists and mainstream parties are unable to escape the frame of coloniality. Importantly, the concept of fantasy can help us even further to explain why the position of the threatening populist remains. Here we can discern the enjoyment by mainstream European political actors in sustaining the fantasy of a benevolent, gender-equal, and civil European culture, one which is under threat from 'external' populist forces.

In this chapter, I investigate the alleged differences in gender policies between populists and the mainstream. I will engage with a variety of cases across left- and right-wing populism, and contrast these with the liberal mainstream. Importantly, this chapter will not only demonstrate that the mainstream is similar to populists when it comes to gender equality but also situate this in a phantasmatic frame. This chapter argues that the very presence of the populist as the main threat to a gender-equal Europe provides a sense of enjoyment for the European mainstream. It sustains the fantasy that Europeans are good at gender equality. Crucially, this phantasmatic frame of superiority must be connected with the frame of coloniality. Europeans feed a fantasy that their subjectivity is built on equality, when, in history and the present, the modern European subject is steeped in coloniality which is tightly linked to oppressive masculinity. Coloniality thus nourishes two simultaneous fantasies of gender equality and civility. Importantly, the chapter demonstrates that populism, in its current European form, does not signify very strong challenge to the status quo in terms of how gender politics is performed and enacted, but that the problem of gender inequality cannot be externalized since it comes from within.

This chapter will proceed as follows: first, I will give an overview of contemporary scholarship on gender and populism, which is a burgeoning field. Second, I will discuss how gender politics is one of the key interfaces of coloniality using decolonial feminism, as described in Chapter 1. Third, I will engage empirical examples to demonstrate how left-wing populism and the liberal European centre are rearticulating gender politics influenced by coloniality. In particular, I will focus on the policies of Podemos in Spain, the BSW in Germany, and security policies within the EU. Throughout, I will explain how we can see the construction of the populist as the simultaneous construction of the fantasy of the gender-equal and civil European.

Contemporary scholarship on the gendered politics of populism

The focus on gender in populism studies is growing and identifies many of the issues previously raised. One of the key focuses concerns the demand side of populism, namely the voter demographic. Can we say that men to a higher degree vote for populist parties? The evidence is not straightforward, with Spierings and Zaslove arguing that the difference in voting behaviour (which does exist between men and women) cannot be fully explained by looking at socioeconomic status, for instance. Instead, we must look at the populist attitudes of voters, but even then we cannot create a watertight correlation between gender and voting behaviour (Spierings & Zaslove, 2015, 2017). There is also significant scholarship on the performance and leadership of populist parties, and how these are gendered practices (Meret, 2015; Norocel, 2018).

There are also quite a few discussions on how leadership in populist movements is often perpetuating the idea of the charismatic leader, who exhibits strong power and governs the parties according to their own wishes. This is what Mudde has referred to as Männerpartien, parties for and by men (Mudde, 2007). There are, however, several contemporary cases of populist parties being led by women, such as Marine Le Pen in France (former leader of Rassemblement National) and Pia Kjaersgaard in Denmark (former leader of Dansk Folkeparti), as well as Alice Weidel in Germany (Alternative für Deutschland). These women are, nonetheless, often supporting social and family policies which confirm a belief in traditional gender roles; the parties are not in favour of increased paternity leave, and see women as destined to care for the home and family (Mudde and Kaltwasser, 2015; Norocel, 2018). Both Kjaersgaard and Le Pen have expressed hostilities towards feminist movements.

At the same time, some would argue that it is neither here nor there whether a party is led by a man or a woman, that populism has little to do with gender, and that populists rarely concern themselves with gender issues.

While it may be true that populists do not have the most elaborate gender policies, does this mean that there is no connection? This is narrative which is strongly rooted in populism research. Even the more critical segments of the field tend to reinforce the stereotype that men with little income are the most likely to become populist, such as Miller-Idriss (2017). As such, it is men who are marginalized that are turning to populism, since they are looking for a sense of 'remasculation', and this is reinforced by Mudde and Kaltwasser (2015) who have argued that regaining masculinity, not racism, is the driving force behind the far right. The 'lost' masculinity is often explained as having lost one's job or income, due to increases in immigration.

This statement deserves some scrutiny. As was also discussed in Chapter 2, we can see that the narrative that it is the lowest brackets of society that vote for populists is not immediately clear. The voter composition of the populist parties in Europe is much more nuanced, and often carries significant elite support (Benquet & Bourgeron, 2022; De Cleen & Ruiz Casado, 2024; Karavasilis, 2025; Schoor, 2019). Many studies argue that populist voters are in fact quite wealthy and can therefore not be said to have 'lost' much at all. One of the most seminal studies on the topic is from Norris, who has analysed several elections of populist parties, including Trump and the Brexit vote, and she has discovered that the economic factors, while influential, are not the strongest determinants of populist voters: age and gender are much more so (Norris & Inglehart, 2019). As turnout rates are normally much lower for younger voters, this further eschews the importance of that demographic for populist parties in national elections (Norris & Inglehart, 2019). Similarly, Mondon and Winter argue that the reporting on populist successes often peddles the narrative of the 'revolt of the white working class' (2018, p 2). This narrative, however, disregards the diversity of the working class, and Mondon and Winter challenge the idea that the 'left behind by globalisation' are the prime populist voters. This ignores the very strong levels of support for nativist and nationalist policies among the wealthier segments of society and pits the ignorant working class against the enlightenment cosmopolitans, further sedimenting the experience of exclusion in these communities. As such, the narrative that it is poor men who are to blame for the rise of populism is riddled with caveats.

There is ample research on the very direct and often spectacular nature of right-wing populist movements. For instance, Miller-Idriss has in several works described how masculinity in the German far right is often tightly knit with a nationalist narrative. In order to be a 'proper' male, one must also adopt the traditional markers of the warrior. She argues that the desire for male senses of belonging (which are so often offered through the military) is highly present in the construction of the right-wing identity (Miller-Idriss, 2017). These markers are often expressed through clothing, and reinforce a sense of 'idealized images of soldiers, a sense of service to the nation and its people, [and] valorization of heterosexuality and national reproduction through fatherhood and childrearing' (Miller-Idriss, 2017, p 206). This is also supported by Simi et al (2013) who connect the traditional markers of the military with right-wing groups. This also relates to the use of femonationalism to further political causes, such as the example of Giorgia Meloni in Italy and her strong belief in the 'natural family' (De Giorgi et al, 2023).

There are also narratives which complicate matters further. Through research by Keskinen (2018) we can learn that the right wing often make claims to feminism in their politics, most notably around the issue of violence against women. Keskinen has written extensively on the Finnish case, and how the Finnish populist right has employed the narrative of protecting women from violent assaults. The debate was from the beginning fraught with falsehoods and inaccurate statistics, but the far right nonetheless managed to build a picture of a non-European invasion threatening the gender-equal way of life of ordinary Finnish people. The whole debate rested on an assumption that Finnish men were incapable of assault, whereas foreign men were natural predators eager for 'blond women' (Keskinen, 2018). This type of triangulation has allowed the far right to capitalize on sentiments of pride of gender equality so common in Scandinavia. This can be seen in further research, which has argued that right-wing movements are often 'instrumentally inclusive', meaning that their commitment to gender equality or LGBT rights is simply a strategy to reach new voters, but there is no deeper belief in these values (Turnbull-Dugarte & López Ortega, 2024).

In sum, the scholarship on populism and gender zooms in on social mechanisms with which we are familiar. What emerges is a picture where the external and malevolent populists propagate a politics which is damaging to the very foundation of European democracy. However, such a narrative cannot be left uncontradicted, but we must ask ourselves whether this is really an external phenomenon, and if there are not similar traits and thoughts in the European mainstream. To do so, this chapter now turns to decolonial feminism and will further explain that the narrative around gender politics and populism is also steeped in the fantasy of separation between the good European liberal centre and the bad and misogynist populist.

Gender as another interface of coloniality

There is ample scholarship on how patriarchy governs the world, often in tandem with capitalist principles (Johnston & Meger, 2024), where it becomes obvious that our modern state structure is reliant on patriarchy (Connell, 1990). As explained in Chapter 1, the figure of the husband/father is what carries society forward. For instance, the core issue of rationality has, in practice, become tightly intertwined with *masculinity*. Women have been seen as incapable of rational thought, and therefore unfit for political life. Importantly, politics is seen as homosocial (Mackay et al, 2010), indicating that men favour the actions of other men due to gender identification and trust. Politics is thus masculinized – it is favouring those characteristics which are most associated with male behaviour, such as *competition* and *argumentation* (Jones et al, 2009), in opposition to cooperation and consensus. This is not to say that there is an essential idea of feminine or masculine traits – the categories are used to identify hierarchical behaviour, while still recognizing that such behaviour is socially contingent (Butler, 1990; Cho et al, 2013). Importantly, the issue of representation goes beyond the definition as leadership and refers to the many other impediments to female empowerment in politics (Verge & de la Fuente, 2014). Women are often precluded from full participation due to the prioritization of the 'male experience regarding authority, competitiveness, ambition, and certain forms of rationality' (Verge & de la Fuente, 2014, p 71). Furthermore, the possibility of feminizing politics and placing greater emphasis on cooperation is often seen as inefficient and utopian.

The assumption made by significant parts of the scholarship on populism that populists somehow threaten or diverge from the mainstream and status quo is not without its problems. As we know, there is ample work in feminist scholarship which demonstrates the exact opposite – it is politics as usual that harbours the most widespread and damaging practices which results in gender inequality. Using Quijano's idea of the colonial matrix of power (Quijano, 2000, 2007), we must interrogate how gender is another prism through which coloniality functions. As Lugones argues, we cannot 'keep on centering our analysis on the patriarchy; that is, on a binary, hierarchical, oppressive gender formation that rests on male supremacy without any clear understanding of the mechanisms by which heterosexuality, capitalism, and racial classification are impossible to understand apart from each other' (Lugones, 2007, p 187). Lugones identifies concomitant problems in contemporary scholarship: white feminists do not take coloniality seriously, and decolonial scholars do not always take gender seriously. The only way forward is to join the two together. These insights have enabled the development of decolonial feminist scholarship, which rejects the idea that gender can be studied without also studying race or capitalism.[1]

Decolonial feminism is not a monolithic field and contains several different interpretations both of coloniality and gender. Quijano is by no means the end all, and is heavily criticized by feminist scholars for treating gender as a biological reality and not as a social construct, and is therefore regarded as closer to the more Eurocentric idea of gender (Mendoza, 2015). It must also be noted, of course, that the most recognized names in decolonial studies (Dussel, Quijano, Maldonado-Torres, and Mignolo) are all men (Velez & Tuana, 2020). Similarly, there is some debate on whether patriarchy and gender hierarchies were non-existent in the colonies prior to the arrival of the Europeans (Lugones, 2007) or whether there were indeed some form of gendered social relations but that these were made worse by colonization (Segato, 2022). Regardless, however, there is agreement that there is a particular form of gendered politics associated with coloniality, and that this is concurrent with the other forms of violence committed in the name of European superiority. As such, it sees gender as much broader than Quijano's idea of 'sex' or the 'sexual', and that there are gender relations which need not be governed by coloniality (Lugones, 2007, p 189), but at the same time there are hegemonic understandings of gender, primarily through the lenses of dimorphism, heterosexuality, and patriarchy. Lugones aims to keep Quijano's understanding of race and coloniality but wants to develop what she terms the modern/colonial gender system. We are still operating on the basis that modernity/coloniality functions across labour, sex, collective authority, and intersubjectivity. As such, Quijano presents coloniality as 'a conception of humanity ... according to which the world's population was differentiated in two groups: superior and inferior, rational and irrational, primitive and civilized, traditional and modern. Primitive referred to a prior time in the history of the species, in terms of evolutionary time' (as cited in Lugones, 2007, p 192), but the gender aspect of this needs to be specified. Lugones here draws on the concept of intersectionality (Cho et al, 2013) to argue that it is indeed only when we fuse race and gender that we can fully understand current power relations. We cannot comprehend the reality for women by solely looking at their racialized identity – their gender is likely to exacerbate inequality. Importantly, this is a product of coloniality – the introduction of the European state system also meant the exclusion of women from spaces where they had previously been included (Oyěwùmí, 1997, p 123): 'the transformation of state power to male-gender power was accomplished at one level by the exclusion of women from state structures. This was in sharp contrast to Yoruba state organization, in which power was not gender-determined.' As such, there were two simultaneous processes of inferiorization, one of non-whites and one of women. The binaries of civilized/uncivilized and rational/emotional must thus be differentiated between genders, not simply race. Colonization therefore also meant the destruction of social relations not based on patriarchy.

Decolonial feminism can thus offer us an explanatory lens which is not currently available through populism studies or mainstream feminist theory. Coloniality – of which gender is but one part – can help us see through the blurring of the lines between populism and the mainstream; the muddy waters are not so muddy after all. Since both populists and mainstream politics are situated within the field of coloniality, it is not very strange that there are similar modes of thinking. However, the function of the 'populist' and the reason why we keep seeing threats to gender equality as an external problem, is the enjoyment that this brings to the European mainstream, and the sustention of the fantasy that Europe promotes and cherishes gender equality.

It has been made abundantly clear in previous research that right-wing populists are indeed promoting a view of gender which is fully accepting the truths offered by the colonial world view. What has been less investigated is how these views permeate other political actors, too. In the remainder of this chapter, I will provide a series of illustrative examples to demonstrate that left-wing populism and the mainstream also perpetuate the modern/colonial gender system. Crucially, the breakdown of the dividing lines between right-wing populism, left-wing populism, and the mainstream demonstrates that the difference between the 'People' and the 'Elite' is but a chimera.

The examples chosen are not case studies, but illustrations of how the discursive field of coloniality still exerts a strong grip on all of these areas. Importantly, I will focus especially on how the divisions and antagonistic constructions between populism and the mainstream only work to cover up the colonial underpinnings of European politics. Populism, in other words, does not significantly challenge the status quo. The assumption that it would, I argue, is a phantasmatic structure – to see the main threat to equality in Europe as being the malevolent 'populists' sustains the fantasy, and thus the enjoyment, of seeing Europe as benevolent, civil, gender-equal. To unveil this fantasy, we must interrogate how also so-called 'progressive' populisms and the liberal mainstream also sediment the modern/colonial gender system.

The modern/colonial gender system in left-wing populism

First, we can consider how easy it has been for European politics to mainstream the far-right populist demands (Brown, 2024; Brown et al, 2021). Through an invocation of the so-called migration crisis, European governments have continuously supported the demands for strengthened borders, for clearer policies on integration, and for outright reductions in new arrivals. Underlying this change of policy is a firm belief in the modern state system, where nation-state borders must be upheld to create order. The nation-state is, in fact, a constant re-articulation of who is worthy as a citizen, and who is not; who is included, and who is not. Populism, in this sense, does not demand anything which is external to contemporary European politics; it is simply reaffirming the very foundations upon which it was built. The literature on masculinity and populism is quick to condemn far-right populists as Islamophobic when they argue that minorities must abide by 'traditional' values. Nonetheless, many European states have for a long time demanded that new arrivals adapt to certain cultural patterns, such as the defence of secularism in France. This predates any of the contemporary populist movements and is a core component of European democracies. As is so common in liberal thought, European constitutional values are seen as not only separate but superior to any other values, be those religious or philosophical. As such, while it is clear that many of the policies advocated by the populist right are deeply racist and xenophobic, it becomes difficult to argue that this is unusual or novel for European democracies.

Second, coloniality is also tightly interlinked with that of masculinity as default. From leaders to citizens, modern democracies are built on the male persona (Dean & Maiguashca, 2018). Leadership is often equated with signs of power, of self-confidence, and with a certain aggressive air, all traditionally masculine attributes. This style of leadership, as I argued earlier, is common on the populist right, but also equally present on the populist left, and within the mainstream. Here, we can use the figure of the modern/colonial gender system to see how the masculine as default is not an external problem, but forms part and parcel of how politics is enacted in Europe.

One of the key players in left-wing populist politics in Europe is Spanish Podemos, founded in 2014 by several university professors, who have been in a coalition government with the social democratic PSOE (Partido Socialista Obrero de España).[2] Podemos is often said to embody how left-wing populism has become possible in Europe, by taking inspiration from left-wing populist examples in Latin America. Nevertheless, I argue that there are several instances where Podemos struggle to break free from coloniality.

Podemos are in many ways governed by a masculine logic. To a large degree, the feminist policies of Podemos are a clear improvement for party politics in Spain – Podemos state clearly that they are a party committed to feminist principles, and this has become even more accentuated with the high profile of Irene Montero as equalities minister in the Sanchez cabinet. Montero has championed several high-profile policies, such as increasing rights for victims of sexual abuse, trans rights, and abortion rights (Borraz, 2023; Kohan, 2022; Público, 2022). As such, Podemos do support stronger protection for victims of domestic violence, and are in favour of stronger rights for women in the labour market (Iglesias et al, 2017). There has nevertheless been quite a substantial amount of criticism of Podemos from feminist activists and scholars, who take issue both with Podemos' way of doing politics and how they still articulate representation in a distinctly masculine way. The critics argue that Podemos, and in particular Pablo Iglesias, take their cues from the masculine playbook and that the party in general favour an adversarial rather than a cooperative logic (Caravantes, 2019, 2020).

When looking more closely at Iglesias, there is evidence that he belongs to a more old-fashioned form of left-wing organizing, which is not particularly famous for the commitment to feminist principles. Iglesias has openly argued that 'feminists screw better' (Alemán, 2018), a statement for which he was widely criticized. Iglesias wanted to signal that he calls himself a feminist, but still argued that this commitment resulted in a 'feminist masculinity', indicating that the need for men to assert masculinity was still present. There is, according to Iglesias, a need to move beyond the *macho ibérico*, which is a certain flavour of *machista* politics local to the Iberian peninsula: often short, balding, and obsessed with money (Colmeiro, 2017). The new Spanish masculinity, on the other hand, is 'a male subjectivity premised on ethical probity, intellectual rationality, left-wing values, hypermodernity, and a misidentification with patriarchal values' (Ryan, 2017, p 80). However, this rejection of a certain type of masculinity over another does not deny the distinctly masculine elements of Iglesias discourse, which have been labelled as alpha male behaviour (Kantola & Lombardo, 2019). Iglesias' preference for intellectual debate, which can be seen in his frequent appearances on television talk shows where he can demonstrate his political acuity, goes hand in hand with the modern Spanish masculine ideal as the well-educated and aggressive intellectual (Caravantes, 2019). In addition, Podemos' strong emphasis on winning and beating their adversaries (Eklundh, 2019) plays right into the conflictual mindset of a Schmittian ontology, as described in Chapter 3. As such, Podemos has quite a difficult relationship with feminism, and, as argued by Caravantes and Lombardo, exhibit

> gendered elements which include the predominance of male leaders, the relegation of women and feminism to the background, and the exclusionary effects of the leaders' personalization. The competitive ethos, the factional dynamics transmitted top-down and the hierarchization that separates the party's leadership from the membership are particularly detrimental to the invoked feminist agenda. (Caravantes & Lombardo, 2023, p 913)

Iglesias has also become known for kissing fellow left-wing politicians on the lips and has claimed this as part of his modern and emancipated masculinity (Caravantes & Lombardo, 2023, p 913). The socialist fraternal kiss – perhaps most famously incarnated between Soviet leader Leonid Brezhnev and GDR head Erich Honecker at the 30th anniversary of the GDR in East Berlin in 1979 – is rather a reaffirmation of the homosocial bond, and indicates recognition between equals (Citron, 2016). Since Iglesias has not made it his habit to kiss his female colleagues on the lips as a greeting, the gesture strengthens the idea of politics as a male-dominated arena. Critics have also questioned the strong factionalism between Iglesias and the party's then political secretary, Iñigo Errejón. The leadership challenge launched at Iglesias resulted in much in-fighting and damaged the reputation of Podemos as a collaborative and cooperative organization. Errejón had to leave his seat in Congress in 2024 after he was the subject of several sexual harassment allegations. The legal proceedings against Errejón are still ongoing at the time of writing (PAÍS, 2025), but definitely casts a shadow over the feminist credentials of left-wing populism. Ultimately, Podemos does not detach representation from its masculine historical articulation but reiterates the exclusionary elements. As mentioned in Chapter 1, rationality and reasonable behaviour are key instances of coloniality. As Mbembe argues, the Western world equates power with virility and 'to be taken even remotely seriously, it is important at some point to show that "one has balls"'(Mbembe, 2019, p 61). The importance of rationality for the development of particularly masculine codes of political behaviour is pertinent when understanding how Podemos present themselves.

Another example of the gendered politics of left populism concerns the German party of Sahra Wagenknecht, which are less keen to label themselves as a feminist party, or a party for women. Wagenknecht, a former leader of the left-wing Die Linke, has now started her own homonymic party called the *Bündnis Sahra Wagenknecht – Vernunft und Gerechtigkeit* (Sahra Wagenknecht Alliance – Reason and Justice, BSW). The BSW have been criticized for their socially conservative policies which are mixed with a generous dose of critiques of the EU and economic elites. Throughout their initial manifesto, there is no mention of gender relations, how women may be affected by poverty to a higher degree than men, or any other gender related policy area. This is not an omission – one of the party founders, Thomas Giesel, has argued that gender politics has gone too far and that he can 'understand that gender gets on people's nerves', because 'people just don't care' (Mbembe, 2019, p 60). Wagenknecht develops this further when she argues that 'women in our group in particular are happy to live in a country that has by and large overcome patriarchy and they don't want to see it being reintroduced through the backdoor' (Wagenknecht, 2024, p 36). Here she connects migration to the worsening of women's rights, much in line with a similar reasoning so common on the populist right. The fantasy of the benevolent and gender-equal Europe is strong at work here, and which is why we must see migration policies in the light of the modern/colonial gender system. Or, in the words of Mbembe: 'The manipulation of questions of gender for racist ends, by way of illustrating the Other's masculine domination, is almost always aimed at concealing the reality of phallocracy at home' (Mbembe, 2019, p 60).

Even though the BSW clearly push for left-wing policies in some areas, it must be noted that their policies on migration and the preservation of the German native population are anything but, rather forming part of the modern/colonial gender system, which it is easy to find on the populist right. The populist left, in this instance, suffers from a similar dominance of coloniality as the populist right. The BSW and Wagenknecht in particular appeal to voters with 'immigration-sceptical, economically left, and culturally conservative attitudes' (Thomeczek, 2024). We can also see that she is labelled as left populist and with strong authoritarian tendencies (Thomeczek, 2024). Indeed, the BSW are tough on immigration, and do not agree with a generous immigration policy. This has caused commentators to argue that voters who are attracted by the rhetoric of the Alternative für Deutschland (AfD) would also be attracted to the BSW (Mudde, 2024). The rather awkward term 'conservative left' – which is frequently applied to the BSW – demonstrates the 'muddled waters' mentioned by Mudde regarding gender politics. According to Wagner, many Germans are ideologically close to the BSW with a strong focus on left-wing economic views and right-wing cultural views (Volmer & Wagner, 2024; Wagner et al, 2023).

As such, the BSW are seen as a contradictory and puzzling phenomenon – why on earth would a left-populist party commit to policies which are most often labelled as right wing? The left and right populist are, indeed, strange bedfellows. The populist frame does a lot of heavy lifting here: as we have seen so many times before, populism becomes the defining factor in understanding similarities between parties that may, at first sight, be radically different. The problem with the concept of populism (as well as populist actors), as explained in the previous chapters, is that it constructs a division between the People are the Elite which is much more tenuous than what is commonly acknowledged. Even though the rhetoric of the BSW contains strong populist elements, is it really the case that the policies proposed indicate a challenge to the status quo? Is it really the case that they challenge common norms and reject the field of discursivity, or do they reinforce coloniality?

In many ways, the BSW are simply reiterating the status quo of the German state. In terms of economic policy, they do criticize some large multinational corporations, such as Amazon or Blackrock, but they do not reject the fundamental commitment to capitalism, and speak in favour of protecting German small and medium enterprises (Bündnis Sahra Wagenknecht, 2024). The BSW sound precisely like a mid-century social democratic European party, when they argue in favour of a strengthened industrial policy which shall provide the 'backbone of wealth' (Bündnis Sahra Wagenknecht, 2024). They also have an unwavering belief in innovation, science, and start-ups that, apart from bringing economic growth, will solve the climate crisis. The BSW do not believe that the climate crisis warrants any major lifestyle changes, but that it should be solved with new technologies. There is also a recognition that international trade brings advantages for the German economy, which is not rich in raw materials (Bündnis Sahra Wagenknecht, 2024). Most of these policies echo the very right-wing mainstream and are not particularly innovative. One could argue that this is simply another articulation of capitalism.

Socially, the BSW are aware of the cost-of-living crisis and blame some of this on the increased privatization of social services. This is negative, not only because of the human cost but because 'a highly productive economy needs qualified and motivated employees' (Bündnis Sahra Wagenknecht, 2024, p 3). At the same time, there is a significant hostility towards immigration, and the party says outright that 'migration is not the solution for the problem of poverty in the world' (Bündnis Sahra Wagenknecht, 2024, p 4). The migrant population is posited as a threat towards the 'native' population, which live in an antagonistic zero-sum game over resources.

It becomes clear when engaging with these politics that coloniality and the modern/colonial gender system still sits at the forefront, in terms of economic policy, migration policy, and gender. The willingness to favour the market (albeit the internal market) and to see citizens as cogs in the capitalist machine indicates that there is no rupture between the European centre and the BSW. Similarly, on migration, the BSW are positing migrants as a threat to native Germans, and that they ultimately fight for resources.

Coloniality and gender in mainstream European politics

We have thus several examples of how the modern/colonial gender system prevails in both right-wing and left-wing populism. But for the purpose of this book, the main focus lies in making the connections between the 'People' and the 'Elite', between the outside populist and the inside mainstream, more visible. These connections, I argue, can be explained through the lens of coloniality. Furthermore, the sustention of the harmful populist as the Other in European politics carries the fantasy that Europeans are by nature civil and gender-equal. This is despite the fact that European politics is far from it, and rather built on exclusionary politics, as described in Chapter 1. The deep rifts between the mainstream and the populists are a chimera.

One of the most prevalent examples of coloniality in mainstream European politics comes into force on Europe's borders. Here, we can see the enforcement of European identity which is done in the name of European superiority. That the border politics of the EU are highly gendered has been studied at length in critical and feminist international relations (IR) scholarship, as well as in the more critical strands of European Integration (Manners, 2002). The EU is articulated as a global actor which is deeply influenced by its historical identities, but there are also tensions with regards to gender. There is ample research demonstrating that the EU is clearly concerned with gender equality (Chappell & Guerrina, 2020), which reaffirms the argument of this book that there is a strong phantasmatic investment in this particular identity. However, recent events point to a strong racialized and gendered policy process, which has been the focus of much research within critical strands in IR. This research has focussed mostly on the security and migration policies of the EU, which are allegedly the most obvious sites where coloniality comes into play. As mentioned in the introduction and as so aptly observed by Hoijtink et al (2023), the High Representative of the Union for Foreign Affairs and Security Policy Josep Borrell is a clear example of this, as we can see from one of his speeches in 2022:

> Europe is a garden. We have built a garden. Everything works. It is the best combination of political freedom, economic prosperity and social cohesion that the humankind has been able to build – the three things together. And here, Bruges is maybe a good representation of beautiful things, intellectual life, wellbeing. The rest of the world … is not exactly a garden. Most of the rest of the world is a jungle, and the jungle could invade the garden. (Borrell, 2022)

To be fair on Borrell, he continues this speech by saying that we cannot build walls around the garden, because the 'wall will never be high enough in order to protect the garden' (Borrell, 2022). However, this provides a textbook case of coloniality, in every sense of the word. Borrell leaves no doubt that he believes in the superiority of Europe and its people, and that those people must be protected from the non-Europeans. Europe is not simply a political unit, but the beautiful against the ugly, the intellectual against the stupid, and wellbeing against misery. Some might argue that these are simply words, but the line of reasoning remains throughout policy enactment on Europe's borders.

This connects to the EU's 'civilising mission' (Onar & Nicolaïdis, 2013), which is a direct example of the phantasmatic investment in European superiority. As such, when we talk about 'normative power Europe' – which is often seen by EU studies scholars as a convincing explanation for the type of international actor the European Union is – we must acknowledge that this type of power is built on a conviction that Europe is superior. We cannot understand the civilizing mission without also remembering Europe's historical civilizing missions, and the violence that ensued in their wake. The superiority is further echoed by Borrell when he states that:

> There is a big difference between Europe and the rest of the world – well, the rest of the world, understand me what I mean, no? – is that we have strong institutions. The most important thing for the quality of life of the people is institutions. The big difference between developed and not developed is not the economy, it is institutions. Here, we have a judiciary – a neutral, independent judiciary. Here, we have systems of distributing the revenue. (Borrell, 2022)

Such a belief in the excellence of the EU's institutions is reminiscent of colonial times when the presence of Europeans on other continents was justified with reference to the supremacy of their governance. It is also a carbon copy of what Habermas has argued throughout his works, that strong processes and institutions will lead to democracy, and that these institutions have to be liberal, in a European sense (Habermas, 1996), as discussed in Chapter 1. This perspective is also prevalent in general EU security policies. As argued by Sachseder and Stachowitsch (2023), the Common Security and Defence Policy (CSDP) is riddled with ideas which promote the EU's security policy as the 'white man's burden' (Narayan, 1995). The EU, on the other hand, is afforded all the qualities of a civilized European: masculine, enlightened, and rational. This is seen through a focus on 'resilience' against the Other who is often labelled as 'chaotic', 'in turmoil', or simply 'violent' (Sachseder & Stachowitsch, 2023, p 413). Furthermore, the EU is associated with 'rationality, technocratic neutrality, and professionalism' (Sachseder & Stachowitsch, 2023, p 415). Similarly, we can see instances of the modern/colonial gender system in the EU's security collaboration with Tunisia, where the way that training is provided by the EU to Tunisian security officials retains strong gender divisions and contributes to a militarized understanding of a gendered division of labour (Musina, 2023).

While security and border policies are indeed important, there are also other policy areas where European mainstream parties are clearly governed by the modern/colonial gender system. One of the most noted policies in this area concerns the prohibition of wearing a head covering, such as the hijab and the niqab, in several European countries, such as France. These policies were not, in fact, instituted by any populist party, but implemented by the conservative President Sarkozy. Other similar examples in the region include the Norwegian mandatory 'citizen education' for new arrivals, similar to the more extreme Danish policy of making nursery attendance compulsory for children from 'ghetto' areas (now called parallel societies) (Witcombe, 2019). This policy was instituted in 2018 by the right-wing coalition government between two liberal and one conservative parties, but no populists. The policy endeavours to ensure that the 'child can be introduced to Danish traditions, celebrations, standards and values' (Witcombe, 2019), but is only directed towards areas with high levels of immigrants and ethnic minorities from 'non-Western' countries. No similar policy exists for parents who do not live in a 'ghetto' area. More recently, the UK government's decision to accept a 'biological' definition of gender identity which should decide which bathroom facilities you are allowed to enter is another example of how the modern/colonial gender system is alive and well (Brocklehurst, 2025). In essence, both the UK Supreme Court and the Equalities and Human Rights Commission in the UK have accepted a view of gender which is one of the most socially conservative globally.

What we can see in the earlier paragraphs is a deep wish to externalize the phenomenon of the populist. The problem is always someone else: it is the uneducated working class; it is the rural voters afraid of migration; it is weak individuals charmed by mad demagogues. Contrary to this, I propose that populism is internal rather than external to European democracies. In many senses, populism constitutes the mirror image of European democracy and modernity, and could be seen as internal to liberal democracy, instead of external to it. According to many critical scholars, among them feminist and decolonial theorists, European modernity is founded upon the very characteristics so common in populism. The male attributes which are commonly found in right-wing populism are, in fact, not too far removed from the regular modus operandi of 'mainstream' politics.

Importantly, it is not enough to argue that there are similarities between populism and the mainstream. While I have demonstrated earlier that both left-wing populism and the liberal mainstream exhibit similar traits to right-wing populists, we must also ask *why* we are so committed to seeing a separation between the populists and the 'normal' mainstream. I argue that the fantasy of a separation works to conceal the real problem (Žižek, 2015), namely the violent and exclusionary history and present of European politics. If violence, authoritarianism, misogyny, and inequality can be blamed on someone else, then this exonerates the liberal centre. As such, there is a strong desire to maintain the figure of the populist as the source of all the ills of Europe. As a counterpoint, the concept of coloniality enables us to look beyond the fantasy of separation to see the common commitment to European superiority across the political spectrum.

Conclusion

We started this chapter by seeing how much of the current commentary on populism and gender expresses bewilderment. How can we possibly explain the very varying stances towards gender from populists? How can we understand the 'strange bedfellows' between feminists and populists, when they should be mortal enemies? How is it possible for populists, the very antithesis of European gender equality, to capitalize on gender issues? This chapter has argued that by looking into the fantasies constructed within the frame of coloniality, we can explain the very varied empirical picture.

We first saw how the scholarship on right-wing populism and gender is quite substantial, and how much of this work is focussed on how right-wing populists fulfil a certain stereotype of the insecure white male who feels like his place in modern society is threatened. While there is some truth to this picture, it does not fully answer our questions posed earlier. There are some studies which point to the intersections between race and gender, but, overall, contemporary scholarship on populism does not engage much with coloniality. As such, it becomes difficult for some to see how 'good' narratives of gender equality and LGBT rights can be appropriated by right-wing populists.

To remedy this, I turn to decolonial feminism to provide a framework through which we can understand how the mainstream and the populists are equally committed to (or restricted by) coloniality. By understanding how patriarchy and gender inequality is largely a phenomenon tied to Euopean modernity, the similarities and overlaps between populism and the mainstream are not strange or surprising. Here, there are no 'strange bedfellows', since these perspectives have shared a bed already for centuries. The devaluation of women, much like the devaluation of the non-white, 'savage' population in the colonies, functions according to a similar pattern.

The similarities and overlaps become obvious when we start looking for them. All of a sudden, the masculine presentation of Podemos' leadership or the hostile views on immigration from the BSW are not strange – they are natural conclusions of the European world view steeped in coloniality. What is more, this world view is perpetuated by the centre mainstream actors, such as Borrell when he speaks about Europe's garden. This is not to say that there are no exceptions to this behaviour – there are many instances where European political actors do not directly engage in coloniality (as will be further discussed in the Conclusion). However, the main point of this chapter is to demonstrate that coloniality is still a dominant perspective, and even the parties and politicians who we might think are the furthest away from this perspective still do not manage to escape it.

Why, then, do we keep saying that populism forms such a substantial threat to European democracy? Where does the unwillingness to recognize the similarities come from? Here, I have argued that the reason that populism as a concept is so popular is due to the enjoyment that the European mainstream draws from the distinction between themselves and the populists, between good and evil. The fantasy that Europe is a force for good and not a violent oppressor of other peoples holds the whole continent in a firm grip. We simply cannot conceive of the populist as a natural conclusion of European politics. This fantasy has several different layers, and but is not simply about creating political community. By creating European superiority, there is also a justification of mastery.

5

Good Populisms? Inclusionary Politics on the Left

In this final chapter, we arrive at what is the final beacon of hope for many in today's political landscape: maybe there is a version of populism which does not have to be bad? Maybe it is possible to speak to the voters attracted by the populist appeal, and still promote an emancipatory or progressive agenda? There are, indeed, numerous examples of where this has been attempted. The increasing line of left-populist parties in Europe argue that they are trying to do precisely this – save Europe from itself. This can be seen in several examples of left populism in Europe, for instance Podemos, Syriza, the BSW (as discussed in Chapter 4), La France Insoumise in France led by Jean-Luc Mélenchon, and the UK Labour Party under Jeremy Corbyn.

There is ample literature which argues that populism can and should be used for left-wing politics, and that the two are entirely compatible (Gerbaudo, 2017; Mouffe, 2018). This has also given rise to a host of scholarship on the so-called inclusionary populisms in Europe (Markou, 2017; Mudde & Rovira Kaltwasser, 2012). The question of the commitment to the People as the primary vehicle of politics has also been widely debated, where it has been argued that left-wing parties are able to rearticulate the People for progressive purposes (Custodi, 2020; Custodi & Padoan, 2022), and not as an exclusionary, ethnic definition.

The aims of the European left-wing populists are clear: they wish to pose a counterweight to the neoliberal policies of the EU (which is why many label them as soft Eurosceptics), they wish to imagine the People of Europe as more inclusionary, and they wish to increase democratic accountability. For many of them, there are clear inspirations and synergies with the wave of left populism in the early 21st century in Latin America. The so-called Pink tide indicates the wave of left-wing, populist politicians who were in power in Brazil, Venezuela, Argentina, and many more in the early 2000s (Biglieri & Cadahia, 2021; Casullo, 2019). Building on a resistance to neoliberal globalization, European left-wing populists, like their Latin American counterparts, want to stand up to unequal power relations.

As described in Chapter 2, there is a substantial portion of the literature on left-wing populism which would argue that it is the answer to our problems. We can consider how, for instance, Mouffe (2018), is convinced that the only way to counter the populist right is by developing similar strategies on the left. Similarly, Marchart (2018) is also arguing that populism can be either left or right, along similar lines of reasoning as Stavrakakis (2014). Biglieri and Cadahia (2021) also maintain that populism can be a tool to achieve the goals of the left. These thinkers all follow the Laclaudian promise of an articulation of a political identity which manages to act against the hegemonic order (Laclau, 2005). However, as discussed in Chapters 2 and 3, there are lingering problems with seeing current incarnations of populism as instances of the political, a moment where there is a real challenge to the status quo.

To what extent does the populist left in Europe manage to leave behind what I have argued are intrinsic elements of any contemporary populist project – a design steeped in coloniality? Do they manage to challenge the status quo and offer a progressive alternative? Surprisingly, we will find that in this area of populism studies any discussion of coloniality is curiously absent. While there is some discussion of how left populism may be restricted by structural factors (Anastasiou, 2019, 2020), there are almost no signs of a critical interrogation of how Europe's past, and the tenets it provides, may prove stronger than the wish for progressive parties to promote equality, apart from a select few (Custodi, 2023c; Kleinberg, 2023). In short, are Europe's left-wing populists more European than they are left? Is left-wing populism possible, in theory and practice?

This chapter takes inspiration from the early works on populism in Latin America that question the progressive potential of left-populist movements (Ianni, 1972). Similar thoughts can be seen in contemporary scholarship where, for instance, Žižek, is highly sceptical of populism as a vehicle of the left (Žižek, 2015, 2017). Comparable perspectives are also present in the extensive literature on how neoliberalism strengthens authoritarian movements on the right (Mattei, 2025; Slobodian, 2025). These scholars, however, can be positioned firmly in the Marxist tradition, and see populism as a distraction from class politics. While this is a valid perspective and, in many cases, very accurate, it only tells one part of the story.

This chapter argues that by using the concept of coloniality and its phantasmatic frames we can better understand the workings of left-wing populism in Europe. However, the conclusions are not particularly cheery. As will be demonstrated, the phantasmatic investment in the myth of European superiority, and in the myth of a political community based on territory, still exerts a strong impact on European left-wing populists. This can be seen in particular in how left-wing populists relate to the nation-state as the main form of political community and how they exhibit the same reliance on rationality as mainstream parties.

Importantly, the chapter will demonstrate that left-wing populism in Europe offers little in terms of challenging the status quo – the influence of coloniality is still very present. The chapter will argue how the fantasy of separation between the populist and the mainstream serves to externalize the violent underpinnings of coloniality. By painting the populist as different from the European mainstream, we sustain the fantasy that Europe is benign, equal, and inclusionary. The fault lines can be seen through primarily two interfaces.

Firstly, as described in Chapter 1, rationality is one of the main interfaces of coloniality, where political subjectivity is afforded to rational individuals. There is, however, a core assumption within liberal thought that rationality is closely intertwined with liberal values, which are by extension European values (Habermas, 1996; Rawls, 2005). This is also what justifies exclusion from the political community. Following this, we have seen an increased assumption that the European mainstream is rational, whereas the populist is emotional, something which will be dispelled in this chapter. It will show how even left-wing populists exhibit commitments to rationality which echo coloniality: conflictual relations, taking power, and a belief in the superiority of deliberation. As such, the chapter seeks to highlight the contradicting aims of a left-wing agenda and a focus on 'rationality'.

Secondly, we are often told that the European mainstream is post-national, whereas the populist is stuck in a regressive form of nationalism. While there are important distinctions made between populism and nationalism in the field (Anastasiou & Custodi, 2024; De Cleen & Stavrakakis, 2017; Katsambekis & Stavrakakis, 2017), when we consider coloniality these differences become less acute. If we follow decolonial theory, what matters is not so much the labels or lines that we use within Europe to distinguish political communities but that those European political communities are situated in relation to a non-European Other (Maldonado-Torres, 2007; Mbembe, 2019; Quijano, 2000). As such, this chapter aims to focus on how these political communities are shaped by an underlying world view which sees Europe as superior, and argues that this is present in European populism, nationalism, and liberalism alike. As such, there is no 'benign' form of nationalism, patriotism, or populism in Europe, regardless of how 'civic' or 'inclusionary' they claim to be. This chapter thus contends that the dividing lines between the populists and the mainstream are not as strong as is often claimed. Instead, we can only make sense of the obvious similarities between the populist and the mainstream if we consider coloniality.

The chapter will begin with an interrogation of contemporary scholarship on Euroscepticism, and how this field often plays into the idea that populists are Eurosceptics, and therefore diametrically opposed to the European mainstream. In the following sections, the chapter will demonstrate how the dichotomies constructed between the populists and the mainstream are much weaker than previously thought. The chapter first shows how left-wing populists also subscribe to an idea of rationality which is embedded in coloniality, of Europe as the civil continent. Second, it will be demonstrated that the racialized politics of the European nation-state are present in many instances of left-wing populism. The forms of civic nationalism and patriotism so heralded in Europe are, I argue, not different from other articulations of European superiority. Both of these dichotomies in the end serve to uphold the phantasmatic structure of Europe as civil and benign.

European mainstream vs. Eurosceptic populists

The term Eurosceptic carries a lot of weight in contemporary European politics, and in some ways epitomizes how some actors and perspectives – often those who are deemed more violent and exclusionary – are seen as essentially un-European. When investigating the relationship between Euroscepticism and populism, it is often assumed that the two are closely related, even though Euroscepticism is influenced by the position on the political spectrum (Taggart & Szczerbiak, 2008). It is often argued that Euroscepticism is located at the extremes (De Vries & Edwards, 2009; Halikiopoulou et al, 2012; Hooghe et al, 2002) and that populist parties are likely to be more radical (Rooduijn & Akkerman, 2017). This has resulted in a viewpoint that populist parties are more likely to be Eurosceptic than mainstream or centrist parties (Gómez-Reino Cachafeiro & Plaza-Colodro, 2018, p 347; Plaza-Colodro et al, 2018).

This said, the connection between Euroscepticism and populism on the left is not identical to that on the right. Much research on this nexus has taken a distinctly Northern European perspective, where right-wing populist parties have typically been more dominant than their left-wing counterparts. As such, recent literature on left-wing populism and Euroscepticism is a welcome addition to the field, which also nuances the idea of this relationship (Damiani & Viviani, 2019; Della Porta et al, 2017; Gómez-Reino Cachafeiro & Plaza-Colodro, 2018; Plaza-Colodro et al, 2018; Rooduijn, 2018). It is widely assumed that the left-wing resistance to the European Union stems from a mostly economic perspective (Rooduijn & Akkerman, 2017). The EU is seen as a neoliberal vehicle which has made market competition its main motto, something which is strongly disputed on the left (Bailey, 2019; Kagarlitsky, 2017). The narrative is strongly related to the 2008 financial crisis and the following austerity policies implemented in much of Southern Europe, which is to blame for subsequent decline of living standards and a loss of faith in democratic institutions (Kagarlitsky, 2017; Lapavitsas,

2019). Left-wing populist parties in Southern Europe are more likely to be opposed to relinquishing economic sovereignty, which is seen as a key component of a fair and equal society for its people (Damiani & Viviani, 2019; Plaza-Colodro et al, 2018). This focus on economic sovereignty instead of necessarily national sovereignty is seen as a distinct difference from right-wing populism, where the resistance to the EU would emerge from a culturalist perspective, and a conviction that other European countries – and other countries in general – pose a threat towards the welfare of the domestic population.

Nevertheless, there are traces of protecting the national population also within the populist left. Some researchers would argue that the commitment to nationalism is more a commonality than a difference between populisms left and right (Halikiopoulou et al, 2012), whereas others would maintain that left-wing populists are not concerned with national sovereignty, but with popular sovereignty (Damiani & Viviani, 2019; Gerbaudo & Screti, 2017). There is a clear sense that left-wing populism can offer some kind of internationalism while still being committed to nation-state politics (De Cleen et al, 2020), what has been termed transnational populism (Moffitt, 2017; Panayotu, 2021).[1] When discussing left-wing positions towards Brexit, for instance, this is seen as stemming from a careful balance of protecting the domestic working population while at the same time resisting neoliberal Europe and remaining in solidarity with the working class in other countries. For instance, what has been referred to as constructive ambiguity (Bailey, 2019), indicates the at times contradictory position taken by the UK Labour Party in relation to European integration, where the party tries to distance itself from the nationalist right, while at the same time expressing Eurosceptic sentiments.

The issue of nationalism and Euroscepticism in the European populist left is thus not subject to scholarly agreement. The evidence on how left-wing populist parties relate to European integration is highly varied across time and space, and does not necessarily fit into how we have traditionally defined Euroscepticism (Keith, 2017). This empirical impasse is the core focus of this chapter, and in the following sections I will argue that the explanation for this lies in the strong will to separate the populist left (or right) from the European mainstream. These explanations do not consider coloniality, which, it is argued, should be seen as the main explanatory frame in European politics. The division is, instead, a phantasmatic structure which serves to sustain the idea that Europeans are civil and equal.

Instead of looking at definitional problems or trying to categorize varieties of populism, analysis must engage with how the terms populism and Euroscepticism are *performing* a certain fantasy which benefits from creating a separation of political actors. As argued in Chapter 2, there is a tendency within populism studies to focus on what is commonly referred to as the measuring problem, but this aim has often been criticized for focussing on 'degreeism' (Pappas, 2019). These strands of research try to define populism as either a nominal or ordinal category, in other words *whether or not* an actor/speech/ideology is populist, or *to what extent* we can say that this actor/speech/ideology is populist (Rooduijn & Akkerman, 2017). However, this can also lead to problems in defining populism against non-populism, where mainstream actors can, in fact, exhibit very high degrees of populist rhetoric (March, 2017, p 287; Pauwels, 2011). Others have pointed out that using populism as an ordinal category is the most useful approach, since this allows us to place actors on a scale, comparable to the left-right spectrum (Ostiguy, 2017). Ultimately, Chapter 2 concluded that we are increasingly struggling to separate the populist from the mainstream, the People from the Elite.

We need to also note how the term populism itself carries normative value and is not an analytical concept devoid of political ideology. This has been researched in the emerging literature on anti-populism, where it is argued that many of the current studies on populism are implicitly or explicitly seeing populism as a threat to democracy (Stavrakakis, 2014; Stavrakakis et al, 2018). These works argue that this misses the democratic potential of left-wing populism, which, according to these scholars, has an inclusionary and egalitarian mission. We can also think of the concept of populism as a signifier. This signifier can be used for political purposes, and populism as a term has become a way for the established political elite to label other actors as unwanted elements (Dean & Maiguashca, 2020; Glynos & Mondon, 2019). Discourses on populism are thus of equal import to the phenomenon itself (De Cleen et al, 2018; Degano & Sicurella, 2019). In other words, populism is not only a nominal or ordinal category, but a *performative* category, which is in and of itself highly political (Eklundh, 2020). Importantly, this performative function is only sustained due to the phantasmatic investment in the evil populist as the threat to European democracy, and precludes attention to coloniality.

The need to erect strong barriers between the newcomers to European politics and the old guard is not done in a vacuum. Underlying the wish to label populists and Eurosceptics as outsiders lies an unwillingness to see how these actors are in many senses more similar to the political mainstream than many would like to admit. In fact, these dichotomies are not as strong as first thought, and by softening the barriers between the political inside and outside, we can demonstrate how populists and Eurosceptics are, in fact, central to the populist condition.

Two dichotomies in particular are central to mark populists and Eurosceptics as outsiders: the emotional populists – rational EU, and the nationalist populists – post-national EU. The first dichotomy argues that populists and Eurosceptics are highly emotional and antagonistic, in contrast to the rational EU which is based on consensual decision-making practices. The second dichotomy relates to the national–post-national divide, where current research has struggled to place left-wing populism into extant categories. Are they nationalist and oppositional to the EU in a different, and perhaps better, way than the populist right? I argue that the focus on popular sovereignty seen within the European populist left is not principally at odds with the European project as an articulation of coloniality. As such, coloniality breaks down the divisions between 'good' and 'bad' populisms, between inclusive and exclusive, civic and ethic. Engaging with the cases of left-wing populism and Euroscepticism in Spain and the UK, the following sections will outline how these dichotomies are difficult to uphold empirically.

Rationality as an interface of coloniality

As argued in Chapter 2, one of the key distinctions often made between populists and non-populists is the emotional character of the former (Müller, 2016). In the growing literature on emotions and populism, populist actors are branded as more emotional than their mainstream counterparts, and there is an implicit assumption that there is a clear division between the rational mainstream and the emotional populist (Breeze, 2019; Skonieczny, 2018). There is also research which tries to determine what kinds of emotions populists are employing to increase their electoral support (Salmela & von Scheve, 2017; Wirz, 2018). Norris and Inglehart are convinced that populists are in direct opposition to liberal democracy, which must, for all means and purposes, be based on rational decision-making (Norris & Inglehart, 2019). Also in Mudde's ideational approach we can see how populism, when labelled as a thin ideology, is considered to be less sophisticated and lacking intellectual refinement (Mudde, 2004), which can be seen as another expression of how populists are less rational than the mainstream. Also, within the more critical sections of populism studies does it become evident that populism is indeed not entirely based on rational thought. For instance, Ostiguy is convinced that populism signifies the 'low' against the mainstream 'high', when populists are labelled as 'coarse' and 'uninhibited' against the 'well-behaved', 'proper', and 'refined' politics of the mainstream (Ostiguy, 2017, p 80). Moffitt has also supported this distinction, when arguing that populism has a 'tabloid style', and that it is often associated with bad manners (Moffitt, 2016). This should be seen in opposition to establishment politicians, who are more often displaying 'rigidness, rationality, composure, and the use of technocratic language' (Moffitt, 2016, p 43).

This becomes particularly accentuated when analysing populist attitudes towards the EU. The difference in the *ways* of doing politics is seen as acutely steep, where the European project is seen to be based on a Habermasian idea of consensus-making which is at its core incompatible with the populist emotional response. As Habermas has argued (1984, 1996), decision-making must take place between rational political subjects who recognize one another as such. This recognition is what will ultimately enable consensus; if political subjects can evaluate the validity of one another's truth claims, there will be a possibility to identify the common good for the community. Consensus can only be built between rational subjects, and if subjects are more emotional than rational, then consensus will not be possible, since the common good cannot be identified. The emotional–rational dichotomy is thus also central to the division between a consensual EU and antagonistic populists. Not only are populists disturbing the consensual process, but it is also inherently impossible to include them since they do not possess what are thought to be necessary characteristics of valid political subjects: capacity of rational thought and reasoned debate.

Importantly, the capacity of rationality is absolutely central to coloniality, since it is so closely connected with the idea of civility, as discussed in Chapter 1. If we look at how rationality has been used historically, it is essentially a tool to keep unwanted elements far away from political decision-making. Rationality was reserved for the white, property-owning man. Importantly, decolonial theory argues that the introduction of rationality as a condition for political deliberation precludes any open competition for power (Dussel, 1977; Maldonado-Torres, 2007). As such, the space of power is not empty waiting to be filled by the most deserving candidate – it has already been filled by the individuals who set the criteria for how the appointment process should unfold. It is thus crucial for any decolonial analysis to critically interrogate how rationality has become and still is one of the main characteristics associated with good political leadership today.

This chapter argues that the emotional–rational dichotomy between the emotional populists and the rational EU demands further analysis – it is the phantasmatic construction of a separation. It is often claimed that left-wing populists are based on a cult of personality. The problem with this narrative is that it tends to tie instances of vertical party structures and strong leadership to an emotional or irrational element of left populism. In reality, the vertical structures and the focus on clear and strong leadership are strategic decisions made by left populists in order to gain electoral power. This, I argue, is by no means a process which defies rational behaviour, but which is deeply steeped in a European model of political representation (Eklundh, 2019, 2022), used liberally by parties throughout the continent. Similarly, as was described in Chapter 4, the constant focus on winning and on gaining power is also taken straight out of the masculine playbook, another interface of coloniality (Caravantes, 2019, 2020; Caravantes & Lombardo, 2023). As Iglesias put it: 'we have to assume and internalize that Podemos can and should lead the government of our country' (Iglesias et al, 2017, p 28).

Many would like to argue that the focus on Pablo Iglesias or Jeremy Corbyn is but a mere demagogical device intended to manipulate the masses, and at first glance this can seem accurate. Podemos has since its foundation in 2014 been strongly tied to its leader, even printing his picture on the ballot for the 2014 European Parliament elections in Spain. The argument for this was that Podemos needed to create a space for representation for the previously unrepresented (Barberá González & Martín del Fresno, 2019; Chironi & Fittipaldi, 2017). In the words of Pablo Iglesias, for Podemos 'the task, then, was to aggregate the new demands generated by the crisis around a mediatic leadership, capable of dichotomizing the political space' (Iglesias, 2015, p 14). Moreover, he argued that it was paramount to construct a popular identity around a leader: 'This populace ... was not "representable" within the traditional left-right categories of the political space. In the context of high dissatisfaction with the elites, our objective of identifying a new "we" that included the TV nation initially came together around the signifier "Pablo Iglesias"' (Iglesias, 2015, p 17).

As such, while social movements matter and can create support for individual causes, real political change comes from taking part in institutions (Errejón & Mouffe, 2016). There are some examples of how Podemos sees itself as the more 'mature' version of the 15M movement which preceded it, one which has more political capability: 'if we do not commit errors of immaturity, we can consolidate ourselves as the principal force of socio-political opposition and advance our social and electoral positions in order to try to win the next municipal, autonomous, and general elections' (Iglesias et al, 2017, p 12). Iglesias himself was to be the carrier of this new representative reality, and even though people would not necessarily care about politics, or identify themselves along the left-right spectrum, they would know the 'guy with the ponytail' from his appearances on television. Podemos have from the start been clear that their political project is about taking power; it is about taking a place in the institutions that make political decisions.

This reasoning has also been seen in the British Labour Party under Corbyn. Even though, as described earlier, the party has made a clear effort to connect with grassroots movements and broaden and involve the membership, there are clear instances of where the leadership in and of itself becomes the articulating signifier for the whole movement (Blakey, 2016; McTernan, 2016). There are diverging opinions on whether Corbyn himself supported the focus on his own persona as leader, but the fact remains that both Momentum and the party itself were, like Podemos, interested in taking power and taking a place in extant institutions: 'Momentum wants to see a more democratic Labour Party with the policies and collective will to build a more democratic, equal and decent society in government' (Schneider, 2015). There are also strong traces of the vertical structures of the trade unions within Corbynism, which supports clear hierarchical and representative orders (Maiguashca & Dean, 2019, p 148; Wainwright, 2018).

In addition, the practice of focussing on large rallies and the omnipresent chant of 'Oh, Jeremy Corbyn', indicates a strong investment in Corbyn as the representative leader (Worth, 2020).

In sum, when looking at the populist left, it is often difficult to establish whether they are clearly emotional or rational. They are therefore often referred to as hybrid parties owing to the mixed empirical picture (Chironi & Fittipaldi, 2017; Della Porta et al, 2017). This inability to neatly align left populism along predetermined categories stems from an inability to see how the definition of populism – and its distinction between the emotional and the rational – created a phantasmatic structure. In other words, the main effect of this distinction is to create a separation between the populists of the political mainstream, when, in fact, left populism is clearly part and parcel of what European party politics stands for. The desire to label populism, left and right, as an outside phenomenon contributes to the phantasmatic structure of Europe as a rational, inclusive, and civil community, which is embedded in coloniality. The problem is thus always on the outside, and the mainstream is exonerated from taking responsibility for its problems.

The European nation-state as an interface of coloniality

The second separation between populists and the mainstream is the assumption that populists are nationalist, and the mainstream EU is post-national. Left-wing populists are said to be more focussed on popular rather than national *sovereignty*, which should, according to their supporters, create a deep rift between the ethic nationalism of right-wing populism and the civic nationalism of the populist left. There are, however, problematizing factors in this dichotomy.

As mentioned earlier and in Chapter 2, the separation is well established in the literature, and Rovira Kaltwasser has even claimed that the main opposition to right-wing populism does not come from left-wing populists, but what can be termed the cosmopolitan elite (Rovira Kaltwasser, 2017). It has been argued that right- and left-wing populists both see the nation-state as the primary arena for politics (Halikiopoulou et al, 2012). Similarly, left radical parties in Europe are generally seen as sceptical to the neoliberal project of the EU (Keith, 2017). There is an increased acceptance that left-wing and right-wing populists are not identical when invoking the concept of sovereignty, and that they are based on two different sets of political community. Based on a distinction between sovereignty based on an *ethnos* or a *demos*, scholars argue that the main subject of right-wing populism is the *ethnos* – a collectivity connected to culture, ethnicity, or race (Akkerman, 2003, p 15). In contrast, the main subject of left populism is the *demos*, the people who are included in a political community based on a notion of citizenship (De Cleen & Stavrakakis, 2017). It is by no means denied that the articulation of the People can often be done within the limits of the Nation, but left populism also opens a space for a People which is not based on blood lines (Anastasiou & Custodi, 2024; Custodi, 2020; Karavasilis et al, 2024; Stavrakakis et al, 2017) and a left return to the nation-state is rather a critique of capitalism and neoliberalism (Charalambous, 2013). There is a clear aim to theoretically oppose the right-wing monopoly of the term sovereignty and to reclaim popular sovereignty for the left. This has been done extensively by scholars who believe that the way forward for left populism is to create a national-popular, often inspired by a Gramscian notion of how to create a successful counter-hegemony (Gerbaudo, 2017; Mouffe, 2018).

As I have discussed in previous chapters, however, these discussions on whether movements are nationalist or populist become secondary when we consider the concept of coloniality. When seeing the exclusionary and violent history of liberalism, as described in Chapter 1, what use is there to quibble about whether the main threat to European democracies comes from populism or nationalism? This book contends that the main threat comes from within and cannot be externalized.

As such, the lines between national sovereignty, popular sovereignty, and the European mainstream are not as clear as is often claimed. In contrast to much of the literature on left populism and Euroscepticism, this chapter contends that the focus on the People and the Nation, and European liberal democracy have developed in tandem and cannot be easily separated, as discussed in Chapter 1. Most of all, there is a tendency not to discuss how European political actors left, right, and centre are all reliant upon an idea of the People which is based on difference – one which favours a conflictual outlook on human relations, which is embedded in coloniality. Both popular and national sovereignty are historically designed to delimit the inside of politics to the outside of politics, a pattern still visible today.

Drawing on scholarship on the genealogy of sovereignty, it can be argued that the national and popular versions are not conceptually distinct, but part and parcel of a European identity project which relies on an articulation of a People which is tied to a particular territory. The creation of a sovereign People which has the power in a modern state is always done through a *racialized* conception of that People (Meister, 2009, p 120). Drawing on Foucault's idea of 'race war' (Foucault, 2003), we can argue that there is no state sovereignty without the creation of racialized difference, whether that difference is based on cultural or biological ideas of race.

Race in this sense is the 'hidden' element in the nation that makes its people 'equal' and enables national to produce a 'fictitious entity', a 'populism', that substitutes in a post feudal world for the rule of family aristocracy (Meister, 2009, p 121). Western conceptions of democracy, in other words, do not rely on a strong sense of equality, but on difference (Rancière, 1999). The People are never constituted through an aggregative or deliberative process, as is so often claimed in democratic theory, but based on exclusionary forces which count some over others. Mann (2012) has taken this argument further and contends that democracies always host a potentiality for genocide; the very fact that the People should be purified from groups who do not share the 'foundational values' of the political community can result in everything from political disagreement to ethnic cleansing. Importantly, this difference is gradational and not substantial. This dark side of democracy is essential to understanding the problematic facets of popular sovereignty, which is nothing but a 'dominion by a people over land as a permanent defense against racialized persecution' (Meister, 2009, p 133).

The narrative that left-wing populism is different from its right-wing counterpart and also distinct from post-national constellations rests upon the distinction between national and popular sovereignty. Popular sovereignty, however, is often deeply influenced by the problematic foundations of European political thought even though it is believed to represent a beacon of equality and popular power. As explained in Chapter 1, in *The Racial Contract* (Mills, 1999), Mills exposes how Western democracies are built upon an idea of the People as carrying certain characteristics. These characteristics are by no means happenstance and form part of a wider pattern of how European countries have designed a political system in order to favour some people over others, preferably to be implemented worldwide. The very famous scholars which we hold in high regard for having developed our modern ideas on popular sovereignty were, in fact, often the strongest defenders of slavery and of racial discrimination. Popular sovereignty is thus still riddled with its historical ties with class, racial, and gender discrimination: coloniality.

The problem of inclusion into and exclusion from the popular sovereign is to a high degree centred on the reason–emotion dichotomy, as described earlier, but must also be connected to how reason is often highly racialized. Even if left-wing populists do not outrightly refer to a 'white' *demos*, popular sovereignty in Europe has historically been associated with characteristics reserved for whites. This was possible due to the belief that the experience of the European white man was universal – politics had to be done the way that the ruling classes at the time thought it should be done (Dussel, 1994; Wynter, 2003). Importantly, the figure of the Savage – who is unable to enter into the social contract – serves as a justification for limiting access to political decision-making. The European People, therefore, is not a neutral vehicle devoid of social hierarchies.

The strong focus on rationality in the European populist left indicates an acceptance of the rules of the game, a game which is designed upon exclusionary principles. Mills (1999, 2017) and Eze (1995, 1997) argue that racial hierarchies are still centre stage when discussing democracy and political subjectivity, and that much of this stems from an overreliance of rationality in democratic theory. Rationality was often seen by the contractualists as the defining feature of the civilized man, reserved for the white population. Modern-day democratic theory would never argue that rationality is reserved for whites, but this is nonetheless what the practice has ended up reinforcing. Democratic theory anchored in rational thought, it is claimed, is a raceless enterprise; rationality can be bestowed on any human being. Nonetheless, as so eloquently argued by Toni Morrison, there are times when claiming racelessness is itself a racial act (Morrison, 1992, p 46). In other words, to argue that popular sovereignty can be separated from national sovereignty, and that a left-wing populist sovereignty is not influenced by the concept's historical heritage, is a more problematic stance than admitted. Similarly, Balibar has argued that

> The idea of a popular sovereignty (collective decision-making, representation of the interests of the mass of citizens, and control of the rules by the ruled), that could be dissociated by its statist forms remains enigmatic, if not inconceivable. Its genealogy is masked more than it is illuminated by the current opposition between national sovereignty and the 'postnational constellation'. (Balibar, 2004, p 134)

Some may argue that even though national and popular sovereignty are historically tied together, surely the European Union is a project which refutes national boundaries and thus overcomes the sovereign problem? However, Balibar argues that the racialized difference which underlies the concept of national and popular sovereignty is not limited to nationalism, but rather an 'excess of nationalism': 'There actually is a racist 'internationalism' or 'supranationalism' which tends to idealize timeless transhistorical communities such as the 'Indo-Europeans', 'the West', 'Judeo-Christian civilisation' and therefore communities which are at the same time both closed and open' (Balibar, 1989, p 59).

As such, there is no guarantee that a post-national project like the European Union would not suffer from the same racialized articulation of the connection between a certain People and a certain territory. Such articulations in fact become blatantly obvious in EU communication in 'promoting the European way of life: protecting our citizens and our values' (European Commission, 2025), where the People of Europe are tied to both a specific place, and particular cultural habits, or in the fierce protection of Europe's borders. As we saw in Chapter 4, the 'European garden' so fondly described by Borrell is under a constant threat from foreign cultures and habits. The more recent return to strong national borders even within the Schengen area would also support that the nation-state as an exclusionary community is far from the European mainstream. Nevertheless, the sovereignty of the people of Europe is constructed upon a fictitious identity which creates a clear demarcation between what is thought to be the rightful ruler of this place, and any potential illegitimate challengers to this dominance. This type of racialized identity formation is identical in the rhetoric of the EU to the populist incarnations throughout the continent. At the same time, the fantasy of an inclusive and equal Europe is strong at work, where the EU is described as a union of equality, tolerance, and social fairness (European Commission, 2025).

As such, the boundaries between the post-national EU and the nationalist populists become increasingly blurred, which reveals that the boundaries are phantasmatic constructions. There is a denial within the mainstream to recognize their racist and exclusionary practice, and this is something which is seen as belonging to the 'political extremes' such as populists. However, racism does not only surface as direct speech, but can also be identified as practices of the state, security policies, or simply arguments around 'cultural' habits, where people want to 'stick with their own' (Wade, 2015). It is also increasingly evident that racist practices form part and parcel of the political mainstream, while defending the 'rights of the People' or freedom of expression (Mondon & Winter, 2020).

How does the difficulty in separating the three forms of political community – a post-national EU, a national sovereign, and a popular sovereign – present itself in analyses of left-wing populism? In Podemos and the UK Labour Party under Corbyn the lines are increasingly challenging to separate, which explains the difficulty of scholars to pinpoint them as supporting one or the other. It is obvious that popular sovereignty is an important concept (Damiani & Viviani, 2019; Gerbaudo & Screti, 2017). Podemos have made it their mission to call for a renegotiation of democracy where the People are better represented, and where unelected bureaucrats in the EU should not have the power to make decisions which so clearly affect the lives and livelihood of ordinary Spaniards (Iglesias, 2015; Iglesias et al, 2017). At the same time, the notion of the Fatherland (patria) has become increasingly important for Podemos (Caravantes & Lombardo, 2023), and invokes patriotism and Spain as a nation to construct a political community:

> We have a democratic, not a nationalist, idea of the fatherland, which identifies the fatherland as the people. We are trying to illustrate how those who are using the word national are also, at the same time, selling our national sovereignty for cheap. We are therefore trying to restore our economic and political sovereignty, a necessary action to restore the country and the interests of the majority. (Iglesias as cited in Marco, 2015)

Similarly, Custodi argues that Podemos invokes a particular notion of the Fatherland which is based on welfare policies, popular mobilization, and pluralism (Custodi, 2020, 2023a, 2023b; Custodi & Padoan, 2022). While there are strong concerns in the Spanish left on whether to use a term so strongly attached to the Francoist dictatorship, this has not seemed to be a hindrance for Podemos (Custodi, 2023c). There are also several analyses which engage with how Podemos have tried to recreate the national-popular (Briziarelli, 2016; Mazzolini, 2020), a Gramscian concept, as a political strategy. While the national-popular cannot be equated to nationalism, it is worthwhile to consider how Gramsci (just like Schmitt or Bataille, as described in Chapter 3) was concerned with how the left could build a political structure as successful as fascism. As I have previously argued, there is a need to recognize the problematic assumptions in copying the political strategy of fascist movements in Europe. This chapter takes these arguments one step further and argues that while there are certainly differences between the rhetoric of the populist left and populist right, any articulation of a specific People tied to a specific territory reinforces an idea that attributes citizenship to a community of birth, which would encompass both populism and nationalism.

In addition, when analysing the most commonly used words in all of Podemos' Facebook communication between 2014 and 2017, it was found that España (Spain), was consistently in the top five words used (Eklundh, 2019, p 224). Podemos have justified this focus on Spain the nation as a core function of political community by saying that the nation-state is still the main area where politics is enacted, and that democracy must be achieved by involving the citizens of Spain. While their rhetoric says nothing about blood lines, there is an implicit assumption that the nation as political community will provide the quickest route to more democratic decision-making (Agustín, 2020, p 107). At the same time, Podemos are by no means advocating for a Spanish exit from the European Union. As such, there is a simultaneous belief in the European project, further demonstrating how the distinctions between popular sovereignty, national sovereignty, and a post-national Europe are losing their edges.

In the UK Labour Party under Corbyn, a similar disintegration of these limits can be discerned. Analysts and scholars alike disagree on Corbynism's stance towards the European Union, and dispute whether Corbyn is a staunch nationalist or a supporter of international solidarity. This analytical stalemate, I argue, stems from the blurred lines between post-nationalism, national sovereignty, and popular sovereignty – the lines are part of a phantasmatic structure which serves to conceal the violent and exclusionary nature of the European mainstream. If the underlying common assumptions of these analytical distinctions is not discussed – coloniality – analyses will inevitably struggle to make a strong empirical case.

Some of the literature on Labour under Corbyn does not identify Corbyn as a populist, and argues that he did not invoke the necessary signifiers of populism, such as the People, popular sovereignty, or anti-elitism (Maiguashca & Dean, 2019; March, 2017). Nevertheless, some argue that Corbynism is the development of a 'national-popular' following the Gramscian tradition. A national-popular seeks to challenge the hegemonic order and create a counter-hegemonic narrative (Gramsci, 2005). Importantly, the national-popular should be constructed from below, through popular movements, and 'provide a basis for national-popular consciousness *within* current countries as a means to counter neoliberalism' (Worth, 2020, p 91). As mentioned earlier, there are concerns with how Gramsci is inspired by the success of fascism. This framework comes as a critique of the anti-globalization movement, and argues that to be truly effective, national politics is the main front of struggle (Gerbaudo, 2017). The strong emphasis on the connection with social movements and civil society within Corbynism would, according to Worth, indicate a nascent national-popular construction within the Labour Party (Worth, 2020).

The discussion becomes even more accentuated with regards to Brexit. Within the Labour Party, there were several factions under Corbyn, some who supported Brexit (or so-called Lexit), and some who were ardently pro-Remain (Bailey, 2019). The Lexit faction was much concerned with the neoliberal stance of the European Union, and argued that only an exit from the union could deliver true left-wing policies for the UK (Worth, 2017). This was supported by the Bennite tradition of Euroscepticism, which assumed that the working class in the north of England would be against freedom of movement for EU workers (Diamond, 2018). Even though Labour under Corbyn did in the end endorse freedom of movement, this was, and still is, a hotly debated topic. Corbyn argued in January 2017 that 'Labour is not wedded to freedom of movement for EU citizens as a point of principle, but I don't want that to be misinterpreted, nor do we rule it out' (Lucas, 2017). Other key figures of the left, such as former union leader Len McCluskey, have argued that Britain needs to put the brakes on the 'influx of cheap labour', echoing historical resistance to foreign workers and warning that not doing so would incur the dissent of the white working class (Bloodworth, 2019). This indicates a clear racialization of the political community. On the other hand, some factions of the Labour movement, such as Momentum or Another Europe is Possible, struggle with the traditionally Eurosceptic left, and do not want to be equated with reactionary forms of nationalism or xenophobia. As such, Corbynism should be seen as 'an attempt, in part, to galvanize these grassroots initiatives within a political movement that is decidedly uncertain with regards to the Brexit question' (Bailey, 2019, p 265).

The lines between popular sovereignty, national sovereignty, and support for a post-national EU are indistinct also in the British left. This inability to neatly place Corbynism into either of these categories stems from an unwillingness to recognize the historical contingency between them. In the current European context, can we ever invoke popular sovereignty without retorting to nationalism, and can we say that being pro-European means being truly anti-racist? This chapter answers both questions in the negative. The popular sovereign is historically and presently articulated within a nationalist framework which takes difference as its starting point and is always racialized. The European mainstream, and support for the European way of life, is by no means freed from these distinctions, and also relies upon core assumptions of what it means to be European. European democracy is constructed around difference, not equality, which is endemic to parties on the left, right, and centre.

Conclusion

This chapter has engaged with the possibilities for left-wing populism to offer a political alternative that goes beyond the exclusionary politics of its right-wing counterpart. The conclusion is not particularly optimistic. As has been shown, two of the most prominent left-wing populist alternatives in recent times in Europe, Podemos and the UK Labour Party under Corbyn, have both struggled to break free from coloniality. In a sense, this is surprising since they should signify two of the most 'successful' cases of a left-populist project. Nevertheless, it is less surprising if we consider the strong influence of coloniality still present in European politics today.

As in Chapter 4, we have seen how left-wing populism, right-wing populism, and the mainstream centre all rely on assumptions which could be drawn entirely from the colonialist playbook. There is a preference for masculinized views on leadership and a strong emphasis on rational thinking and maturity. There is often an unwillingness to question the current status quo regarding migration (Karavasilis et al, 2024). This book argues that not only is this true for populisms left and right, but it is also true for the mainstream and that the only way that we can explain these similarities is through the decolonial lens. As described in Chapter 1, without seeing the historical development of liberal democracy for what they actually were – exclusionary and often violent – we cannot fully grasp the underpinnings of contemporary European politics. This is a politics which does not hesitate to build higher and higher walls against the non-European jungle, and one which does not doubt its own superiority.

In this context, it becomes futile to maintain the strong distinctions between the European populist and the mainstream. Populism, in this sense, forms part of a phantasmatic structure. It becomes the way for the European mainstream to uphold the belief that Europeans are not what all the populists are accused of being – racists, bigots, threats. There is, in other words, a strong sense of enjoyment for the mainstream – to think of themselves as pure, innocent, good. This fantasy of separation thus conceals some of the deeper and underlying mechanisms: that Europe's problem with violence and exclusion comes from within.

Where does this leave left-wing populism? We have seen that there are diverging opinions in the literature on the emancipatory potential of left-wing populism. While Marxist theorists – historically and in the present – argue that populism will always result in class conflict sooner or later, much of contemporary discourse theory would like to retain the hope that there is a form of populism which can be the quintessential expression of the political, a true challenge to the status quo. When considering coloniality this becomes increasingly difficult to maintain in the European context. Looking at the practices of populism, not only on the right but also on the left, we can see that they are more often than not simply offering more of the same instead of breaking the hegemonic order.

This leaves populism as a concept in a pickle. We can no longer reasonably argue that contemporary politics is organized around the People versus the Elites when the People and the Elites are working for the same political project. In this sense, populism ceases to be an expression of the political. The cases that we call populist in Europe today do not challenge the status quo but are simply an elongation or exaggerations of it, a European modernity on steroids. In the Conclusion, I will comment further on the potential for emancipation in Europe, and beyond.

Conclusion

The 2024 European elections highlighted a stark and troubling reality: the rise of populist movements across the European Union is not an isolated phenomenon but a deeply rooted aspect of European political life. The election results, with right-wing populists claiming 187 of the 720 seats in the European Parliament, underscored a phenomenon that cannot be dismissed as a passing trend. While much of the discourse surrounding this rise frames it as a reaction to economic struggles and migration issues, it is increasingly clear that the popularity of populism in Europe is not simply a symptom of economic failure or poorly managed crises. Rather, it demonstrates that populism, rather than being an exception, is very appealing to the European voter, even though so many would like to argue that it is an abomination. This book has presented an alternative reading of this conundrum, namely that what we refer to as populism is actually part and parcel of what Europe is. The idea that Europe, as the birthplace of the Enlightenment and the home of modern democratic values, should be different from populism is a prevalent but ultimately flawed narrative. In practice, Europe has long struggled with the contradictions inherent in its political systems.

In this book, I have argued that the demarcation between the populists and the mainstream is nothing but a phantasmatic structure. We hold on to the figure of the populist for dear life so that the elements on European politics which are not so palatable – its harsh migration policies, its lack of solidarity with people beyond the continent and its lingering patriarchal order – can be blamed on someone else. It is always the populist, never the centre, that is the source of evil. This fantasy works to conceal the uncomfortable truths about Europe and its violent and exclusionary history. The history and present of European politics must, therefore, be seen through the lens of coloniality.

The notion that populism is an external threat to European democracy overlooks the reality that it is an integral part of the continent's political DNA. The idea presented in this book of an 'inherent populist condition' within Europe suggests that rather than being a passing phase or an anomaly, populism is a deeply ingrained feature of European political culture. Europe's commitment to human rights, democratic governance, and equality must therefore be seen as a contested, evolving project, not a completed achievement.

Ultimately, Europe's political problem is not one of populism's sudden emergence but of coloniality's longstanding and structural presence. The challenge ahead is not to resist the rise of populist movements but to confront the deep-seated issues they highlight and work towards a more inclusive and genuinely democratic Europe.

The rise of populism across Europe forces us to confront uncomfortable questions about the foundations of European politics and its claims to be a beacon of democracy and equality. This book argues that the conventional division between populism and democracy, and the conflation of liberalism with democracy, are oversimplifications that fail to stand up to scrutiny. Rather than accepting the mainstream narrative that positions populism as an external threat to European democracy, it suggests a more critical rethinking of the very principles that have historically underpinned European political thought.

In this regard, this book departs from Chantal Mouffe's assertion that liberalism and democracy are 'joined at the hip', and proposes a critical disentangling of these two concepts. Over the past two decades, it has become commonplace to argue that right-wing populist policies have been 'mainstreamed', signalling a dangerous shift where populism supposedly infiltrates and threatens liberal democracy. This perspective is valid to an extent – centrist policies have indeed drifted to the right in many Western democracies. However, what is often overlooked in these discussions is the possibility that the so-called 'liberal centre' (Brown, 2024; Brown et al, 2021; Gillespie, 2024) never truly embodied the democratic ideals it claimed to uphold. In fact, as discussed in Chapter 1, this book suggests that the very policies we associate with liberal democracy have always been intertwined with undemocratic elements, particularly in their treatment of inequality, class, and race. In order to make this argument, this book turned to decolonial theory.

Liberalism, as a political philosophy, has long been rooted in the preservation of inequality. For instance, figures such as John Stuart Mill, despite their support for individual freedoms, expressed deep mistrust of the masses and feared the consequences of democratic participation by what they saw as uneducated and unworthy groups. Mill's warning against the 'dictatorship of the majority' was not just a theoretical observation; it reflected a genuine concern about the potential for democracy to challenge the status quo, particularly the privileges of the aristocracy and the property-owning elite. Mill's work, and that of other liberal thinkers, reveals an essential tension within liberalism – a tension that is fundamentally anti-democratic in nature. The idea that liberalism and democracy are inherently compatible becomes difficult to sustain when we examine the historical realities of liberal thought.

This book further challenges the conventional understanding of liberalism by examining its colonial foundations in Chapter 1. The liberal values celebrated in Europe have often been intertwined with colonial power dynamics, reinforcing hierarchical structures that denied equality to vast segments of the population. The European conception of the 'People' has always been defined in opposition to a colonial 'Other', and this exclusionary framework continues to shape political life in the contemporary era (Dussel, 1977; Maldonado-Torres, 2007; Quijano, 2007). The failure to acknowledge the colonial roots of European political systems, and their implications for the politics of race and inequality, has left a blind spot in our understanding of Europe's populist condition.

Rather than treating populism as an aberration or an external threat to European democracy, this book argues that what we think is populism is, at the end of the day, the very centre of European politics. The contradictions between Europe's claims to democracy and its historical practices of exclusion and inequality are not simply unfortunate byproducts but fundamental features of the system. Understanding the 'populist condition' requires us to engage critically with the concept of coloniality and to recognize how European politics has always been shaped by exclusionary practices – whether in the form of gender, class, or racial hierarchy.

Ultimately, Europe's populist condition is not a fleeting disruption but a manifestation of deeper, unresolved tensions within its political and social structures. In addition, I argue, our current political debate (Mounk, 2019; Müller, 2016) is working overtime to cover up these tensions with discussions about how populism is a 'threat' to Europe. To address these tensions, European politics must confront its colonial past, disentangle liberalism from democracy, and reckon with the ways in which inequality and exclusion have always been central to the European project. The rise of populism in Europe, then, is not an anomaly but a symptom of the persistence of these contradictions. Only by confronting them head-on can we hope to build a more inclusive and genuinely democratic future for Europe.

Deconstructing the People–Elite distinction

As I have shown in Chapter 2, the study of populism in contemporary European politics presents a complex and often contradictory landscape. While much of the scholarship surrounding populism has been preoccupied with defining it – whether as an ideology, a political strategy, a style, or a discourse – the debates have largely focussed on distinguishing populism from 'mainstream' politics. However, as the political influence of populist movements expands, particularly in Europe, it is increasingly clear that populism is no longer an exception but a dominant feature of the political landscape. Thus, it is time to reconsider the distinction between populism and the 'Elite' and to accept that populism has become the norm, not the anomaly, which some scholarship has begun to do (De Cleen & Ruiz Casado, 2024; Rojas-Andrés et al, 2024; Schoor, 2019), as described in Chapter 2. This book has pointed out that we need to take this point even further and question the People–Elite distinction altogether. This can be done successfully if considering coloniality.

Some approaches to populism are better suited for this type of dismantling. The discursive approach to populism, championed by figures such as Ernesto Laclau (2005, 2007), provides a more nuanced perspective by arguing that populism is not confined to the fringes of the political spectrum but is an inherent part of any political project. Populism, according to Laclau, is essentially the creation of a political identity, one that can emerge across the political spectrum whenever there is a challenge to the status quo. This conception of populism, as a tool for constructing political identities and challenging established power structures, is crucial in understanding its widespread appeal and its ability to adapt to various political contexts. Populism, in this sense, is not inherently radical or extreme, but a logic which is present in the creation of any political identity.

Yet, despite the growing recognition of populism's centrality to modern political life, there are significant blind spots in the existing research on populism. One of the main challenges is the persistent belief that populism is a genuine challenge to the existing system. This book, however, contends that populism in Europe does not represent such a revolutionary force. Instead, it argues that what we call populism is simply the latest iteration of a political order shaped by coloniality, a system of thought that has long structured European society. Far from disrupting the status quo, populism, in its current form, reflects a deepening of the colonial logics of modernity – what might be termed 'modernity on steroids'. These logics, grounded in exclusion, inequality, and conflict, continue to underpin populist movements and the mainstream, whether on the left or the right of the political spectrum.

While some recent scholarship has sought to frame populism, especially left-wing populism, in a more positive light – arguing that it can be compatible with democratic values and equality (Biglieri & Cadahia, 2021; Mouffe, 2018) – this book challenges that view. In Chapter 2, I took inspiration from Marxist theorists who have argued that populist projects transcending class boundaries, sooner or later, will be broken up by conflicting class interests (Ianni, 1972; Lazzarato, 2021; Žižek, 2015, 2017). While this analysis is compelling, I also argued that it does not sufficiently engage with coloniality. A critique of populism, therefore, cannot be made with reference to class politics alone, but must also consider how the colonial heritage shapes left-wing populism in Europe. I argue that left-wing populism in Europe, despite its focus on inclusion and critique of elites, remains entangled in the same colonial and exclusionary frameworks that underpin right-wing populism.

This is not merely a theoretical concern but a practical one: even in its most radical and inclusionary forms, populism continues to rely on a vision of society that views difference as a source of conflict.

I also made the point that in populism studies, the commitment to conflict as the source of the social is problematic. This vision, rooted in the thought of political theorists like Carl Schmitt, cannot be reconciled with a future founded on equality and democratic participation. Schmitt's theories, with their emphasis on the natural antagonism between groups, have been surprisingly influential in shaping populist thought. His ideas, which played a central role in the rise of Nazi ideology, continue to inform much of contemporary populist theory, even among scholars who claim to be on the left.

The enduring influence of Schmitt's ideas, especially his commitment to the idea of irreconcilable differences between groups, highlights a crucial flaw in the current populism literature. Despite its professed commitment to democracy, the populist logic of difference as conflict remains rooted in coloniality, and as such, it is fundamentally incompatible with a future built on equality. Populism in Europe, whether left-wing or right-wing, continues to perpetuate the idea that society is divided into antagonistic groups, and that political engagement must be framed as a struggle between these groups. This logic is not conducive to a vision of democracy based on equality, mutual respect, and inclusion.

The reliance on exclusionary logics and the emphasis on conflict rather than cooperation make populism, in its current form, incompatible with the values of equality and democracy. To move towards a more inclusive and democratic Europe, it is necessary to rethink the political order in ways that transcend the coloniality of difference and conflict. The future of European democracy depends on our ability to imagine and build a political system that is based on cooperation, mutual recognition, and a commitment to equality – values that are fundamentally at odds with the vision of society offered by coloniality.

As such, this book takes issue with the contemporary field of populism studies which is not sufficiently sensitive to coloniality. The continued commitment to antagonism, and the strong belief that populism challenges the status quo, limits the analysis of populism in Europe today. By constantly referring to it as a challenge to the status quo, either in a positive or negative sense, we are failing to grasp how populism, in many ways, simply repeats the same elitist and liberal modes of political life which Europe has been plagued by for centuries. This book thus challenges the dominant understanding of populism in Europe, urging a deeper engagement with its colonial roots and its inherent contradictions. Only by confronting the colonial foundations of European politics and moving beyond the logic of difference and conflict can we hope to create a political system that is truly democratic and inclusive.

The fantasy of the benevolent Europe

The rise of populism in Europe cannot be fully understood without grappling with the role of coloniality in shaping political identities and desires. This book contends that, to further comprehend the appeal of populism – both as a concept and as a political alternative – we need to delve deeper into the role of affect and fantasy. Why is populism so popular? The growing popularity of populism in Europe reflects not only a reaction against perceived threats to identity and culture but also an expression of desires that shape the political landscape. Equally, we need to understand why the figure of the populist as a scapegoat for Europe's ills is such an appealing notion to the liberal mainstream.

In Chapter 3 I discussed how psychoanalytic theory offers a crucial lens through which to understand these desires. While psychoanalysis was originally conceived as a theory of individual identity (Lacan, 2007; Stavrakakis, 2002, 2007), it has increasingly been extended to the collective, with a focus on how communities form and how desire drives political dynamics. Political identity, it turns out, is not just about rational arguments or ideological consistency – it is rooted in affective attachments that shape what individuals and communities identify with. This dimension is central to understanding why populism has such resonance – both as a concept and as a political alternative – particularly in a European context that prides itself on its inclusivity but is simultaneously attracted to exclusionary policies.

In this regard, the emerging field of critical fantasy studies provides a valuable framework for understanding the affective dimensions of politics (Glynos, 2008, 2021; Ronderos 2020). This field challenges the tendency to treat emotions as peripheral to 'rational' political life. Instead, emotions, and particularly affect, are seen as the very essence of politics. Politics is not just about cold calculations and policies; it is fundamentally about the fantasies and affective attachments that make political identities and actions meaningful. As Glynos and Howarth argue (2007), the logics approach can help us understand how these affective attachments shape political opportunities and movements, particularly in the context of populism. By exploring how fantasy structures political identity and desire, we gain insight into the appeal of populism, both as a concept and as a political alternative.

Crucially, critical fantasy studies also help us avoid the mistake of reducing populist politics to an excess of emotion or irrationality, a common critique levelled at populist movements. What the concept of fantasy allows us to understand is the function that populism serves in European politics: it creates a clear division between an 'inside' and an 'outside' of politics. Here, I draw on Žižek to explain how fantasy can work to conceal the underlying mechanisms at play (Žižek, 2017, 2008). The mainstream European political order continues to uphold a fantasy of civilizational superiority, rooted in colonial ideas of European exceptionalism (Fanon, 2021; Mbembe, 2019). To maintain this fantasy – that Europeans are inherently good, inclusive, and democratic – the realities of exclusion, inequality, and violence that are foundational to European history must be externalized. Populism, in this framework, becomes the scapegoat for the mainstream, the 'Other' that allows Europeans to maintain the illusion of their inherent civility. In this sense, populism is not so much a radical departure from mainstream politics, but rather a mirror image of it, reflecting the same desires, fears, and anxieties, but in a more overt and exaggerated form. As such, the concept of populism, the idea that it exists as an external force, becomes a vehicle for enjoyment for the European liberal mainstream. On the other hand, populism as a political alternative is attractive to voters since it speaks to a logic which is already familiar to them: European superiority.

Thus, while mainstream political forces and populist movements may seem to be diametrically opposed, they are in fact part of the same political logic, which is rooted in the coloniality of modern European politics. Both are united by a shared fantasy of European superiority, and both rely on the exclusion of certain populations to maintain this fantasy. The populist, far from being a challenger to the mainstream, plays a crucial role in upholding the very structures of power and identity that the mainstream seeks to protect.

We must therefore move beyond simplistic notions of ideological opposition. Instead, we must engage with the affective and phantasmatic dimensions of political life. Populism is not just an aberration or a fringe movement: it is an integral part of the political order in Europe, one that reflects the deep desires that underpin European identity. By acknowledging the role of coloniality in shaping European politics, we can better understand how populism functions not as an external challenge to European values but as a manifestation of the same desires, anxieties, and fantasies that continue to shape the European political landscape. Only by addressing these underlying dynamics can we hope to move beyond the colonial logics that sustain both mainstream and populist politics in Europe.

Gender as an interface of coloniality

It also crucial that we interrogate how coloniality presents itself in our current political juncture. In this book, I looked in particular at how gender and the nation-state are interfaces of coloniality. As described in Chapter 4, the relationship between gender and populism is far more complex than it initially appears, revealing significant contradictions and deeper systemic issues. Feminist theory offers a powerful lens through which to examine the interplay of gender and populism in European democracies, providing crucial insights into why these dynamics persist and how they are intricately connected. While populists in Europe often claim to champion gender equality and even LGBT rights, these positions are frequently instrumental and serve as strategic tools to bolster their image and garner votes. However, as recent scholarship suggests (Turnbull-Dugarte & López Ortega, 2024), their commitment to these values is neither deep nor consistent, but often opportunistic and designed to contrast with immigrant communities or other minority groups deemed 'backward' in the populist narrative.

Moreover, feminist theory exposes the broader paradox within right-wing populism. On one hand, women like Marine Le Pen and Giorgia Meloni have risen to prominent leadership roles, demonstrating that populist movements are not necessarily devoid of female representation. On the other hand, these movements frequently espouse chauvinistic policies that seek to reinforce traditional gender roles, such as encouraging women to stay home and withdrawing support for reproductive rights. This apparent contradiction raises a vital question: how do women align themselves with political ideologies that seem inherently opposed to their rights? The concept of femonationalism offers a compelling explanation here, showing that women themselves can be active participants in promoting nationalist, exclusionary, and patriarchal agendas. Furthermore, studies suggest that while male voters still form the majority of populist supporters, increasing numbers of women are aligning with right-wing populist parties, indicating a trend that requires deeper exploration.

The discussion of gender within populism cannot overlook its colonial dimensions, which can help us shed light on the 'muddy waters'. Decolonial feminist theory sheds light on how patriarchy, as it exists today, is inseparable from its colonial heritage (Lugones, 2007; Mendoza, 2015). European states, often portrayed as paragons of gender equality, are not neutral arbiters but are deeply embedded in systems that historically profited from gendered and racialized inequalities. Whether through unpaid labour in the domestic sphere, capitalist exploitation, or the promotion of militarized masculinity, gender inequality has been foundational to the functioning of European democracies. This historical reality calls into question the sharp divide often drawn between populist ideologies and mainstream politics. If violence, exclusion, and gender inequality are integral to the very construction of European states, it becomes evident that populism does not represent an aberration but rather a reflection of deeper systemic issues within democratic societies. In Chapter 4, I discussed how this is present even in left-wing populist parties and can be seen through their masculine repertoire.

Ultimately, this book challenges the notion that a commitment to patriarchy and exclusionary politics is unique to populist movements. While mainstream political actors often portray themselves as civilized, inclusive, and equal, feminist scholarship argues that masculinity and power dynamics are central to the entire political game. The constructed difference between populism and the mainstream is thus, as this work asserts, part of a phantasmatic structure. Both exist within the same discursive order of coloniality, where gender inequality and patriarchal values continue to shape political narratives and systems. Importantly, the widespread myth that Europe represents a 'gender-equal paradise' is one that must be dismantled if we are to achieve a more just and equitable future.

By integrating feminist critiques, we gain a clearer understanding of how populism and mainstream politics operate within similar frameworks of exclusion and inequality. These insights are essential not only for analysing the appeal of populism but also for confronting the broader challenges that persist within European democratic systems. Only by recognizing these deep-rooted connections can we begin to imagine and work towards a truly inclusive and equitable society.

Left-wing populism as a way forward?

In Chapter 5, the book introduced the nation-state as another interface of coloniality. The chapter showed how even left-wing populists struggle to move beyond the reliance on the nation as the main form of political community. As such, the tensions found in right-wing populism – such as its claims to protect European values while promoting exclusion and chauvinism – are mirrored in the struggles of left-wing populism to articulate a coherent and truly inclusive vision. While left-wing populism seeks to differentiate itself through its emphasis on equality, justice, and resistance to neoliberalism, its conceptualization of 'the People' remains entangled in problematic political traditions, including nationalism, patriotism, and managed borders. These tensions expose the limits of left-wing populism and highlight how its European heritage continues to hinder its emancipatory potential.

The successes of left-wing populist movements such as Podemos in Spain, Syriza in Greece, and La France Insoumise in France illustrate both their potential and their contradictions. While these parties have, at times, articulated a vision of politics that challenges exclusion and inequality, they remain tethered to the very same frameworks that they attempt to resist. Their reliance on concepts like nationhood, sovereignty, and patriotism – albeit reframed with some progressive content (Custodi, 2020) – demonstrates how difficult it is to escape the structural legacies of European coloniality. For example, Podemos' invocation of patriotism or Mélenchon's steadfast commitment to French republican values highlights how left-wing populists, much like their right-wing counterparts, still draw on nationalistic rhetoric to mobilize support. This raises a crucial question: can populism, even in its left-wing form, ever truly overcome the chauvinist and exclusionary tendencies inherent in European politics?

The book's final analysis underscores that these contradictions are not incidental but structural. The violent history of liberal democracy in Europe, combined with the colonial origins of 'the People', makes the emergence of a fully inclusionary and egalitarian populism unlikely. Left-wing populists, despite their progressive aspirations, remain more European than they are left-wing, as their political identities are shaped by the same colonial and rationalist frameworks that inform mainstream and right-wing politics. Even in moments of optimism – when conditions seem favourable for an egalitarian populism to take hold – these movements struggle to articulate a vision that escapes Europe's exclusionary legacy. Whether it is the left's ambivalence towards migration or its reliance on managed borders, these choices reflect deeper systemic limitations that are difficult to overcome.

Importantly, this book challenges the assumption that left-wing populism represents a clear alternative to the exclusionary politics of the right. While policy differences exist, the underlying frameworks – constructed through the violent and exclusionary history of European democracy – persist across the political spectrum. Antagonisms continue to be framed in terms of 'the People' against an external Other, rather than addressing the structural inequalities and exclusions that shape political identity itself. As such, populism, whether on the left or the right, remains constrained by the coloniality. In their failure to truly challenge the status quo and move beyond the logic of coloniality, left-wing populists also fail to be truly progressive.

Ultimately, this analysis serves as a reminder that the problems attributed to populism – chauvinism, exclusion, and nationalism – are not anomalies but core features of European political systems. Any emancipatory project must confront these historical and structural realities if it is to become anything more than a reimagining of the same exclusionary politics under a different guise. Until then, the contradictions of left-wing populism will persist, offering a partial critique of the system it inhabits while remaining bound to its most problematic legacies.

Remarks on the future

In the end, I would like to offer a few remarks on the future, not only for populism, but for the study of political parties and movements. Throughout the writing process, I have been asked time and again if I think there is a future for populism, both as a concept and as a political alternative. People have asked whether we can still use the concept to understand what is going on around us, and also whether populism could ever, in other political contexts outside of Europe, offer a way towards a more equal society. Third, I have also got a lot of sometimes desperate pleas for a way forward for emancipatory politics. Let me deal with these queries in turn.

First, I have presented a rather critical account of populism studies, but one which is still largely reliant on many of the insights from discourse theory and the legacy of Laclau. Nevertheless, we must consider the future for the concept of populism, as a field and as an analytical figure. As this book has demonstrated, there is little that indicates that examples of populism do what we think they do, which signals a schism between the concept and the empirical phenomenon: Populism does not seem to challenge the logic of coloniality.

This poses several problems. One of them, which I have discussed at length in Chapter 3, is the continued conflation between populism and the political, as seen in the discursive approach to populism. In the future, I think that this conflation will become untenable. Since, as I have demonstrated, there are so many ways that populists do not actually challenge the status quo and subvert current hierarchies, using populism as an example of the political becomes misleading. This is a problem for Laclau, but it is also a problem for the field as a whole and all the many studies which continue to do so.

Here, we are faced with two choices. Either we can keep the concept of populism as a useful analytical tool, but then we must be prepared to accept that what we are currently calling populism in Europe is politics as usual, built on a logic of coloniality. The parties and movements that we would like to call populists should then not be thought of as challenging the status quo. Or we can discard the concept of populism altogether and accept that it has a history which is not conducive to subversion. Perhaps it is impossible to salvage a concept which has been so tightly intertwined with reactionary politics.

Whichever choice we make, there are profound political implications. Importantly, it is paramount that we recognize the centrality of coloniality for politics in Europe, and that analyses do not shy away from reading political parties and movements as reinforcing colonial logics. In addition, it is only by employing the concept of coloniality that we can understand the popularity of populism in the first place, and the need to externalize what we think are 'bad' political actors. A first step towards an equal society must be to interrogate the fantasy that Europeans promote equality. There must be an acknowledgement that the mainstream in Europe does nothing of the sort and is often creating hierarchies between deserving citizens and unwanted elements. It is not until this fantasy is made visible that we can start working towards a different future.

The second question, with which I have been battling for some time, regards whether the problem with populism as a part of coloniality is only a problem in Europe. This is a tough one, since in many other places, most notably in Latin America, populism has in many instances been seen as furthering a progressive agenda. This, however, is a truth with modification. Even in other geographical contexts we can question how much populism is a progressive vehicle, and whether it manages to overcome, for instance, neoliberal hegemonies.

For me, however, this is not the main point. Rather than seeing the populist condition as geographically tied to Europe, I want to maintain that it is an idea. Just like the main tenets of coloniality – European superiority as read through a higher capacity to be a rational thinker – it is an idea which knows no geographical boundaries. As described by so many post- and decolonial theorists, the success of coloniality many times rests upon its ability to travel outside of Europe: it is not only Europeans who consider Europe in this favourable light (Dussel, 1977; Fanon, 2021; Mbembe, 2019). This means that populism in other geographical contexts is also at risk of being part of coloniality, but to show that it definitely is would require another book.

Third, can we envision a way forward for emancipatory politics? This book has focussed on explaining the populist condition, which is a diagnosis, not a treatment. But there are some obvious paths ahead which stand out after this analysis. Any future emancipatory project must be able to traverse the fantasy (Žižek, 2015). This means going beyond the phantasmatic structure in which we are currently situated, that populism is the main threat to an otherwise benign Europe. This would entail breaking the assumption that populism is an important part of politics and turn the gaze inwards. No longer can we externalize our problems, but we must face the European commitment to coloniality.

The future must also be able to conceptualize difference as non-antagonistic. For too long, critical political and democratic theory in Europe has been held hostage to the idea that difference means antagonism, which is by no means a necessary conclusion, as described in Chapter 3. What would be truly subversive today is to afford political subjectivity to those who have none, whose voices are not heard (and those are typically not the voice of 'populists', but can be seen in, for instance, the trans movement or fights against militarism). Such possibilities exist in the wealth of social movements and civil society organizations, political actors who are rarely deemed important enough for the 'big questions'. These, I argue, are the real examples of 'the political'.

Notes

Chapter 1

[1] One may think that this is a thing of the past, but as recent discussions on colonialism have demonstrated, there are significant portions of contemporary scholarship who believe in the benevolent nature of the colonial enterprise. Perhaps most noted is the (now infamous) article in *Third World Quarterly* from 2017, entitled 'The case for colonialism'. The article has now been retracted, but its mere presence, albeit short-lived, speaks for itself.

[2] This is not an attempt at rehabilitating the democratic credentials of Boris Johnson, who, on multiple occasions, has demonstrated an indubitable fondness for the British Empire and has been very apologetic about the unspeakable crimes committed in its name (El-Enany, 2020).

[3] This is not to say that the entire scholarly field studying deliberative forms of democracy are suffering from the same problem. We must recognize the advances made in deliberative democracy to confront injustices, which has been spearheaded by feminist critiques (Young, 2014). Recently, there are also signs of acknowledging the colonial and Eurocentric heritage (Asenbaum et al, 2024). Nevertheless, the point remains that contemporary public debate about populism and liberalism are more often than not attuned to these advances.

Chapter 2

[1] The next two subsections contain content from a previously published article. Used with permission of Michigan University Press, from 'Populism or the European Condition', Emmy Eklundh and Henrique Tavares Furtado, *Journal for the Study of Radicalism*, 16(2), 2022; permission conveyed through Copyright Clearance Center, Inc.

[2] Mudde here follows the argument of thin ideologies from Michael Freeden (1996), who primarily argued that nationalism is a thin ideology. It must also be mentioned that feminism is a thin ideology, according to Freeden, something which we will discuss more at length in Chapter 5.

[3] This is very evident when we consider the example that Adhemar de Barros was the subject of one of the most spectacular heists in 1970s Brazil, when a group of left-wing militants (VAR-Palmares) broke into his home to find millions of dollars (Furtado, 2022, p 98; Singer, 2009).

Chapter 4

[1] This chapter recognizes that there are other feminist theories, most notably in postcolonial feminism (Spivak, 2011), that differ from the decolonial approach. Primarily, postcolonial feminism does not believe that capitalism or the modern state system developed the same way in the colonized world as it did in Europe, whereas decolonial theory is much quicker to argue that capitalism as we know it could not have been possible without colonization

(Mendoza, 2015). For the purpose of the arguments made in this book, however, both posit a healthy alternative to the mainstream literature on the gendered politics of populism, even though decolonial theory serves as a main source of inspiration.

2 The next two pages contain content about Podemos taken from a previously published article: Emmy Eklundh (2022), 'Questioning European Democracy? Versions of representation in the 15M movement and Podemos', *Journal of Iberian and Latin American Research*, 28(3). Copyright © 2010 Association of Iberian and Latin American Studies of Australasia (AILASA), reprinted by permission of Informa UK Limited, trading as Taylor & Francis Group, www.tandfonline.com on behalf of 2010 Association of Iberian and Latin American Studies of Australasia (AILASA).

Chapter 5

1 It must of course be recognized that this transnational populism can equally take a right-wing turn, as it so often does, and is not by default a left-wing political project (Hall, 2024; Wojczewski, 2023).

Bibliography

Aboy Carlés, G. (2023). El populismo latinoamericano en perspectiva. *Revista Mexicana De Sociología, 85*(e2), 169–196. https://doi.org/10.22201/iis.01882503p.2023.e2.60987

Agamben, G. (2005). *State of Exception*. University of Chicago Press.

Agius, C. (2022). 'This is not who we are': Gendered bordering practices, ontological insecurity, and lines of continuity under the Trump presidency. *Review of International Studies, 48*(2), 385–402. https://doi.org/10.1017/S0260210521000590

Agustín, Ó. G. (2020). *Left-Wing Populism: The Politics of the People*. Emerald Publishing.

Aiolfi, T. (2022). Populism as a transgressive style. *Global Studies Quarterly, 2*(1), 1–12. https://doi.org/10.1093/isagsq/ksac006

Akkerman, T. (2003). Populism and democracy: Challenge or pathology? *Acta Politica, 38*, 147–159. https://doi.org/10.1057/palgrave.ap.5500021

Alemán, J. (2018). *Jorge Alemán 07—Conversación con Pablo Iglesias*. Youtube.Com. https://www.youtube.com/watch?v=b2w5LXpHH4Q&ab_channel=PuntodeEmancipación

Almond, G., & Verba, S. (1963). *The Civic Culture: Political Attitudes and Democracy in Five Nations*. Princeton University Press.

Anastasiou, M. (2019). *Popular or Hegemonic Subject? On the Limits of Democratic Populism, 9*.

Anastasiou, M. (2020). The spatiotemporality of nationalist populism and the production of political subjectivities. *Subjectivity, 13*(3), 217–234. https://doi.org/10.1057/s41286-020-00104-x

Anastasiou, M., & Custodi, J. (2024). The populism-nationalism nexus. In G. Katsambekis & Y. Stavrakakis (eds) *Research Handbook on Populism*. Edward Elgar Publishing. https://www.elgaronline.com/edcollchap/book/9781800379695/book-part-9781800379695-10.xml

Anderson, B. (1983). *Imagined Communities: Reflections on the Origin and Spread of Nationalism*. Verso.

Angelos, J. (2024). Is Germany's rising superstar so far left she's far right? *Politico*. 26 August. https://www.politico.eu/article/germany-superstar-sahra-wagenknecht-far-left-far-right/

Ardanuy Pizarro, M., & Labuske, E. (2015). El músculo deliberativo del algoritmo democrático: Podemos y la participación ciudadana. *Teknokultura*, *12*(1), 93–109. https://doi.org/10.5209/rev_TK.2015.v12.n1.48887

Arditi, B. (2005). Populism as an internal periphery of democratic politics. In F. Panizza (ed) *Populism and the Mirror of Democracy*. Verso.

Asenbaum, H., Curato, N., Ibhawoh, B., Johnson, G. F., McCaul, J., & Mendonça, R. F. (2024). Can deliberative democracy be decolonized? A debate. *Centre for Deliberative Democracy & Global Governance Working Paper Series*, *2024*(1).

Ausserladscheider, V. (2022). Constructing a neoliberal exclusionary state: The role of far-right populism in economic policy change in post-war Austria. *Comparative European Politics*. https://doi.org/10.1057/s41295-022-00315-3

Ausserladscheider, V. (2024). *Far-Right Populism and the Making of the Exclusionary Neoliberal State* (1st ed. 2024.). Springer Nature Switzerland. https://doi.org/10.1007/978-3-031-64467-2

Bailey, D. J. (2019). Neither Brexit nor remain: Disruptive solidarity initiatives in a time of false promises and anti-democracy. *Contemporary Social Science*, *14*(2), 256–275. https://doi.org/10.1080/21582041.2018.1559349

Balibar, E. (1989). Racism as universalism. *New Political Science*, *8*(1–2), 9–22. https://doi.org/10.1080/07393148908429618

Balibar, E. (2004). *We the People of Europe: Reflections on Transnational Citizenship*. Princeton University Press.

Barberá González, R., & Martín del Fresno, F. (2019). El populismo de izquierdas en el discurso de Pablo Iglesias. *Revista de Comunicación de La SEECI*, *November*, 141–158. https://doi.org/10.15198/seeci.2019.49.141-158

Bartelson, J. (1995). *A Genealogy of Sovereignty*. Cambridge University Press. https://doi.org/10.1017/CBO9780511586385

Bataille, G. (with Botting, F., & Wilson, S.). (1997). *The Bataille Reader*. Blackwell.

Bataille, G., & Lovitt, C. R. (1979). The psychological structure of fascism. *New German Critique*, *16*, 64. https://doi.org/10.2307/487877

BBC. (2016). *Labour leadership: Corbyn says his 'social movement' will win elections*. 23 July.

Benquet, M., & Bourgeron, T. (2022). *Alt-Finance: How the City of London Bought Democracy*. Pluto Press.

Berlin, I., & Hofstadter, R. (1968). To define populism. *Government and Opposition*, *3*(2), 137–180. https://doi.org/10.1111/j.1477-7053.1968.tb01332.x

Berman, S. (2017). The pipe dream of undemocratic liberalism. *Journal of Democracy*, *28*(3), 29–38. https://doi.org/10.1353/jod.2017.0041

Bhambra, G. K. (2017). Brexit, Trump, and 'methodological whiteness': On the misrecognition of race and class. *British Journal of Sociology*, *68*, S214–S232. https://doi.org/10.1111/1468-4446.12317

Biglieri, P., & Cadahia, L. (2021). *Seven Essays on Populism: For a Renewed Theoretical Perspective*. Consortium Books.

Blakey, H. (2016). 'Corbyn-mania': Cult of personality or political movement? *Open Democracy*.

Bloodworth, J. (2019). Jeremy Corbyn is caught in Labour's immigration wars. *Foreign Policy*. November.

Bonansinga, D. (2020). Who thinks, feels: The relationship between emotions, politics and populism. *Partecipazione e Conflitto*, *13*(1), 83–106. https://doi.org/10.1285/i20356609v13i1p83

Borge Bravo, R., & Santamarina Sáez, E. (2016). From protest to political parties: Online deliberation in new parties in Spain. *Medijske Studije*, 7(14), 104–122. https://doi.org/10.20901/ms.7.14.8

Borraz, M. (2023). *El Congreso aprueba la reforma del aborto con el voto en contra del PP y Vox*. ElDiario.es. 16 February. https://www.eldiario.es/sociedad/congreso-aprueba-reforma-aborto-voto-pp-vox_1_9952845.html

Borrell, J. (2022). *European Diplomatic Academy: Opening remarks by High Representative Josep Borrell at the inauguration of the pilot programme | EEAS*. https://www.eeas.europa.eu/eeas/european-diplomatic-academy-opening-remarks-high-representative-josep-borrell-inauguration-pilot_en

Bortun, V. (2024). It's time for a 'material turn' in populism studies. *The Loop*. 19 March. https://theloop.ecpr.eu/its-time-for-a-material-turn-in-populism-studies/

Breeze, R. (2019). Emotion in politics: Affective-discursive practices in UKIP and Labour. *Discourse and Society*, *30*(1), 24–43. https://doi.org/10.1177/0957926518801074

Briziarelli, M. (2016). To 'feel' and to 'understand' political struggle: The national-popular rhetoric of Podemos. *Journal of Communication Inquiry*, *40*(3), 287–304. https://doi.org/10.1177/0196859916634084

Brocklehurst, S. (2025). *UK Supreme Court rules legal definition of a woman is based on biological sex—BBC News*. 16 April. https://www.bbc.co.uk/news/live/cvgq9ejql39t

Broughton, J. (2003). *Descartes's Method of Doubt*. Princeton University Press. https://doi.org/10.1515/9781400825042

Brown, K. (2024). Perceptions of the 'mainstream' and the mainstreaming of the far right: From Ed Sheeran to Keir Starmer. *Journal of Political Ideologies*, 1–22. https://doi.org/10.1080/13569317.2024.2408241

Brown, K., & Mondon, A. (2020). Populism, the media, and the mainstreaming of the far right: The Guardian's coverage of populism as a case study. *Politics*, *26*(3), 279–295.

Brown, K., Mondon, A., & Winter, A. (2021). The far right, the mainstream and mainstreaming: Towards a heuristic framework. *Journal of Political Ideologies*, 1–18. https://doi.org/10.1080/13569317.2021.1949829

Bruff, I. (2014). The rise of authoritarian neoliberalism. *Rethinking Marxism*, *26*(1), 113–129. https://doi.org/10.1080/08935696.2013.843250

Bruff, I., & Tansel, C. B. (2019). Authoritarian neoliberalism: Trajectories of knowledge production and praxis. *Globalizations*, *16*(3), 233–244. https://doi.org/10.1080/14747731.2018.1502497

Bündnis Sahra Wagenknecht. (2024). *Bündnis Sahra Wagenknecht Gründungsmanifest*. https://buendnis-sahra-wagenknecht.de/wp-content/themes/bsw/assets/files/BSW_Gruendungsmanifest.pdf

Butler, J. (1990). *Gender Trouble: Feminism and the Subversion of Identity*. Routledge.

Caiani, M., & Della Porta, D. (2011). The elitist populism of the extreme right: A frame analysis of extreme right-wing discourses in Italy and Germany. *Acta Politica*, *46*(2), 180–202. https://doi.org/10.1057/ap.2010.28

Canovan, M. (2005). *The People*. Polity Press.

Caravantes, P. (2019). New versus old politics in Podemos: Feminization and masculinized party discourse. *Men and Masculinities*, *22*(3), 465–490. https://doi.org/10.1177/1097184X18769350

Caravantes, P. (2020). Tensions between populist and feminist politics: The case of the Spanish left populist party Podemos. *International Political Science Review*. https://doi.org/10.1177/0192512120931209

Caravantes, P., & Lombardo, E. (2023). The symbolic representation of the 'People' and the 'Homeland' in Spanish left populism: An opportunity for feminist politics? *Journal of Contemporary European Studies*, *31*(3), 902–915. https://doi.org/10.1080/14782804.2022.2090322

Casullo, M. E. (2019). *¿Por qué funciona el populismo? El discurso que sabe construir explicaciones convincentes de un mundo en crisis*. Siglo XXI editores.

Casullo, M. E. (2020). The body speaks before it even talks: Deliberation, populism and bodily representation. *Journal of Deliberative Democracy*, *16*(1), 27–36. https://doi.org/10.16997/jdd.380

Casullo, M. E., & Ostiguy, P. (2017). *Left Versus Right Populism: Antagonism and the Social Other*. 10 April. Political Studies Association.

Chappell, L., & Guerrina, R. (2020). Understanding the gender regime in the European External Action Service. *Cooperation and Conflict*, *55*(2), 261–280.

Charalambous, G. (2013). Nationalism, Euroscepticism and the radical left and right: A short response to Halikio poulou's, Nanou's and Vasilopoulou's (2012) study. *Extremis Project, 2013*.

Chatterjee, P. (2004). *The Politics of the Governed: Reflections on Popular Politics in Most of the World*. Columbia University Press.

Chironi, D., & Fittipaldi, R. (2017). Social movements and new forms of political organization: Podemos as a hybrid party. *Partecipazione e Conflitto*, *10*(1), 275–305. https://doi.org/10.1285/i20356609v10i1p275

Cho, S., Crenshaw, K. W., & McCall, L. (2013). Toward a field of intersectionality studies: Theory, applications, and praxis. *Signs: Journal of Women in Culture and Society, 38*(4), 785–810. https://doi.org/10.1086/669608

Citron, L. (2016). The politics of the kiss. *New Statesman*. 11 February.

Colmeiro, J. (2017). Old traditions and revolutionary tendencies: Performing different masculinities in Spanish cinema. In L. Ryan & A. Corbalán (eds) *The Dynamics of Masculinity in Contemporary Spanish Culture*. Routledge, pp 19–35.

Connell, R. W. (1990). The state, gender, and sexual politics: Theory and appraisal. *Theory and Society, 19*(5), 507–544.

Cowling, M., & Martin, J. (eds) (2002). *Marx's Eighteenth Brumaire: (Post) modern Interpretations*. Pluto Press.

Custodi, J. (2020). Nationalism and populism on the left: The case of Podemos. *Nations and Nationalism, June*, 1–16. https://doi.org/10.1111/nana.12663

Custodi, J. (2023a). How should we analyse the patriotism of the populist left: A response to Josep Lobera and Juan Roch. *Nations and Nationalism, 29*(1), 113–116. https://doi.org/10.1111/nana.12880

Custodi, J. (2023b). *Radical Left Parties and National Identity in Spain, Italy and Portugal: Rejecting or Reclaiming the Nation*. Springer Nature Switzerland. https://doi.org/10.1007/978-3-031-48926-6

Custodi, J. (2023c). The Spanish case. What is Spain? Franco's legacy and Podemos' patriotism. In *Radical Left Parties and National Identity in Spain, Italy and Portugal*. Springer Nature Switzerland, pp 87–126. https://doi.org/10.1007/978-3-031-48926-6_4

Custodi, J., & Padoan, E. (2022). The nation of the people: An analysis of Podemos and Five Star Movement's discourse on the nation. *Nations and Nationalism*, nana.12865. https://doi.org/10.1111/nana.12865

Damiani, M., & Viviani, L. (2019). Populism and euroscepticism in podemos and in the five star movement: Faraway, so close? *Partecipazione e Conflitto, 12*(1), 97–216. https://doi.org/10.1285/i20356609v12i1p197

De Cleen, B., & Ruiz Casado, J. A. (2024). Populism of the privileged: On the use of underdog identities by comparatively privileged groups. *Political Studies, 72*(3), 1005–1025. https://doi.org/10.1177/00323217231160427

De Cleen, B., & Stavrakakis, Y. (2017). Distinctions and articulations: A discourse theoretical framework for the study of populism and nationalism. *Javnost, 24*(4), 301–319. https://doi.org/10.1080/13183222.2017.1330083

De Cleen, B., Glynos, J., & Mondon, A. (2018). Critical research on populism: Nine rules of engagement. *Organization, 25*(5), 649–661. https://doi.org/10.1177/1350508418768053

De Cleen, B., Moffitt, B., Panayotu, P., & Stavrakakis, Y. (2020). The potentials and difficulties of transnational populism: The case of the Democracy in Europe Movement 2025 (diem25). *Political Studies, 68*(1), 146–166. https://doi.org/10.1177/0032321719847576

De Giorgi, E., Cavalieri, A., & Feo, F. (2023). From opposition leader to prime minister: Giorgia Meloni and women's issues in the Italian radical right. *Politics and Governance*, *11*(1), 108–118. https://doi.org/10.17645/pag.v11i1.6042

De La Torre, C. (2017). Populism and nationalism in Latin America. *Javnost*, *24*(4), 375–390. https://doi.org/10.1080/13183222.2017.1330731

De Vries, C. E., & Edwards, E. E. (2009). Taking Europe to its extremes: Extremist parties and public Euroscepticism. *Party Politics*, *15*(1), 5–28. https://doi.org/10.1177/1354068808097889

Dean, J., & Maiguashca, B. (2018). Gender, power, and left politics: From feminization to feministization. *Politics and Gender*, *14*(3), 376–406. https://doi.org/10.1017/S1743923X18000193

Dean, J., & Maiguashca, B. (2020). Did somebody say populism? Towards a renewal and reorientation of populism studies. *Journal of Political Ideologies*, *25*(1), 11–27. https://doi.org/10.1080/13569317.2020.1699712

Degano, C., & Sicurella, F. G. (2019). A dialogue on populism? A study of intellectual discourse about populism in the Brexit debate in Italy and the UK. In J. Zienkowski & R. Breeze (eds) (2019). *Imagining the Peoples of Europe: Populist Discourses Across the Political Spectrum*. John Benjamins, pp 43–72.

Della Porta, D. (2015). *Social Movements in Times of Austerity: Bringing Capitalism Back into Protest Analysis*. Polity Press.

Della Porta, D., Fernández, J., Kouki, H., & Mosca, L. (2017). *Movement Parties Against Austerity*. Polity Press.

Della Porta, D., Kouki, H., & Fernandez, J. (2017). Left's love and hate for Europe: Syriza, Podemos, and critical visions of Europe during the crisis. In M. Caiani & S. Guerra (eds) (2017). *Euroscepticism, Democracy and the Media*. Palgrave Macmillan, pp 219–240.

Derrida, J. (1988). The politics of friendship. *The Journal of Philosophy*, *85*(11), 632–644. https://doi.org/10.5840/jphil1988851110

Derrida, J. (2006). Specters of Marx. In *Specters of Marx*. Taylor & Francis Group.

Di Tella, T. S. (1965). Populism and reform in Latin America. *Desarrollo económico (Buenos Aires)*, *4*(16), 391–425.

Diamond, J. (2019). *Guns, Germs and Steel*. Penguin.

Diamond, P. (2018). Brexit and the Labour party: Euro-caution vs. Euro-fanaticism? The Labour Party's constructive ambiguity on Brexit and the European Union. In P. Diamond, P. Nedergaard, & B. Rosamond (eds) *The Routledge Handbook on the Politics of Brexit*. Routledge, pp 167–178.

Dussel, E. (1977). *Filosofía de la Liberación*. Editorial Nueva America.

Dussel, E. (1994). *1492: El Encubrimiento del Otro: Hacia el Origen del Mito de la Modernidad*. Plural Editores.

Dussel, E., & MacEoin, G. (1991). 1492: The discovery of an invasion. *CrossCurrents*, *41*(4), 437–452.

Edelman, L. (2004). *No Future: Queer Theory and the Death Drive*. Duke University Press.

Eklundh, E. (2019). *Emotions, Protest, Democracy—Collective Identities in Contemporary Spain*. Routledge.

Eklundh, E. (2020). Excluding emotions: The performative function of populism. *Partecipazione e Conflitto*, *13*(1), 107–131. https://doi.org/10.1285/i20356609v13i1p107

Eklundh, E. (2022). Questioning European democracy? Versions of representation in the 15M Movement and Podemos. *Journal of Iberian and Latin American Research*, *28*(3), 335–349. https://doi.org/10.1080/13260219.2022.2170729

Eklundh, E., & Ronderos, S. (2025). Studying affect through discourse theory: Towards a methodology of practice. *Journal of Language and Politics*. https://doi.org/10.1075/jlp.24197.ekl

Eklundh, E., Stengel, F., & Wojczewski, T. (2024). Left populism and foreign policy: Bernie Sanders and Podemos. *International Affairs*, *100*(5), 1899–1918. https://doi.org/10.1093/ia/iiae137

El-Enany, N. (2020). Europe's colonial embrace and the Brexit nostalgia for empire are two sides of the same coin. *LSE BREXIT*. https://blogs.lse.ac.uk/brexit/2020/04/29/europes-colonial-embrace-and-brexit-as-nostalgia-for-empire-are-part-of-the-same-story/

El País (2025). *Caso Errejón en EL PAÍS*. El País. 14 March. https://elpais.com/noticias/caso-errejon/

Errejón, Í., & Mouffe, C. (2016). *Podemos: In the name of the People*. Lawrence and Wishart Limited.

European Commission. (2025). *Promoting our European way of life—European Commission*. https://commission.europa.eu/strategy-and-policy/priorities-2019-2024/promoting-our-european-way-life_en

European Parliament. (2024). *2024 Election Results*. https://www.results.elections.europa.eu/en/index.html

Eze, E. C. (1995). The color of reason: The idea of 'race' in Kant's anthropology. *The Bucknell Review*, *38*(2), 200–241.

Eze, E. C. (1997). *Race and the Enlightenment: A Reader*. Blackwell.

Fanon, F. (with Philcox, R.). (2021). *Black Skin, White Masks*. Penguin.

Farkas, J. (2023). News on fake news: Logics of media discourses on disinformation. *Journal of Language and Politics*, *22*(1), 1–21. https://doi.org/10.1075/jlp.22020.far

Flesher Fominaya, C. (2015a). Debunking spontaneity: Spain's 15-M/Indignados as Autonomous Movement. *Social Movement Studies*, *14*(2), 142–163. https://doi.org/10.1080/14742837.2014.945075

Flesher Fominaya, C. (2015b). Redefining the crisis/redefining democracy: Mobilising for the right to housing in Spain's PAH Movement. *South European Society and Politics*, *20*(4), 465–485. https://doi.org/10.1080/13608746.2015.1058216

Foucault, M. (2003). *Society Must Be Defended: Lectures at the Collège de France, 1975–76*. Penguin Press.

Freeden, M. (1996). *Ideologies and Political Theory: A Conceptual Approach*. Oxford University Press.

Freedom House. (2024). *Expanding Freedom and Democracy*. Freedom House. 12 December. https://freedomhouse.org/expanding-freedom-and-democracy

Froio, C., & Gattinara, P. C. (2015). *Neo-fascist mobilization in contemporary Italy. Ideology and Repertoire of Action of CasaPound Italia*. 2, 86–118.

Furtado, H. T. (2022). *Politics of Impunity*. Edinburgh University Press. https://edinburghuniversitypress.com/book-politics-of-impunity.html

Furtado, H. T. (2023). Critique of ontological militarism. *International Political Sociology*, *17*(3), olad012. https://doi.org/10.1093/ips/olad012

Galanopoulos, A., & Venizelos, G. (2022). Anti-populism and populist hype during the COVID-19 pandemic. *Representation*, *58*(2), 251–268. https://doi.org/10.1080/00344893.2021.2017334

Galston, W. A. (2018). *Anti-Pluralism: The Populist Threat to Liberal Democracy*. Yale University Press.

Gellner, E. (1983). *Nations and Nationalism*. Blackwell.

Gerbaudo, P. (2017). *The Mask and the Flag: Populism, Citizenism and Global Protest*. C. Hurst and Co.

Gerbaudo, P., & Screti, F. (2017). Reclaiming popular sovereignty: The vision of the state in the discourse of podemos and the movimento 5 stelle. *Javnost*, *24*(4), 320–335. https://doi.org/10.1080/13183222.2017.1330089

Germani, G. (1979). *Política y Sociedad en una Época de Transición*. Paidós.

Germani, G., & de Yujnovsky, S. S. (1973). El surgimiento del peronismo: El rol de los obreros y de los migrantes internos. *Desarrollo Económico (Buenos Aires)*, *13*(51), 435–488. https://doi.org/10.2307/3466131

Gifford, C. (2015). Nationalism, populism and Anglo-British Euroscepticism. *British Politics*, *10*(3), 362–366. https://doi.org/10.1057/bp.2015.2

Gillespie, L. (2024). On the proximity of the far right and the misuses of the 'mainstreaming' metaphor. *Identities*, 1–20. https://doi.org/10.1080/1070289X.2024.2442197

Glynos, J. (2008). Ideological fantasy at work. *Journal of Political Ideologies*, *13*(3), 275–296. https://doi.org/10.1080/13569310802376961

Glynos, J. (2021). Critical fantasy studies. *Journal of Language and Politics*, *20*(1), 95–111. https://doi.org/10.1075/jlp.20052.gly

Glynos, J., & Howarth, D. (2007). *Logics of Critical Explanation in Social and Political Theory*. Routledge.

Glynos, J., & Mondon, A. (2019). The political logic of populist hype: The case of right-wing populism's 'meteoric rise' and its relation to the status quo. In P. Cossarini & F. Vallespín (eds) *Populism and Passions: Democratic Legitimacy After Austerity*. Routledge.

Glynos, J., & Stavrakakis, Y. (2004). Encounter of the real kind: Sussing out the limits of Laclau's embrace of Lacan. In S. Critchley & O. Marchart (eds) *Laclau: A Critical Reader*. Routledge.

Gómez-Reino Cachafeiro, M., & Plaza-Colodro, C. (2018). Populist Euroscepticism in Iberian party systems. *Politics*, *38*(3), 344–360. https://doi.org/10.1177/0263395718762667

Goodwin, M., & Eatwell, R. (2018). *National Populism: The Revolt Against Liberal Democracy*. Pelican Press.

Gramsci, A. (2005). State and civil society. In *Selections from the Prison Notebooks of Antonio Gramsci*. Lawrence and Wishart Limited.

Grattan, L. (2021). Populism, race, and radical imagination: #FeelingtheBern in the age of #BlackLivesMatter. In P. Ostiguy, F. Panizza, & B. Moffitt (eds) *Populism in a Global Perspective: A Performative and Discursive Approach*. Routledge, pp 136–154.

Grosfoguel, R. (2007). The epistemic decolonial turn: Beyond political-economy paradigms. *Cultural Studies*, *21*(2–3), 211–223. https://doi.org/10.1080/09502380601162514

Habermas, J. (1984). *Communicative Action: Reason and the Rationalisation of Society*. Beacon Press.

Habermas, J. (1996). *Between Facts and Norms: Contributions to a Discourse Theory of Law and Democracy*. Polity Press.

Habermas, J. (with Cronin, C.). (2006). *The Divided West*. Polity.

Halikiopoulou, D., Nanou, K., & Vasilopoulou, S. (2012). The paradox of nationalism: The common denominator of radical right and radical left euroscepticism. *European Journal of Political Research*, *51*(4), 504–539. https://doi.org/10.1111/j.1475-6765.2011.02050.x

Hall, N.-A. (2024). *Brexit, Facebook, and Transnational Right-Wing Populism*. Lexington Books, an imprint of The Rowman & Littlefield Publishing Group, Inc.

Hall, S. (1988). *The Hard Road to Renewal: Thatcherism and the Crisis of the Left*. Verso in association with Marxism Today.

Hall, S. (2017). *The Fateful Triangle: Race, Ethnicity, Nation*. Harvard University Press. https://doi.org/10.4159/9780674982260

Hansen, A. D. (2020). Is antagonism a good name for radical negativity? Review of Oliver Marchart's Thinking Antagonism. *Etica & Politica*, *22*(3), 533–543.

Hartikainen, I. (2021). Authentic Expertise: Andrej Babiš and the technocratic populist performance during the COVID-19 crisis. *Frontiers in Political Science*, *3*(November), 1–17. https://doi.org/10.3389/fpos.2021.734093

Hatakka, N., & Herkman, J. (2022). *Hegemonic Meanings of Populism: Populism as a Signifier in Legacy Dailies of Six Countries 2000–2018*. 44(8), 1523–1540. https://doi.org/10.1177/01634437221104680

Heinisch, R., & Werner, A. (2024). The strange bedfellows of populism and liberalism: The effect of populist attitudes on the perception of the COVID-19 pandemic and policies to contain it. *Comparative European Politics*, 22(4), 433–458. https://doi.org/10.1057/s41295-023-00367-z

Hemmings, C. (2012). Affective solidarity: Feminist reflexivity and political transformation. *Feminist Theory*, 13(2), 147–161. https://doi.org/10.1177/1464700112442643

Hobbes, T. (1991). *Leviathan* (R. Tuck, ed). Cambridge University Press.

Hobbes, T. (2009). *De Cive: Philosophical Rudiments Concerning Government and Society*. Dodo Press.

Hoijtink, M., Mühlenhoff, H. L., & Welfens, N. (2023). Whose (in)security? Gender, race and coloniality in European security policies: Introduction to the Special Issue. *European Security*. https://www.tandfonline.com/doi/abs/10.1080/09662839.2023.2235286

Hooghe, L., Marks, G., & Wilson, C. J. (2002). Does left/right structure party positions on European integration? *Comparative Political Studies*, 35(8), 965–989. https://doi.org/10.1177/001041402236310

Ianni, O. (1972). Populismo y relaciones de clase en América Latina. *Revista Mexicana de Ciencias Políticas y Sociales*, 18(67), Article 67. https://doi.org/10.22201/fcpys.2448492xe.1972.67.82359

Iglesias, P. (2015). Understanding Podemos. *New Left Review*, 93, 5–22.

Iglesias, P., Errejón, Í., Monedero, J. C., Bescansa, C., & Alegre, L. (2014). *#CLAROQUEPODEMOS: Borrador de Principios Organizativos*. https://www.scribd.com/document/240575611/PODEMOS-Resumen-Borrador-Principios-Organizativos

Iglesias, P., Montero, I., & Monedero, J. C. (2017). *Plan 2020: Ganar al PP, gobernar España, construir derechos. Documento Político*.

Ionescu, G., & Gellner, E. (eds) (1969). *Populism: Its Meanings and National Characteristics: Ionescu, Ghita, Gellner, Ernest*. Macmillan.

Jaguaribe, H. (2013). *Estudos Filosóficos e Políticos*. Fundação Alexandre de Gusmão.

Johnston, M., & Meger, S. (2024). Morbid symptoms: A feminist dialectics of global patriarchy in crisis. *European Journal of International Relations*, 13540661241295658. https://doi.org/10.1177/13540661241295658

Jones, S., Charles, N. & Davies, C. (2009). Transforming masculinist political cultures? Doing politics in new political institutions. *Sociological Research Online*, 14(2). https://doi.org/10.5153/sro.1863

Kagarlitsky, B. (2017). Brexit and the future of the left. *Globalizations*, 14(1), 110–117. https://doi.org/10.1080/14747731.2016.1228800

Kant, I. (1960). *Observations on the Feeling of the Beautiful and Sublime*, trans. John T. Goldthwait. University of California Press.

Kantola, J., & Lombardo, E. (2019). Populism and feminist politics: The cases of Finland and Spain. *European Journal of Political Research*, 58(4), 1108–1128. https://doi.org/10.1111/1475-6765.12333

Karavasilis, L. (2025). What we talk about when we talk about 'the elite' in populism studies: Re-examining an often-neglected term in the cases of Die Linke and AfD. *Critical Discourse Studies*, 1–17. https://doi.org/10.1080/17405904.2025.2496630

Karavasilis, L., Custodi, J., & Chazel, L. (2024). *How Do Radical Left Parties Frame the Nation? A Comparison Between Greece, Spain and France* (Version 1.0) [Dataset]. University of Salento. https://doi.org/10.1285/I203566 09V17I3P717

Katsambekis, G. (2020). Constructing 'the people' of populism: A critique of the ideational approach from a discursive perspective. *Journal of Political Ideologies*, 27(1), 1–22. https://doi.org/10.1080/13569317.2020.1844372

Katsambekis, G. (2023). Mainstreaming authoritarianism. *The Political Quarterly*, 94(3), 428–436. https://doi.org/10.1111/1467-923X.13299

Katsambekis, G., & Stavrakakis, Y. (2017). Revisiting the nationalism/populism nexus: Lessons from the Greek case. *Javnost*, 24(4), 391–408. https://doi.org/10.1080/13183222.2017.1330087

Keith, D. (2017). Opposing Europe, opposing austerity: Radical left parties and the Eurosceptic debate. *The Routledge Handbook of Euroscepticism*, 86–99. https://doi.org/10.4324/9781315464015

Keskinen, S. (2018). The 'crisis' of white hegemony, neonationalist femininities and antiracist feminism. *Women's Studies International Forum*, 68(October 2017), 157–163. https://doi.org/10.1016/j.wsif.2017.11.001

Kinnvall, C. (2015). Borders and fear: Insecurity, gender and the far right in Europe. *Journal of Contemporary European Studies*, 23(4), 514–529. https://doi.org/10.1080/14782804.2015.1056115

Kioupkiolis, A. (2016). Podemos: The ambiguous promises of left-wing populism in contemporary Spain. *Journal of Political Ideologies*, 21(2). https://doi.org/10.1080/13569317.2016.1150136

Kioupkiolis, A., & Pérez, F. S. (2018). Reflexive technopopulism: Podemos and the search for a new left-wing hegemony. *European Political Science*, 1–13. https://doi.org/10.1057/s41304-017-0140-9

Kleinberg, R. (2023). *On the Limits of a Left-Populist Nationalism: A Radical Democratic Critique of Jean-Luc Mélenchon's Neo-Republicanism, 2015–2017* [PhD]. University of Essex.

Knott, A. (2020). The new moving right show. *Soundings*, 75(75), 111–123. https://doi.org/10.3898/SOUN.75.07.2020

Kohan, M. (2022). *El Congreso Aprueba la Ley Trans con la Abstención de Carmen Calvo y los Votos en contra de PP, Vox y Ciudadanos*. 22 December. https://www.publico.es/sociedad/congreso-aprueba-ley-trans-abstencion-carmen-calvo-votos-pp-vox-ciudadanos.html

Kundnani, H. (2023). *Eurowhiteness—Culture, Empire and Race in the European Project*. Hurst Publishing.

Lacan, J. (2007). *The Seminar of Jaques Lacan Book XVII: The Other Side of Psychoanalysis by Jacques Lacan* (R. Grigg, Trans.). W. W. Norton.

Laclau, E. (1990). *New Reflections on the Revolutions of Our Time*. Verso.

Laclau, E. (2005). *On Populist Reason*. Verso.

Laclau, E. (2007). *Emancipation(s)*. Verso.

Landa, I. (2012). *The Apprentice's Sorcerer*. Haymarket Books.

Lapavitsas, C. (2019). Learning from Brexit. *Monthly Review*, 26–48. https://doi.org/10.14452/mr-071-05-2019-09_4

Laruelle, M. (2022). Illiberalism: A conceptual introduction. *East European Politics*, *38*(2), 303–327. https://doi.org/10.1080/21599165.2022.2037079

Lazzarato, M. (2021). *Capital Hates Everyone: Fascism or Revolution*. Semiotext(e).

Le Bon, G. (1960). *The Crowd*. Viking Press.

Le Goff, J. (with Goldhammer, A.). (1992). *The Medieval Imagination* (Paperback ed.). University of Chicago Press.

Lefort, C. (1988). *Democracy and Political Theory*. Polity.

Lucas, C. (2017, 11 January). Jeremy Corbyn should tell voters the truth about freedom of movement.pdf. *New Statesman*.

Lugones, M. (2007). Heterosexualism and the colonial/modern gender system. *Hypatia*, *22*(1), 186–209.

Mackay, F., Kenny, M., & Chappell, L. (2010). New institutionalism through a gender lens: Towards a feminist institutionalism? *International Political Science Review / Revue Internationale de Science Politique*, *31*(5), 573–588.

Maiguashca, B., & Dean, J. (2019). Corbynism, populism and the re-shaping of left politics in contemporary Britain. In G. Katsambekis & A. Kioupkiolis (eds) *The Populist Radical Left in Europe*. Routledge, pp 145–167.

Maldonado-Torres, N. (2007). On the coloniality of being: Contributions to the development of a concept. *Cultural Studies*, *21*(2–3), 240–270. https://doi.org/10.1080/09502380601162548

Maldonado-Torres, N. (2008). *Against War: Views from the Underside of Modernity*. Duke University Press.

Mandelbaum, M. (2020). *The Nation/State Fantasy: A Psychoanalytical Genealogy of Nationalism*. Palgrave Macmillan.

Mann, M. (2012). Two versions of 'We, the People'. *The Dark Side of Democracy*, 55–69. https://doi.org/10.1017/cbo9780511817274.004

Manners, I. (2002). Normative power Europe: A contradiction in terms? *Journal of Common Market Studies*, *40*(2), 235. https://doi.org/10.1111/1468-5965.00353

March, L. (2017). Left and right populism compared: The British case. *British Journal of Politics and International Relations*, *19*(2), 282–303. https://doi.org/10.1177/1369148117701753

Marchart, O. (2018). *Thinking Antagonism: Political Ontology After Laclau*. Edinburgh University Press.

Marco, J. M. (2015). La patria es la gente o el nacionalismo, según Podemos. *La Razón*. 25 October.

Markou, G. (2017). The rise of inclusionary populism in Europe: The case of SYRIZA. *Contemporary Southeastern Europe*, *4*(1), 54–71.

Mattei, C. E. (2025). *The Capital Order: How Economists Invented Austerity and Paved the Way to Fascism*. University of Chicago Press.

Mazzolini, S. (2020). *Populism Is not Hegemony: Towards a Re-Gramscianization of Ernesto Laclau*. *23*(3), 765–786.

Mbembe, A. (2019). *Necropolitics*. Duke University Press.

McKean, B. L. (2016). Toward an inclusive populism? On the role of race and difference in Laclau's politics. *Political Theory*, *44*(6), 797–820. https://doi.org/10.1177/0090591716647771

McTernan, J. (2016). The cult of Jeremy Corbyn: The making of a modern sect. *The Evening Standard*. 30 June.

Mehring, R., & Steuer, D. (2019). Carl Schmitt and the politics of identity. In M. Sedgwick (ed) *Key Thinkers of the Radical Right*. Oxford University Press.

Mehta, U. S. (1999). *Liberalism and Empire: A Study in Nineteenth-Century British Liberal Thought*. University of Chicago Press.

Meister, R. (2009). *After Evil: A Politics of Human Rights*. Columbia University Press.

Mendoza, B. (2015). Coloniality of gender and power: From postcoloniality to decoloniality. In L. Disch & M. Hawkesworth (eds) *The Oxford Handbook of Feminist Theory*. Oxford University Press.

Menon, A. (2024). Anand Menon on racism: The UK has made progress, but this year's riots show there's a long way to go. Tortoise. https://www.tortoisemedia.com/2024/10/04/anand-menon-on-racism-uk-has-made-progress-but-far-right-riots-show-theres-a-long-way-to-go/

Meret, S. (2015). Charismatic female leadership and gender: Pia Kjærsgaard and the Danish People's Party. *Patterns of Prejudice*, *49*(1–2), 81–102. https://doi.org/10.1080/0031322X.2015.1023657

Mény, Y., & Surel, Y. (2000). *Par Le Peuple, Pour Le Peuple. Le Populisme Et Les Démocraties*. Fayard.

Mignolo, W. (2011). *The Darker Side of Western Modernity: Global Futures, Decolonial Options*. Duke University Press.

Mignolo, W. D. (2007). Introduction. *Cultural Studies*. https://doi.org/10.1080/09502380601162498

Mill, J. (1937). *Essay on Government*. Cambridge University Press.

Mill, J. S. (1972). Considerations on representative government. In *Three Essays*. Oxford University Press.

Miller-Idriss, C. (2017). Soldier, sailor, rebel, rule-breaker: Masculinity and the body in the German far right. *Gender and Education, 29*(2), 199–215. https://doi.org/10.1080/09540253.2016.1274381

Mills, C. W. (1999). The racial contract. In *Women's Philosophy Review* (Issue 21). Cornell University Press. https://doi.org/10.5840/wpr1999219

Mills, C. W. (2017). *Black Rights/White Wrongs: The Critique of Racial Liberalism*. Oxford University Press.

Moffitt, B. (2016). *The Global Rise of Populism: Performance, Political Style, and Representation*. Stanford University Press.

Moffitt, B. (2017). Transnational populism? Representative claims, media and the difficulty of constructing a transnational 'people'. *Javnost, 24*(4), 409–425. https://doi.org/10.1080/13183222.2017.1330086

Moffitt, B. (2018). The populism/anti-populism divide in Western Europe. *Democratic Theory, 5*(2), 1–16. https://doi.org/10.3167/dt.2018.050202

Mondon, A. (2022). Epistemologies of ignorance in far right studies: The invisibilisation of racism and whiteness in times of populist hype. *Acta Politica*. https://doi.org/10.1057/s41269-022-00271-6

Mondon, A. (2024). Really existing liberalism, the bulwark fantasy, and the enabling of reactionary, far right politics. *Constellations*. https://doi.org/10.1111/1467-8675.12749

Mondon, A. (2024a). Hegemonic defeatism: The mainstreaming of far-right politics in France. *Parliamentary Affairs*, gsae044. https://doi.org/10.1093/pa/gsae044

Mondon, A., & Winter, A. (2018). Whiteness, populism and the racialisation of the working class in the United Kingdom and the United States. *Identities, 26*(5), 510–528. https://doi.org/10.1080/1070289X.2018.1552440

Mondon, A., & Winter, A. (2020). *Reactionary Democracy: How Racism and the Populist Far Right Became Mainstream*. Verso Books.

Morrison, T. (1992). *Playing in the Dark: Whiteness and the Literary Imagination*. Harvard University Press.

Mouffe, C. (2005). *The Return of the Political*. Verso.

Mouffe, C. (2018). *For a Left Populism*. Verso.

Mouffe, C. (ed) (1999). *The Challenge of Carl Schmitt*. Verso. https://www.versobooks.com/en-gb/products/1671-the-challenge-of-carl-schmitt

Mounk, Y. (2018). *Der Zerfall der Demokratie: Wie der Populismus den Rechtsstaat bedroht*. Droemer Verlag.

Mounk, Y. (2019). *The People vs. Democracy*. Harvard University Press. https://www.hup.harvard.edu/books/9780674237681

Mudde, C. (2004). The populist zeitgeist. *Government and Opposition, 39*(4), 542–563. https://doi.org/10.1111/j.1477-7053.2004.00135.x

Mudde, C. (2007). *Populist Radical Right Parties in Europe.* Cambridge University Press.

Mudde, C. (2024). Can Europe's new 'conservative left' persuade voters to abandon the far right? *The Guardian.* 16 January. https://www.theguardian.com/commentisfree/2024/jan/16/conservative-left-europe-far-right-sahra-wagenknecht-germany

Mudde, C., & Rovira Kaltwasser, C. (2012). Exclusionary vs. inclusionary populism: Comparing contemporary Europe and Latin America. *Government and Opposition, 48*(2), 147–174. https://doi.org/10.1017/gov.2012.11

Mudde, C., & Rovira Kaltwasser, C. (2015). Vox populi or vox masculini? Populism and gender in Northern Europe and South America. *Patterns of Prejudice, 49*(1–2), 16–36. https://doi.org/10.1080/0031322X.2015.1014197

Müller, J.-W. (2016). *What Is Populism?* University of Pennsylvania Press.

Musina, D. (2023). Militarising gender: A (contrapuntal) reading of Women, Peace and Security (WPS) applications in EU-Tunisian security assemblages. *European Security, 32*(3), 464–484. https://doi.org/10.1080/09662839.2023.2233961

Narayan, U. (1995). Colonialism and its others: Considerations on rights and care discourses. *Hypatia, 10*(2), 133–140.

Nietzsche, F. W. (with Smith, D.). (1996). *On the Genealogy of Morals: A Polemic: By Way of Clarification and Supplement to My Last Book, Beyond Good and Evil.* Oxford University Press.

Norocel, O. C. (2018). Antifeminist and 'truly liberated': Conservative performances of gender by women politicians in Hungary and Romania. *Politics and Governance, 6*(3), 43–54. https://doi.org/10.17645/pag.v6i3.1417

Norris, P., & Inglehart, R. (2019). *Cultural Backlash: Trump, Brexit, and Authoritarian Populism.* Cambridge University Press.

Onar, N. F., & Nicolaïdis, K. (2013). The decentring agenda: Europe as a post-colonial power. *Cooperation and Conflict, 48*(2), 283–303. https://doi.org/10.1177/0010836713485384

Ostiguy, P. (2017). Populism: A socio-cultural approach. In C. R. Kaltwasser, P. Taggart, P. Ochoa Espejo, & P. Ostiguy (eds) (2017). *The Oxford Handbook on Populism.* Oxford University Press, pp 73–97.

Ostiguy, P., Panizza, F., & Moffitt, B. (eds) (2021). *Populism in a Global Perspective: A Performative and Discursive Approach.* Routledge.

Oyěwùmí, O. (1997). *The Invention of Women: Making an African Sense of Western Gender Discourses.* University of Minnesota Press.

Panayotu, P. (2021). Transnational populism and the European Union: An uneasy alliance? The case of DiEM25. In *Imagining Europe*. Springer International Publishing AG, pp 117–148. https://doi.org/10.1007/978-3-030-81369-7_5

Panizza, F. (2005). *Populism and the Mirror of Democracy*. Verso.

Pappas, T. (2019). *Populism and Liberal Democracy: A Comparative and Theoretical Analysis*. Oxford University Press.

Pateman, C. (1988). *The Sexual Contract*. Polity Press.

Pauwels, T. (2011). Measuring populism: A quantitative text analysis of party literature in Belgium. *Journal of Elections, Public Opinion and Parties*, *21*(1), 97–119. https://doi.org/10.1080/17457289.2011.539483

Peruzzotti, E. (2017). Populism as democratization's nemesis: The politics of regime hybridization. *Chinese Political Science Review*, *2*(3), 314–327. https://doi.org/10.1007/s41111-017-0070-2

Pitts, J. (2005). *A Turn to Empire: The Rise of Imperial Liberalism in Britain and France*. Princeton University Press. https://doi.org/10.1515/9781400826636

Plaza-Colodro, C., Gómez-Reino, M., & Marcos-Marne, H. (2018). Does host ideology shape populist parties' attitudes towards the EU? The links of populism and Euroscepticism in Southern Europe. *Revista Internacional de Sociologia*, *76*(4). https://doi.org/10.3989/ris.2018.76.4.18.003

Portantiero, J. C., & De Ipola, E. (1981). Lo nacional popular y los populismos realmente existentes. *Nueva Sociedad*, *54*, 7–18.

Público. (2022). Así es la ley del 'solo sí es sí' que ha aprobado el Congreso. Público. 25 August. https://www.publico.es/mujer/asi-ley-aprobado-congreso.html

Pufendorf, S. (2005). *On the Law of Nature and Nations*. Lawbook Exchange Limited.

Quijano, A. (2000). Coloniality of power and Eurocentrism in Latin America. *International Sociology*, *15*(2), 215–232.

Quijano, A. (2000a). Colonialidad del poder, eurocentrismo y América Latina. In E. Lander (ed) *La Colonialidad del Saber: Eurocentrismo y Ciencias Sociales. Perspectivas Latinoamericanas*. CLACSO, pp 200–246.

Quijano, A. (2000b). Colonialidad del poder y clasificacion social. *Journal of World-Systems Research*, *6*(2), 342–386.

Quijano, A. (2007). Coloniality and modernity/rationality. *Cultural Studies*, *21*(2), 168–178. https://doi.org/10.1080/09502380601164353

Rancière, J. (1999). *Disagreement: Politics and Philosophy*. University of Minnesota Press.

Rawls, J. (1999a). *A Theory of Justice*. Harvard University Press.

Rawls, J. (1999b). *Law of the Peoples*. Harvard University Press.

Rawls, J. (2001). *Justice as Fairness: A Restatement*. Harvard University Press.

Rawls, J. (2005). *Political Liberalism*. Columbia University Press.

Rawls, J. (2005). *Political Liberalism*. Columbia University Press.

Remnick, D. (2016). An American tragedy. *The New Yorker*. 9 November. https://www.newyorker.com/news/news-desk/an-american-tragedy-remnick-trump-wins-presidency-2016

Restall, M. (2003). *Seven Myths of the Spanish Conquest*. Oxford University Press.

Reynolds, B. (2015). I was a civil rights activist in the 1960s. But it's hard for me to get behind Black Lives Matter. *Washington Post*. 24 August. https://www.washingtonpost.com/posteverything/wp/2015/08/24/i-was-a-civil-rights-activist-in-the-1960s-but-its-hard-for-me-to-get-behind-black-lives-matter/

Rojas-Andrés, R., Mazzolini, S., & Custodi, J. (2024). Does left populism short-circuit itself? Podemos in the labyrinths of cultural elitism and radical leftism. *Journal of Contemporary European Studies*, *32*(4), 960–977. https://doi.org/10.1080/14782804.2023.2269375

Ronderos, S. (2020). Hysteria in the squares: Approaching populism from a perspective of desire. *Psychoanalysis, Culture and Society*, *26*(1), 46–64. https://doi.org/10.1057/s41282-020-00189-y

Ronderos, S., & Glynos, J. (2023). Anti-populist fantasies: Interrogating Veja's discursive constructions, from Lula to Bolsonaro. *Critical Discourse Studies*, *20*(6), 618–642. https://doi.org/10.1080/17405904.2022.2156567

Ronderos, S., & Zicman De Barros, T. (2020). Populismo e antipopulismo na política Brasileira: Massas, lógicas políticas e significantes em disputa. *Aurora. Revista de Arte, Mídia e Política*, *12*(36), 31–48. https://doi.org/10.23925/v12n36_dossie2

Rooduijn, M. (2018). What unites the voter bases of populist parties? Comparing the electorates of 15 populist parties. *European Political Science Review*, *10*(3), 351–368. https://doi.org/10.1017/S1755773917000145

Rooduijn, M., & Akkerman, T. (2017). Flank attacks: Populism and left-right radicalism in Western Europe. *Party Politics*, *23*(3), 193–204. https://doi.org/10.1177/1354068815596514

Rousseau, J.-J. (1984). *Discourse on the Origins and Foundation of Inequality Among Men, trans. Maurice Cranston*. Penguin Press.

Rovira Kaltwasser, C. (2017, 14 May). Populismo vs. cosmopolitanismo. *Diario El Austral*, 9.

Rueda, D. (2021). Is populism a political strategy? A critique of an enduring approach. *Political Studies*, *69*(2), 167–184. https://doi.org/10.1177/0032321720962355

Rummens, S. (2017). *Populism as a Threat to Liberal Democracy* (C. R. Kaltwasser, P. Taggart, P. O. Espejo, & P. Ostiguy (eds); Vol. 1). Oxford University Press. https://doi.org/10.1093/oxfordhb/9780198803560.013.27

Ryan, L. (2017). Memory and masculinity in Almudena Grandes's El Corazón Helado. In L. Ryan & A. Corbalán (eds) *The Dynamics of Masculinity in Contemporary Spanish Culture*. Routledge, pp 80–98.

Sachseder, J., & Stachowitsch, S. (2023). Gendering EU security strategies: A feminist postcolonial approach to the EU as a (global) security actor. *European Security*, *32*(3), 404–424. https://doi.org/10.1080/09662839.2023.2232742

Salmela, M., & von Scheve, C. (2017). Emotional roots of right-wing political populism. *Social Science Information*, *56*(4), 567–595. https://doi.org/10.1177/0539018417734419

Schiwy, F. (2007). Decolonization and the question of subjectivity: Gender, race, and binary thinking. *Cultural Studies*, *21*(2–3), 271–294. https://doi.org/10.1080/09502380601162555

Schmitt, C. (2007). *The Concept of the Political: Expanded Edition*. University of Chicago Press.

Schneider, J. (2015). What the Corbyn campaign did next: Meet Momentum. *Red Pepper*.

Schoor, C. (2019). Where the real people meet the real elite: Exploring mixes of populism with elitism. *Populism*, *2*(2), 184–206. https://doi.org/10.1163/25888072-02021032

Schumpeter, J. (1976). *Capitalism, Socialism and Democracy*. Allen and Unwin.

Segato, R. (2022). Género y colonialidad: En busca de claves delectura y de un vocabulario estratégico descolonia. In K. Bidaseca (ed) *Feminismos y Poscolonialidad*. Ediciones Godot.

Segato, R. L. (2015). *La Critica a La Colonialidad En Ocho Ensayos y Una Antropología Por Demanda*. Prometeo Libros.

Segato, R. L. (2010). Género y colonialidad: En busca de claves de lectura y de un vocabulario estratégico descolonial. In A. Quijano & J.M. Navarrete (eds) *La Cuestión Descolonial*. Universidad Ricardo Palma.

Sieben, P. (2024). Politiker von Wagenknecht-Partei über das Gendern: „Kann verstehen, dass die Leute genervt sind". 18 January. https://www.merkur.de/politik/sahra-wagenknecht-buendnis-bsw-partei-gendern-thomas-geisel-cancel-culture-zr-92782110.html

Simi, P., Bubolz, B. F., & Hardman, A. (2013). Military experience, identity discrepancies, and far right terrorism: An exploratory analysis. *Studies in Conflict & Terrorism*, *36*(8), 654–671. https://doi.org/10.1080/1057610X.2013.802976

Singer, A. (2009). Raízes sociais e ideológicas do lulismo. *Novos estudos CEBRAP*, 83–102. https://doi.org/10.1590/S0101-33002009000300004

Skonieczny, A. (2018). Emotions and political narratives: Populism, Trump and trade. *Politics and Governance*, *6*(4), 62. https://doi.org/10.17645/pag.v6i4.1574

Slobodian, Q. (2025). *Hayek's Bastards: The Neoliberal Roots of the Populist Right*. Penguin.

Sorensen, L. (2021). *Populist Communication: Ideology, Performance, Mediation.* Palgrave Macmillan.

Spierings, N., & Zaslove, A. (2015). Gendering the vote for populist radical-right parties. *Patterns of Prejudice*, *49*(1–2), 135–162. https://doi.org/10.1080/0031322X.2015.1024404

Spierings, N., & Zaslove, A. (2017). Gender, populist attitudes, and voting: Explaining the gender gap in voting for populist radical right and populist radical left parties. *West European Politics*, *40*(4), 821–847. https://doi.org/10.1080/01402382.2017.1287448

Spivak, G. C. (2011). Can the subaltern speak? In *Colonial Discourse and Post-Colonial Theory—A Reader*. Columbia University Press, pp 66–111.

Stäheli, U. (2004). Competing figures of the limit: Dispersion, transgression, antagonism, and indifference. In S. Critchley & O. Marchart (eds) *Laclau: A Critical Reader*. Routledge, pp 226–240.

Stallybrass, P. (1990). Marx and heterogeneity: Thinking the lumpenproletariat. *Representations (Berkeley, Calif.)*, *31*(31), 69–95. https://doi.org/10.2307/2928400

Stanley, B. (2008). The thin ideology of populism. *Journal of Political Ideologies*, *13*(1), 95–110. https://doi.org/10.1080/13569310701822289

Stavrakakis, Y. (2002). *Lacan and the Political*. Routledge.

Stavrakakis, Y. (2007). *The Lacanian Left: Psychoanalysis, Theory, Politics* (1st ed.). University Press. https://doi.org/10.1515/9780748629077

Stavrakakis, Y. (2014). The return of 'the people': Populism and anti-populism in the shadow of the European crisis. *Constellations*, *21*(4), 505–517. https://doi.org/10.1111/1467-8675.12127

Stavrakakis, Y. (2017). Discourse theory in populism research: Three challenges and a dilemma. *Journal of Language and Politics*, *16*(4), 523–534. https://doi.org/10.1075/jlp.17025.sta

Stavrakakis, Y., Andreadis, I., & Katsambekis, G. (2017). A new populism index at work: Identifying populist candidates and parties in the contemporary Greek context. *European Politics and Society*, *18*(4), 446–464. https://doi.org/10.1080/23745118.2016.1261434

Stavrakakis, Y., Katsambekis, G., Kioupkiolis, A., Nikisianis, N., & Siomos, T. (2018). Populism, anti-populism and crisis. *Contemporary Political Theory*, *17*(1), 4–27. https://doi.org/10.1057/s41296-017-0142-y

Stone, J. (2016). British people are proud of colonialism and the British Empire, poll finds. *The Independent*. 21 January. https://www.independent.co.uk/news/uk/politics/british-people-are-proud-of-colonialism-and-the-british-empire-poll-finds-a6821206.html

Suuronen, V. (2021). Carl Schmitt as a theorist of the 1933 Nazi revolution: 'The difficult task of rethinking and recultivating traditional concepts'. *Contemporary Political Theory*, *20*(2), 341–363. https://doi.org/10.1057/s41296-020-00417-1

Taggart, P., & Szczerbiak, A. (2008). *Opposing Europe? The Comparative Party Politics of Euroscepticism. Volume 1, Case Studies and Country Surveys*. Oxford University Press.

Thomassen, L. (2019). Discourse and heterogeneity. In *Discourse, Culture and Organization*. Springer International Publishing, pp 43–61. https://doi.org/10.1007/978-3-319-94123-3_3

Thomeczek, J. P. (2024). Bündnis Sahra Wagenknecht (BSW): Left-wing authoritarian—and populist? An empirical analysis. *Politische Vierteljahresschrift*, 65(3), 535–552. https://doi.org/10.1007/s11615-024-00544-z

Tocqueville, A. de (with Reeve, H.). (2009). *Democracy in America: Volumes I & II* (1st ed.). The Floating Press.

Torre, C. de la. (2015). *The Promise and Perils of Populism: Global Perspectives*. University Press of Kentucky.

Turnbull-Dugarte, S. J., & López Ortega, A. (2024). Instrumentally inclusive: The political psychology of homonationalism. *American Political Science Review*, 118(3), 1360–1378. https://doi.org/10.1017/S0003055423000849

Urbinati, N. (2019). Political theory of populism. *Annual Review of Political Science*, 22(1), 111–127. https://doi.org/10.1146/annurev-polisci-050317-070753

Valentim, V., & Widmann, T. (2021). Does radical-right success make the political debate more negative? Evidence from emotional rhetoric in German state parliaments. *Political Behavior*, 0123456789. https://doi.org/10.1007/s11109-021-09697-8

Velez, E. D., & Tuana, N. (2020). Toward decolonial feminisms: Tracing the lineages of decolonial thinking through Latin American/Latinx feminist philosophy. *Hypatia*, 35(3), 366–372. https://doi.org/10.1017/hyp.2020.26

Venizelos, G. (2023). *Populism in Power: Discourse and Performativity in SYRIZA and Donald Trump*. Routledge. https://doi.org/10.4324/9781003351634

Verge, T., & de la Fuente, M. (2014). Playing with different cards: Party politics, gender quotas and women's empowerment. *International Political Science Review*, 35(1), 67–79. https://doi.org/10.1177/0192512113508295

Volmer, H., & Wagner, S. (2024). *Sahra Wagenknecht hätte kaum einen besseren Zeitpunkt finden können*. n-tv.de. https://www.n-tv.de/politik/Partei-wird-am-Montag-gegruendet-Sahra-Wagenknecht-haette-kaum-einen-besseren-Zeitpunkt-finden-koennen-article24643602.html

Wade, P. (2015). Racism and liberalism: The dynamics of inclusion and exclusion. *Ethnic and Racial Studies*, 38(8), 1292–1297. https://doi.org/10.1080/01419870.2015.1016065

Wagenknecht, S. (2024). Condition of Germany. *New Left Review*, 146, 31–49.

Wagner, S., Wurthmann, L. C., & Thomeczek, J. P. (2023). Bridging left and right? How Sahra Wagenknecht could change the German party landscape. *Politische Vierteljahresschrift, 64*(3), 621–636. https://doi.org/10.1007/s11615-023-00481-3

Wainwright, H. (2018). The remarkable rise of Jeremy Corbyn. *New Labor Forum, 27*(3), 34–42. https://doi.org/10.1177/1095796018791115

Weyland, K. (2021). Populism as a political strategy: An approach's enduring — and increasing — advantages. *Political Studies, 69*(2), 185–189. https://doi.org/10.1177/00323217211002669

Widmann, T. (2021). How emotional are populists really? Factors explaining emotional appeals in the communication of political parties. *Political Psychology, 42*(1), 163–181. https://doi.org/10.1111/pops.12693

Williams, R. A. Jr. (1995). Documents of barbarism: The contemporary legacy of European racism and colonialism in the narrative traditions of federal Indian law. In R. Delgado (ed) *Critical Race Theory: The Cutting Edge*. Temple University Press.

Wirz, D. (2018). Persuasion through emotion? An experimental test of the emotion-eliciting nature of populist communication. *International Journal of Communication, 12*, 25. https://doi.org/10.5167/uzh-149959

Witcombe, N. A. (2019). *Compulsory Childcare in Socially Marginalised Areas in Denmark.* 16 January. https://nordics.info/show/artikel/compulsory-childcare-in-socially-marginalised-areas-in-denmark

Wojczewski, T. (2023). *The Inter- and Transnational Politics of Populism: Foreign Policy, Identity and Popular Sovereignty* (1st ed.). Springer International Publishing. https://doi.org/10.1007/978-3-031-16848-2

Worth, O. (2017). Whither Lexit? *Capital and Class, 41*(2), 351–357. https://doi.org/10.1177/0309816817711558c

Worth, O. (2020). Corbyn, Sanders and the contestation of neoliberal hegemony. In G. Charalambous & G. Ioannou (eds) *Left Radicalism and Populism in Europe*. Routledge, pp 89–105.

Wynter, S. (2003). Unsettling the coloniality of being/ power/ truth/ freedom. *CR: The New Centennial Review, 3*(3), 257–336.

Young, I. M. (2014). Activist challenges to deliberative democracy. *Political Theory, 29*(5), 670–690. http://www.jstor.org/stable/3072534.

Zakaria, F. (1997). The rise of illiberal democracy. *Foreign Affairs, 76*(6), 22–43. https://doi.org/10.2307/20048274

Zanotti, L., & Turnbull-Dugarte, S. J. (2022). Surviving but not thriving: VOX and Spain in times of COVID-19. *Government and Opposition*, 1–20. https://doi.org/10.1017/gov.2022.7

Zicman de Barros, T. (2022). Populism: Symptom or sublimation? Reassessing the use of psychoanalytic metaphors. *Psychoanalysis, Culture and Society, 27*(2–3), 218–234.

Zicman de Barros, T. (forthcoming). *Radical Democracy, Populism and Psychoanalysis*. Edinburgh University Press.

Zicman de Barros, T., & Aiolfi, T. (2025). The transgressive aesthetics of populism. *Politics*. https://doi.org/10.1177/02633957241312601

Žižek, S. (1990). Beyond discourse analysis. In E. Laclau (ed) *New Reflections on the Revolution of our Time*. Verso.

Žižek, S. (1993). *Tarrying with the Negative: Kant, Hegel, and the Critique of Ideology*. Duke University Press.

Žižek, S. (2008). *The Sublime Object of Ideology*. Verso.

Žižek, S. (2015). The need to traverse the fantasy. *In These Times*. 28 December. https://inthesetimes.com/article/slavoj-zizek-on-syria-refugees-eurocentrism-western-values-lacan-islam

Žižek, S. (2017). *In Defense of Lost Causes*. Verso. https://www.versobooks.com/en-gb/products/2038-in-defense-of-lost-causes

Index

References to figures appear in *italic* type. References to endnotes show the page and chapter number and the note number (231ch2n3).

A
affect 8, 67, 115
Agamben, G. 58
agonism 6
Aiolfi, T. 45
Anderson, B. 69
Angelos, James 76
annihilation
  fantasy of 35, 71
  politics of 61
antagonism
  analytical problems with 62–65, *65*
  author's overview of 57
  conceptual problems with 60–62
  difference as 71, 73, 114
  ethico-political problems with 65–66
  of Eurosceptics 97–98
  identities, and 40
  inequality, and 53, 66
  People and, the 11–12, 55–57, 119
  of Populists 99
  scholarship on 7, 58–60
Arditi, B. 37–38, 40
A Theory of Justice (Rawls) 28
authoritarianism 16–17, 35, 36, 37, 38, 93

B
Balibar, E. 104
barbarians 18, 20 *see also* Other, the
Barros, Adhemar de 122ch2n3
Bataille, G. 57, 63–64
Baudet, Thierry 46
Between Facts and Norms (Habermas) 30
Bhambra, G. K. 28–29
Biglieri, P. 44–45, 93
Black Lives Matter movement 26
Borrell, Josep 1–2, 88
Bortun, V. 46
Brexit 11, 96, 107

British Empire 27, 122ch1n1
BSW *see* Bündnis Sahra Wagenknecht (BSW)
bulwark fantasy 49, 69
Bündnis Sahra Wagenknecht (BSW) 76, 85–87, 91

C
Cadahia, L. 44–45, 93
Caiani, M. 46
Canovan, M. 38–39, 50
capitalism 10, 22, 64, 79–80, 86, 87, 122ch4n1
Caravantes, P. 84
'The case for colonialism' 122ch1n1
Casullo, M. E. 45
civility
  coloniality and 31, 37, 44, 76
  democracy and 4, 14–15, 27
  fantasy/myth of 34, 35, 38, 40–41, 70, 87, 116
collective identities 7, 54, 55, 60–61
colonialism 18, 19, 27, 28, 31, 32, 122ch1n1
coloniality
  author's overview of 19–20
  author's summary of 49–50, 110–111
  civility and 31, 37, 44, 76
  critical fantasy studies and 7, 8, 66–69
  democracy and 31
  fantasy/myth of 40–41, 90–91, 115, 116
  gender and 9–10, 22–23, 76, 79–82, 87–90, 116–118
  left-wing populism, and 5, 6, 8, 83, 85–87, 118, 119
  liberalism and 27–28
  modernity and 73
  nation-states and 10–12, 101–108
  phantasmatic structures of political identity 69–70, 93, 96

populism and 4, 6, 46, 64–65, *65*, 73, 98, 108–109, 120–121
power relations in 52, 70
rationality and 15, 20, 36, 70, 85, 94–95, 98–101
Schmitt and 59, 62
system of 64
see also People–Elite distinction
colonial matrix of power 20, 24, 48, 65, 80
colonial Other *see* Other, the
colonization
  capitalism, and 22, 122ch4n1
  democracy, and 3–4, 14
  gender hierarchies and 22–23, 81
  liberal thought on 24
  rationality and 15, 20
communicative action 30, 31
conservative left 86
contractualism 24, 25, 104
Corbyn, Jeremy 99–101, 105, 106–108
corruption 17
critical fantasy studies 7–8, 53, 66–68, 115–116 *see also* fantasy
critical race theory 31
Custodi, J. 105–106

D

De Cleen, B. 47, 48, 49
decolonial feminist theory 10, 22, 80–81, 91, 117, 122ch4n1
decolonial theory
  author's overview of 3–4
  coloniality and 121
  dark side of modernity 19, 90
  fantasy, and European 8
  gender, and 22
  hierarchies 19–20
  Other, and the 94
  patriarchy, and 10
  populism studies and 35
  rationality and 99
De Ipola, E. 41
Della Porta, D. 46
democracy
  civility, and 4, 14–15, 27
  difference and 102–103, 107–108
  history of in Europe 14
  liberalism and 2–3, 13, 31–32, 43–44, 111
  populism and 36–38, 38–39, 42, 89–90
  racial hierarchies and 103–104
  radical democracy 42, 43, 44, 53, 58, 61
  rationality and 4, 26, 103–104
  threat to, populism as 34–36
  transparency, and 17
Derrida, J. 58, 60, 63–64
Descartes 20–21, 26, 30
discursive approach
  aim of 47

antagonism, and 60, 65, *65*
author's overview of 51, 52
author's summary of 73, 120
challenges with 64
critical fantasy studies 67
friend-enemy relation 62
new approach to populism, and 53
political identities 72–73, 113
reality, and 4–5
scholarship 53–57
socio-cultural approach, and 45
dislocation 60–61, 67
Di Tella, T. S. 35
Dussel, E. 19, 20–21, 70, 72

E

economic sovereignty 96
Edelman, L. 69
ego cogito 20, 21
ego conquiro 20, 65, 70
Elite, the
  definitions of 47
  People, as the 5, 34, 82, 97, 109
  see also People–Elite distinction
elitism 15–18, 31–32, 34, 36, 45, 46, 49–50
  see also People–Elite distinction
Emancipations (Laclau) 60
emotional-rational dichotomy 98–99, 101
  see also rationality
empty signifiers 54, 55–56, 57
empty space of power 3, 16, 21–22, 31, 35–36, 46, 49, 70
Engels 56
enjoyment (*jouissance*) 67–69, 70, 72, 76, 81–82, 108–109
Enlightenment 1, 3–4, 16, 25, 26, 65, 110
epochal degodding 21
equality
  antagonism and 66
  fantasy of 76, 85, 87
  liberal democracies and 27–28
  see also gender equality; inequality
Errejón, Iñigo 84–85
Europe
  colonial history of 18–23
  see also fantasy
European elections 1, 2, 100, 110
European Union (EU) 87–89, 95–96, 97–99, 104–106, 107, 110
Eurosceptic 95
Euroscepticism 92, 95–98, 107
Eze, E. C. 39, 103

F

Fanon, F. 68
fantasy
  of annihilation 35, 71
  author's summary of 115–116

bulwark fantasy 49, 69
  of gender equality 76, 85, 87
  of the populist 53, 110
  of separation 72, 73–74
  of superiority 12, 15, 18, 21, 24, 70, 76, 88, 93–94
  of unity 38
  see also critical fantasy studies
fascism 6, 44–45, 57, 63–64, 106, 107
feminist masculinity 83–84
feminist theory
  decolonial feminist theory 10, 22, 80–81, 91, 117
  EU border politics 87
  populism, and 9–10, 80, 90, 116–118, 122ch1n3
  postcolonial feminism 22, 122ch4n1
femonationalism 9, 79, 117
floating signifiers 55–56, 57
For a Left Populism (Mouffe) 41
Foucault, M. 42, 59, 102
France 11, 50, 62, 68, 77, 82, 89, 92, 118
Freeden, Michael 122ch2n2
Freedom House Index 17
Front National (FN) 61–62
fundamental scepticism 21
Furtado, H. T. 71

G

Gellner, E. 69
gender
  border politics of EU 87–89
  coloniality and 9–10, 22–23, 76, 79–82, 87–90, 116–118
  decolonial theory and 22
  fantasy of equality 76, 85, 87
  hierarchies of 22–23, 76, 79–81
  left-wing populism 82–87
  populism and 9–10, 75–76, 77–79, 117
  race, and 22, 23, 24, 81, 90–91
  scholarship on 22–23, 77–79, 87–89, 117
  women-led populist parties 77
gender-critical feminists 31
gender equality 9, 76–77, 79, 81–82, 87, 90–91, 117–118
Germani, G. 35
Giesel, Thomas 85
Glynos, J. 7–8, 66–67, 68, 115
Goodwin, Matthew 7
Gramsci, A. 57, 63–64, 102, 106, 107
Grattan, L. 50
Greece 11, 42, 118
Guns, Germs and Steel (Diamond) 24–25

H

Habermas, Jürgen 30–31, 36, 58, 70, 89, 98–99
Hall, S. 16

Hansen, A. D. 60
head coverings 89
Hegel 56–57, 63
hegemony 40, 55
hegemony of rationality 36
heterogeneity 7, 45, 55–57, 63–64, *65*, 66
hierarchies
  gender hierarchies 22–23, 76, 80–81
  hierarchies of coloniality 3–4, 7, 19–20, 50, 64, 67, 112
  invisibility of 51
  liberalism and 15, 17, 24, 32, 36
  Other and, the 62
  racial hierarchies 26, 103–104
  sovereignty and 42–43
Hobbes, T. 24, 25
Hoijtink, M. 88
Howarth, D. 7–8, 67, 115

I

Ianni, O. 41, 47
ideal theory 29
identities *see* collective identities; political identities
ideologies, thick/thin 5–6, 36, 37, 98, 122ch2n2
Iglesias, Pablo 83–84, 99–100
illiberalism 13–14, 16, 36, 49
immigration 78, 85–86, 87, 91
inequality
  antagonism and 53, 66
  liberalism and 27–28, 44, 49–50, 111
  racial inequality 28–29
  rationality and 28, 36
  see also equality
Inglehart, R. 35, 98
intersectionality 23, 81, 90–91
iron 24
Italy 11, 12, 46

J

Jaguaribe, H. 41
Johnson, Boris 27, 46, 122ch1n2
jouissance see enjoyment (*jouissance*)

K

Kaltwasser, Rovira 75, 78, 101
Kant, Immanuel 26, 29, 30
Katsambekis, G. 37
kisses 84
Kjaersgaard, Pia 77
Kleinberg, R. 50

L

Labour Party 96, 100–101, 105, 106–107, 108
Lacan, J. 37, 40, 54, 56, 67
Laclau, Ernesto
  antagonism 40, 57–58, 71

dislocation 60–61, 67
hegemony 40, 55
heterogeneity 7, 45
populism 5, 12, 42, 50, 53, 54–57, 62–63, 66, 93, 113
psychoanalysis 7
Schmitt's influence 6
La France Insoumise 11, 92, 118
Landa, I. 16, 17
The Law of the Peoples (Rawls) 28
Lazzarato, M. 64
Le Bon, Gustave 27
Lefort, C. 21
left-lepenism 62
left-wing populism
  author's summary of 113–114, 118–119
  coloniality and 5, 6, 8
  and Euroscepticism 95–98
  gender and 82–87
  right-wing populism, and 11–12, 41, 42, 44
  see also Bündnis Sahra Wagenknecht (BSW); Podemos; scholarship; Syriza
Le Pen, Marine 9, 17, 77, 117
Lexit 11, 107
LGBT rights 9, 79, 91, 117
liberal centre 3
liberal democracies
  design problem with 15, 29, 31, 50
  equality, and 27–28
  see also democracy; liberalism
liberalism
  coloniality and 24, 25, 64, 112
  democracy and 2–3, 13, 31–32, 43–44, 111
  elitism and 15–18, 34, 36
  empty space of power 16, 31, 36, 46
  fantasy and 69
  inequality, and 27–28, 44, 49–50, 111
  populism and 14, 53, 72
  race, and 24, 26
  rationality and 30–31
liberal values 4, 50, 94, 112
Locke, John 24, 25
Lombardo, E. 84
London School of Economics (LSE) 34
LSE (London School of Economics) 34
Lugones, M. 22–23, 80, 81
lumpenproletariat 11, 56, 63

M

M5S 11, 12
Machiavelli 18–19
Maldonado-Torres, N. 19, 20–21
Mandelbaum, M. 69
Mann, M. 64, 103
Marchart, O. 44, 61, 65, 93
marriage 25–26

Marx, Karl 6, 19, 40, 41, 54, 56, 63, 93, 109, 113
masculinities
  coloniality and 83
  feminist masculinity 83–84
  lost masculinity 78
  militarized masculinity 10, 74, 117
  oppressive masculinity 76
  of politics 80
  populist parties, of 64, 82
  rationality and 79–80
  toxic masculinity 10
matrix of power *see* colonial matrix of power
Mbembe, A. 61, 68, 71, 85
McCluskey, Len 107
Meister, R. 64
Mélenchon, Jean-Luc 12, 50, 92, 118
Meloni, Giorgia 9, 79, 117
Mendoza, B. 19
Menon, Anand 27
Mény, Y. 62
metallurgy 24
Mignolo, W. 19
migration 1, 2, 5, 82, 85, 87, 90, 108
militarism 61, 71
Mill, James 24
Mill, John Stuart 3, 16, 24
Miller 68
Miller-Idriss, C. 78
Mills, C. W. 28–29, 39, 103
mind-body distinction 20, 21, 26
misanthropic scepticism 21
modernity
  coloniality and 73, 81
  dark side of 19
  impacts of 26–27
  populism as generalized form of politics 40, 51, 52, 90, 91
  rise of 21
  on steroids 5, 113
Moffitt, B. 45, 98
Mondon, A. 48–49, 68–69, 78
Montero, Irene 83
Morrison, Toni 104
Mouffe, Chantal
  agonism 6–7
  left-wing populism 41–44, 93
  liberalism and democracy 2, 50, 111
  populism 53
  Schmitt, on Carl 58–59
Mounk, Yasha 13
Mudde, Cas 36–37, 75, 77, 78, 86, 98, 122ch2n2
Müller, Jan-Werner 35, 36
myth of civility 34, 35, 38, 40–41

N

narratives
  of Europe 1–2

of liberalism 15–16
of populism 1, 13–14, 32, 78–79
of populists 13
of rationality 15
of right-wing populism 82–83
nationalism
  coloniality, and 69, 94–95, 101–102, 107–108
  Euroscepticism and 96, 97
  racial differences and 104, 105, 106
  right-wing populism and 78–79
  sovereignty and 107–108
  thin ideology, as 122ch2n2
  United States 39
national sovereignty 96, 101, 102, 104, 105, 106
nation-states
  coloniality and 10–12, 101–108, 118
  worthiness, and 82
Nazism 6, 8, 53, 58, 59–60, 68, 114
neoliberalism
  European Union and 95, 107
  impacts of 43
  left-wing populism and 11, 42, 92–93, 118
  right-wing populism and 16, 64
  scholarship on 17
New Reflections on the Revolutions of our Time (Laclau) 54, 60
Nietzsche, F. W. 18, 21
Norris, P. 35, 78, 98

O

On Populist Reason (Laclau) 54, 55, 56
ontological militarism 61, 71
Ostiguy, P. 45, 98
Other, the
  author's overview of 3–4
  decolonial theory and 94
  enjoyment, and 68
  hierarchies, and 62
  Medieval Europe, in 18
  original sin, and 21–22
  People, and the 3, 31–32, 112
  political identity and 60, 70, 72
  populism as 116

P

Paget 46
Panizza, F. 38, 40
Pateman, C. 25, 29–30
patriarchy
  coloniality and 10, 117–118
  gender hierarchies 22–23, 76, 79–81
  populism and 85, 91
People, the
  antagonism and 11–12
  coloniality and 87
  definitions of 47

democracy and 102–103
discursive field of coloniality 64–65, *65*
Elites, as the 5, 34, 82, 97, 109
homogenous, as 36
left-wing populism, in 11, 41–42, 43, 92, 118, 119
liberal democracy, in 14–15
Other, and the 3, 31–32, 112
populism and 86
power of 38
privileged boundedness 39
territorial boundaries and 104–105, 106–107
tyranny of the majority 16, 27
see also People–Elite distinction
The People (Canovan) 38
People–Elite distinction 6, 45, 46–50, 55–56, 57, 64, 70, 112–114
The People vs. Democracy (Mounk) 13
phantasmatic structures 68, 69–70, 93, 96, 110
Pink tide 92
Podemos
  coloniality and 108
  gender politics 75, 83–85, 91
  leadership 100
  left-wing populism 11, 12, 50, 92
  patriotism 105–106, 118
  scholarship on 41–42, 50
political identities
  affect and 115
  antagonism and 57
  critical fantasy studies and 8, 53, 67
  discursive studies and 72
  European 18, 73
  Other, and the 60, 70, 72
  phantasmatic structures of 68, 69–70, 110
  populism as 5, 6, 34, 40–41, 113
Political Liberalism (Rawls) 28
popular sovereignty 42–43, 96, 98, 102, 103–106, 107–108
populism
  author's overview of 4–5
  definitions of 36
  the term *populism* 4, 48, 97
  voter turnout 78
  see also coloniality; democracy; gender; left-wing populism; modernity; neoliberalism; People, the; political identities; populism studies; right-wing populism; scholarship
populism of the privileged 47, 48
populism studies
  author's overview of 33–34
  author's summary of 50–51, 114, 120
  coloniality and 93
  democracy and 36–38, 38–39, 42, 89–90
  gender and 77

history of 34–36
liberal narrative, and 32
measuring problem 96–97
new perspectives on 45–46
the term *populism* 4, 48, 97
see also People–Elite distinction
Portantiero, J. C. 41
postcolonial feminism 22, 122ch4n1
power
  coloniality, relations of in 52, 70
  People, of the 38
  superiority and 85
  see also colonial matrix of power;
    empty space of power; hierarchies
privileged boundedness 39
proletariat 56, 63
psychoanalysis 7, 8, 18, 40, 54, 67–68, 73, 115
Pufendorf, S. 25

Q
Quijano, A. 19–20, 22–23, 24, 65, 80–81

R
race
  coloniality and 19, 23
  gender, and 22, 23, 24, 81, 90–91
  ideal theory, and 29
  nationalism and 104, 105, 106
  rationality and 28
  sovereignty and 102–103
race war 102
The Racial Contract (Mills) 103
racial inequality 28–29
radical democracy 42, 43, 44, 53, 58, 61
Rancière, J. 16, 21, 37, 57
rationality
  coloniality and 15, 20, 36, 70, 85, 94–95, 98–101
  democracy and 4, 26, 103–104
  inequality, and 28, 36
  left-wing populism and 12
  liberalism and 30–31
  masculinity and 79–80
Rawls, John 28–30
Remnick, David 13
res cogitans 20
right-wing populism
  democracy and 31–32
  and Euroscepticism 95–98
  gender, and 9–10
  left-wing populism, and 11–12, 41, 42, 44
  mainstreaming of 48, 111
  narratives of 82–83
  neoliberalism and 16
  politics of 2–3
  support for 17, 110
  see also scholarship
Ronderos, S. 68

Rousseau, J.-J. 24, 25, 26, 39
Ruiz Casado, J. A. 47, 48, 49
Rummens, S. 35, 36

S
Sachseder, J. 89
Sanders, Bernie 50
Savages *see* Other, the
scepticism 21
Schmitt, Carl
  influence of 6
  radical democracy 51, 53
  scholarship on 61–62, 63, 66
  theories of 58–60, 70, 114
scholarship
  on antagonism 7, 58–60, 60–66
  on colonialism 122ch1n1
  on coloniality 19–23
  on critical fantasy studies 66–69
  on elitism 17
  on Euroscepticism 95–6
  gaps in populism 5–6
  on gender 22–23, 77–79, 87–89, 117
  on left-wing populism 5–6, 11–12, 41–44, 92, 93
  on neoliberalism 17
  on patriarchy 79–80
  on People–Elite distinction 46–50
  on populism 4–5, 10, 34–36, 36–38, 96–97
  on rationality 30–31
  on right-wing populism 11–12, 14, 16, 44–45
  on sovereignty 101–108
Schoor, C. 46
Schumpeter, J. 27
signifiers, empty/floating 54, 55–56, 57
social contracts 25–26, 39, 103
social heterogeneity 55, 56
socio-cultural approach 45–46
Sorensen, L. 45
sovereignty 43, 96, 101–102 *see also* national sovereignty; popular sovereignty
Spain 11, 77, 83, 98, 100, 105–106, 118
Spierings, N. 77
Stachowitsch, S. 89
Stäheli, U. 60
Stavrakakis, Y. 44, 93
Strauss, Leo 17
subalterns 63, 72–73
Surel, Y. 62
Suuronen, V. 59
Syriza 11, 42, 50, 92, 118

T
techno-populism 46
thick ideologies 5–6, 36, 37
thin ideologies 5, 36, 37, 98, 122ch2n2
Thomassen, L. 63
Tocqueville, A. de 16

toxic masculinity 10
transnational populism 96, 123n1
trans people 14, 31
Trump, Donald 45, 46
tyranny of the majority 16, 27

U

United States 39, 50
universality 19, 30
Urbinati, N. 36

V

values 1, 9, 14, 18–19, 33, 82–83 *see also* liberal values
VAR-Palmares 122ch2n3
Venizelos, G. 46

W

Wagenknecht, Sahra 85
The Washington Post 26
Weidel, Alice 77
'Why do Empty Signifiers Matter to Politics?' (Laclau) 54
Winter, A. 48–49, 78
world-making 18, 19
Worth, O. 107
Wynter, S. 21–22, 73

Z

Zaslove, A. 77
Zicman de Barros, T. 68
Žižek, S. 8, 37, 61, 64, 68, 69, 93, 115

www.ingramcontent.com/pod-product-compliance
Lightning Source LLC
Chambersburg PA
CBHW071712020426
42333CB00017B/2236